# In Another World with My Smartphone ②

Art • **Soto**   Original Story • **Patora Fuyuhara**

Character Design: Eiji Usatsuka

«contents»

In Another World
with My Smartphone.

Vol.2

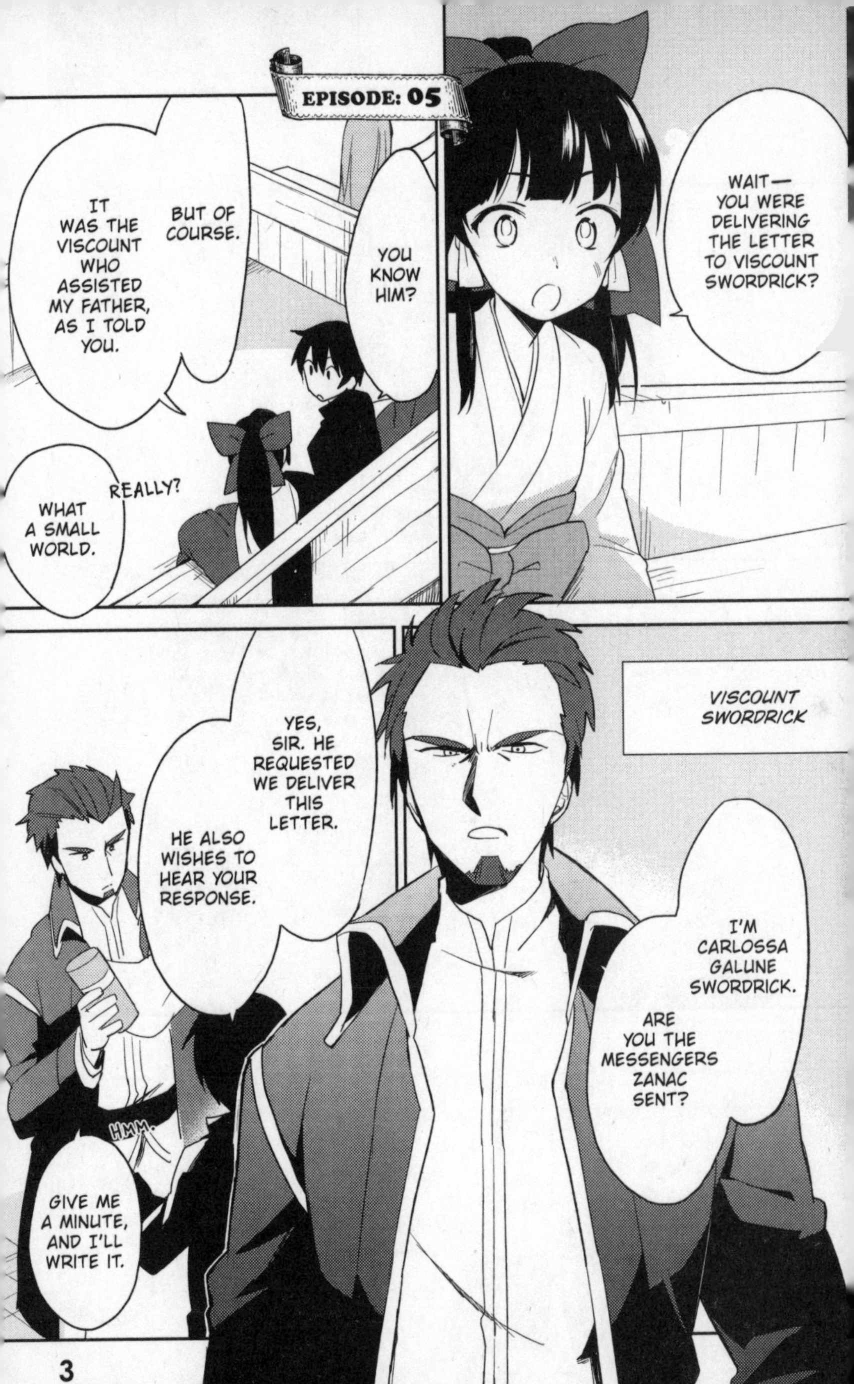
EPISODE: 05
WAIT— YOU WERE DELIVERING THE LETTER TO VISCOUNT SWORDRICK?
YOU KNOW HIM?
BUT OF COURSE.
IT WAS THE VISCOUNT WHO ASSISTED MY FATHER, AS I TOLD YOU.
REALLY?
WHAT A SMALL WORLD.
VISCOUNT SWORDRICK
I'M CARLOSSA GALUNE SWORDRICK.
ARE YOU THE MESSENGERS ZANAC SENT?
YES, SIR. HE REQUESTED WE DELIVER THIS LETTER.
HE ALSO WISHES TO HEAR YOUR RESPONSE.
HMM.
GIVE ME A MINUTE, AND I'LL WRITE IT.

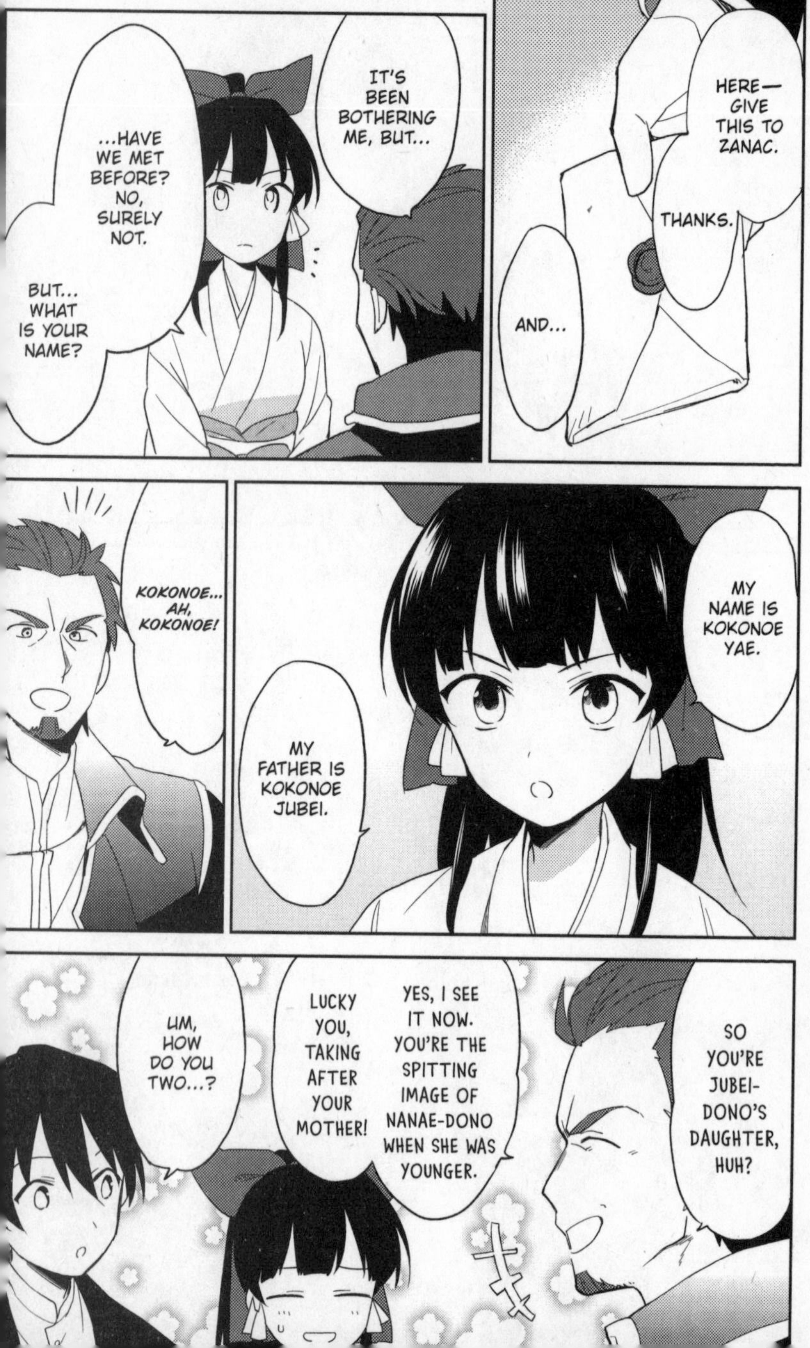
HERE— GIVE THIS TO ZANAC.
THANKS.
AND...
IT'S BEEN BOTHERING ME, BUT...
...HAVE WE MET BEFORE? NO, SURELY NOT.
BUT... WHAT IS YOUR NAME?
MY NAME IS KOKONOE YAE.
MY FATHER IS KOKONOE JUBEI.
KOKONOE... AH, KOKONOE!
SO YOU'RE JUBEI-DONO'S DAUGHTER, HUH?
YES, I SEE IT NOW. YOU'RE THE SPITTING IMAGE OF NANAE-DONO WHEN SHE WAS YOUNGER.
LUCKY YOU, TAKING AFTER YOUR MOTHER!
UM, HOW DO YOU TWO...?

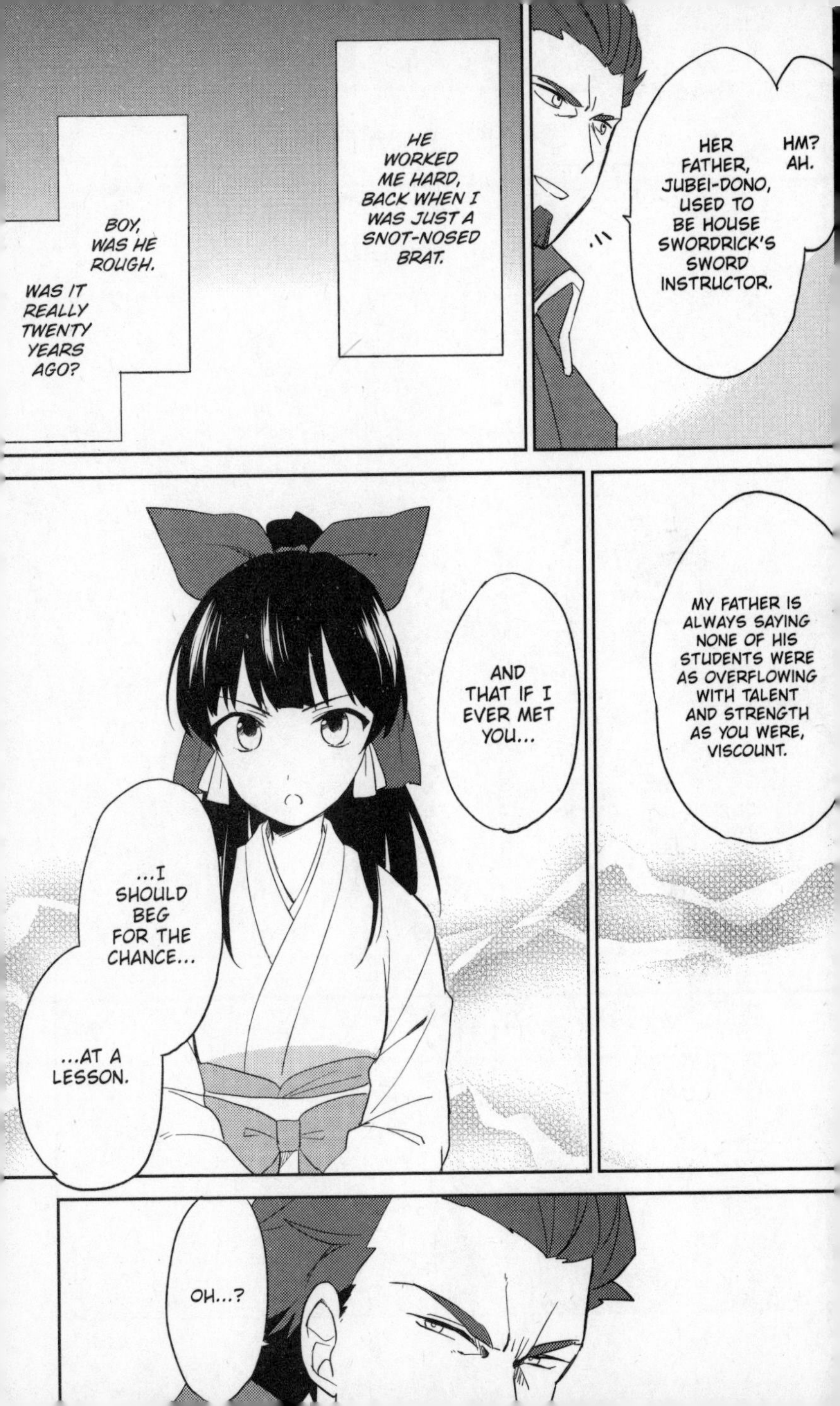
HM? AH.
HER FATHER, JUBEI-DONO, USED TO BE HOUSE SWORDRICK'S SWORD INSTRUCTOR.
HE WORKED ME HARD, BACK WHEN I WAS JUST A SNOT-NOSED BRAT.
BOY, WAS HE ROUGH.
WAS IT REALLY TWENTY YEARS AGO?
MY FATHER IS ALWAYS SAYING NONE OF HIS STUDENTS WERE AS OVERFLOWING WITH TALENT AND STRENGTH AS YOU WERE, VISCOUNT.
AND THAT IF I EVER MET YOU...
...I SHOULD BEG FOR THE CHANCE...
...AT A LESSON.
OH...?

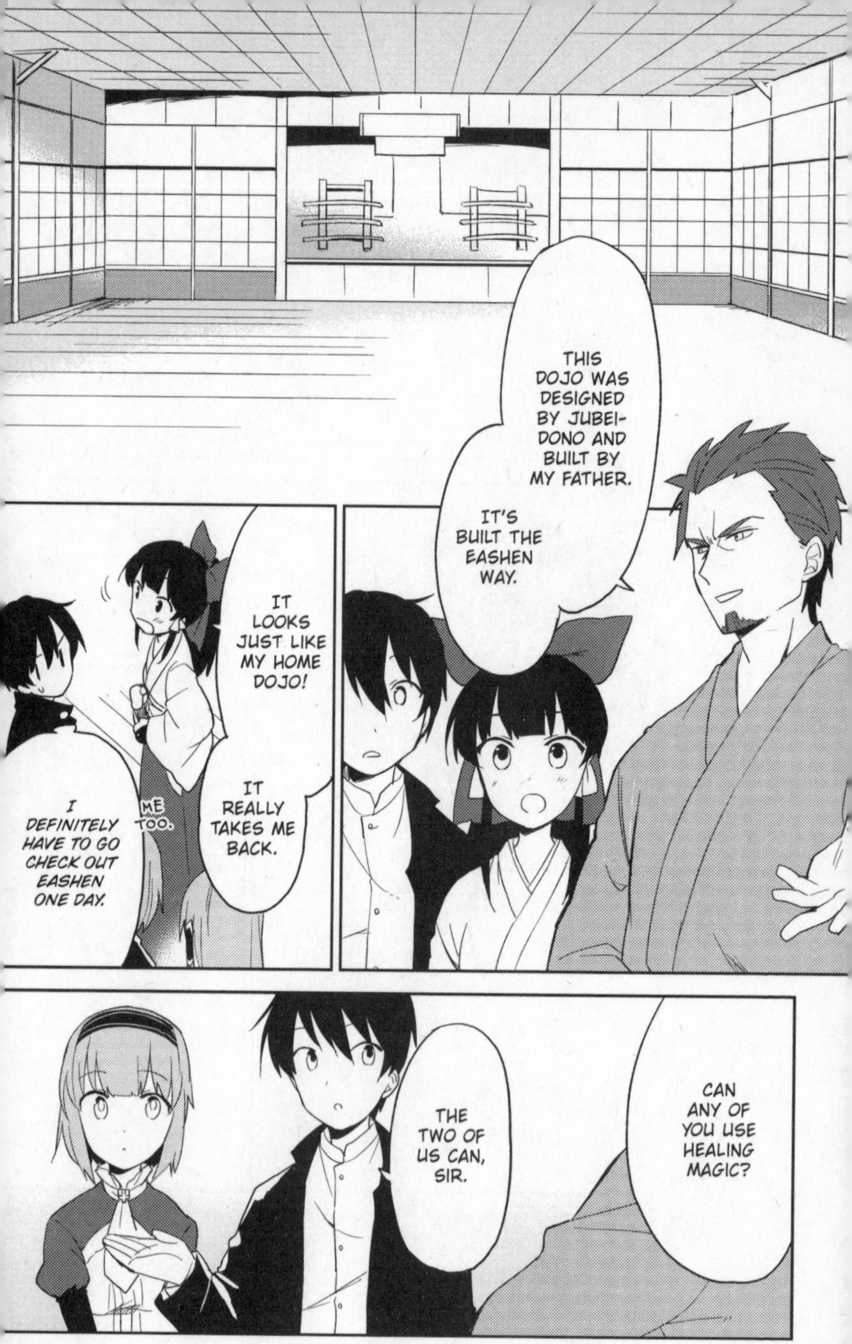
THIS DOJO WAS DESIGNED BY JUBEI-DONO AND BUILT BY MY FATHER.
IT'S BUILT THE EASHEN WAY.
IT LOOKS JUST LIKE MY HOME DOJO!
IT REALLY TAKES ME BACK.
ME TOO.
I DEFINITELY HAVE TO GO CHECK OUT EASHEN ONE DAY.
CAN ANY OF YOU USE HEALING MAGIC?
THE TWO OF US CAN, SIR.

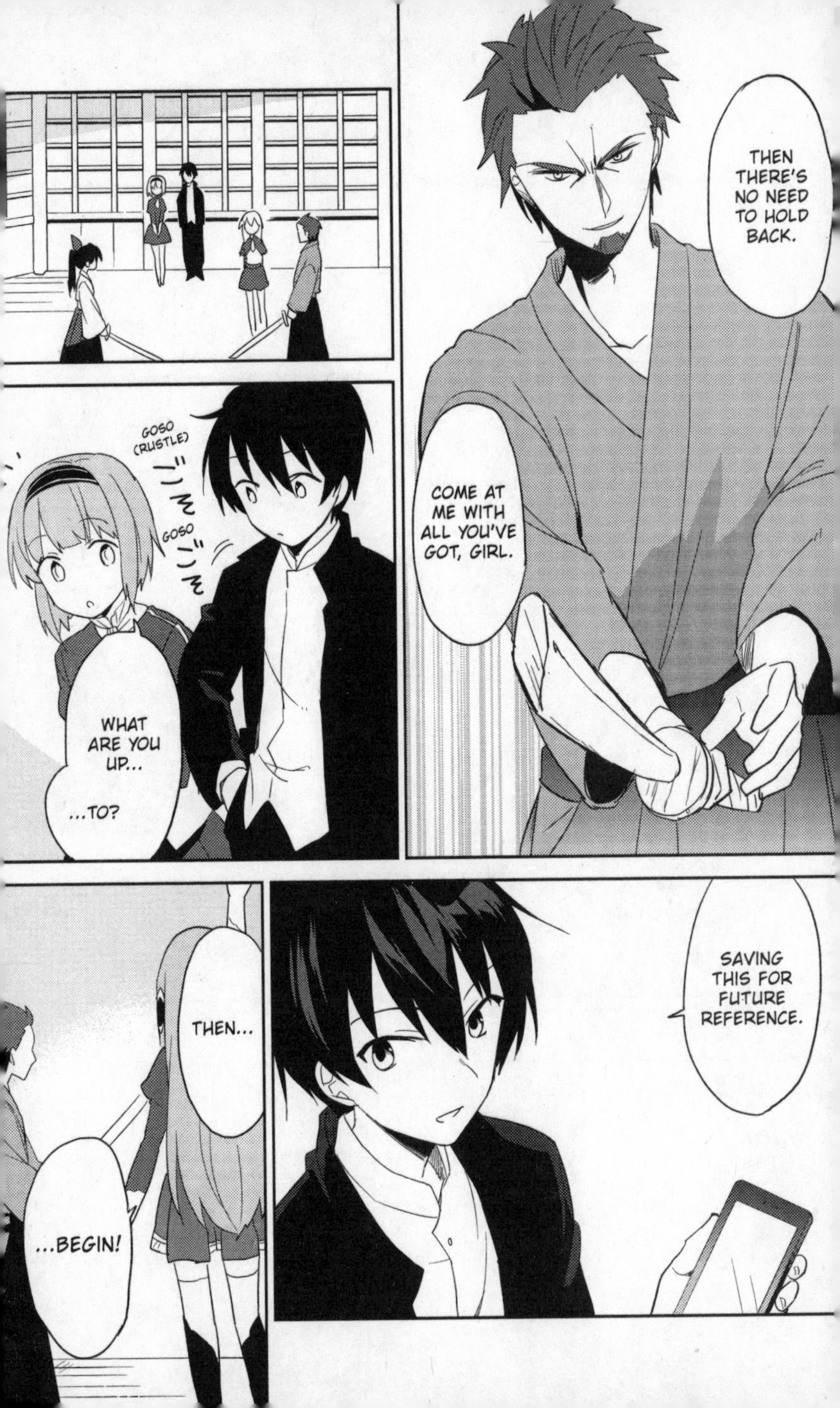

THEN THERE'S NO NEED TO HOLD BACK.
COME AT ME WITH ALL YOU'VE GOT, GIRL.
GOSO (RUSTLE)
GOSO
WHAT ARE YOU UP...
...TO?
SAVING THIS FOR FUTURE REFERENCE.
THEN...
...BEGIN!

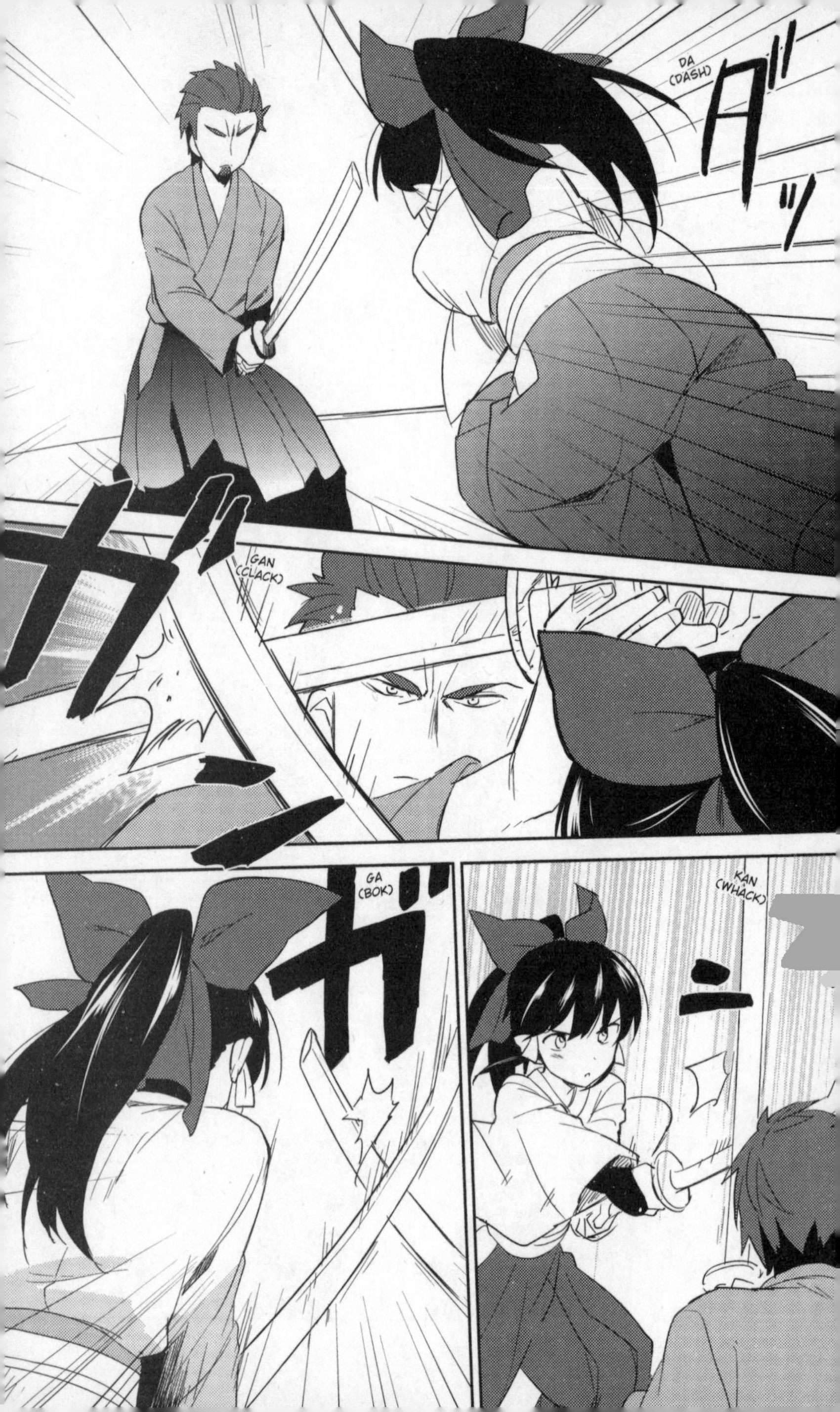
DA
(DASH)
GAN
(CLACK)
KAN
(WHACK)
GA
(BOK)

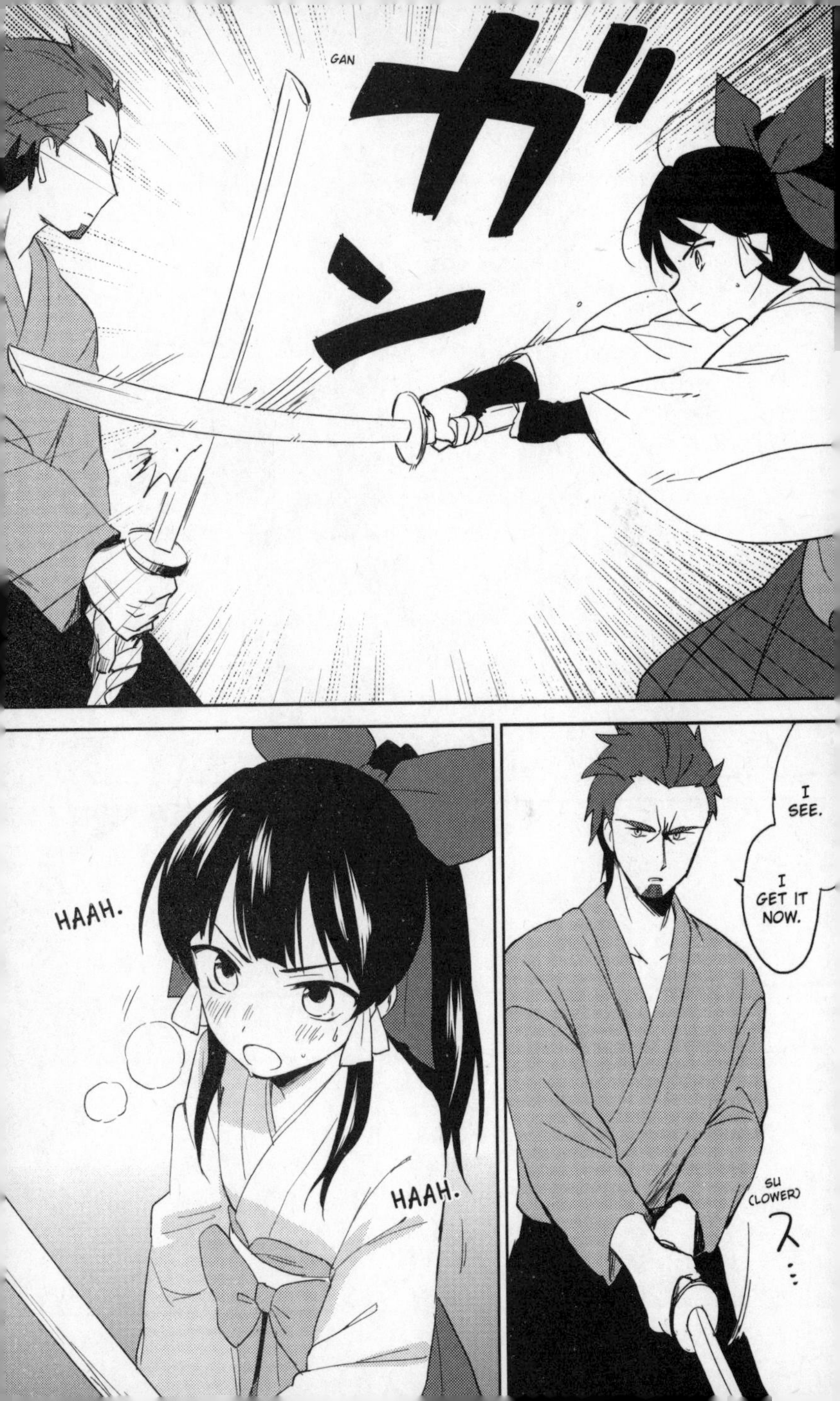
GAN
ガン
I SEE.
I GET IT NOW.
SU (LOWER)
ス…
HAAH.
HAAH.

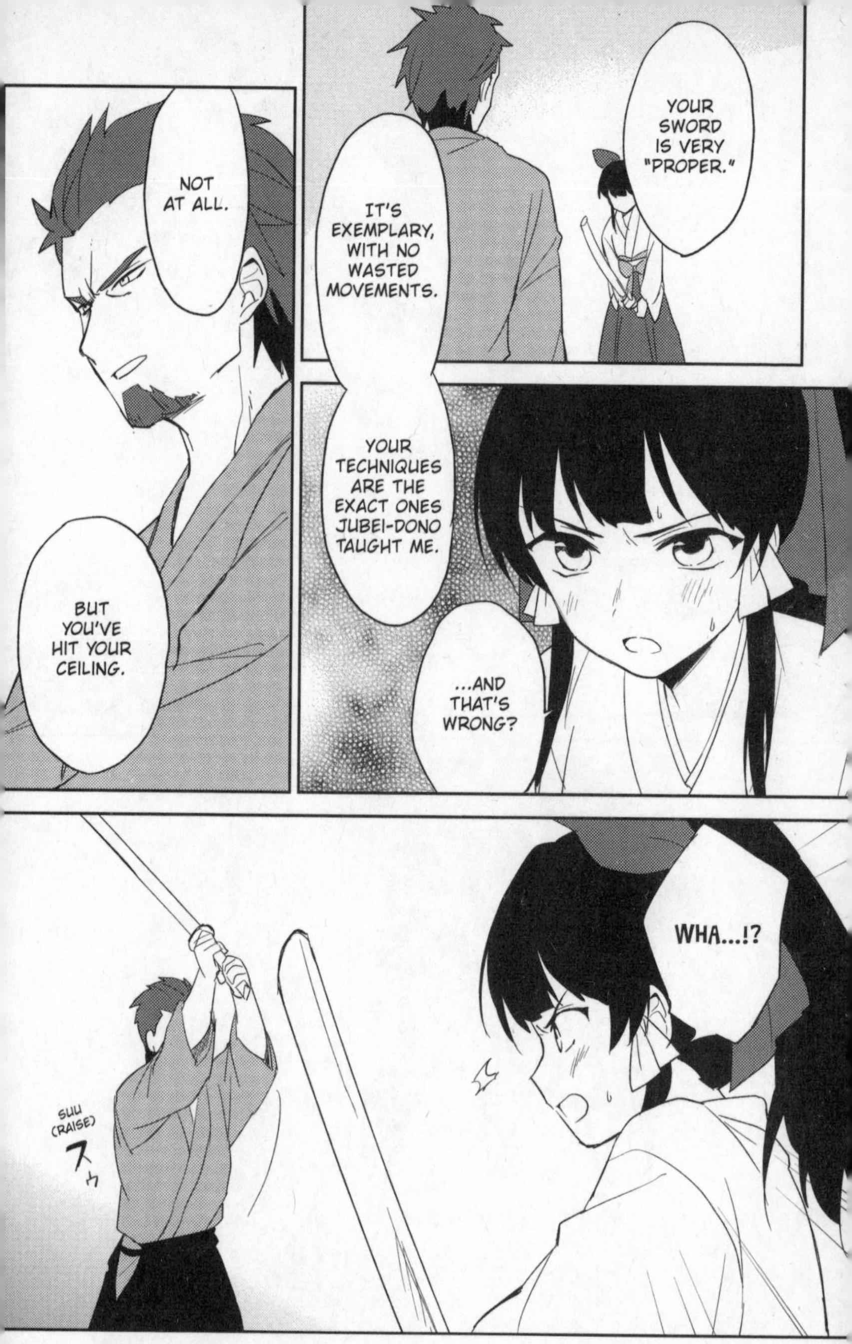
YOUR SWORD IS VERY "PROPER."
IT'S EXEMPLARY, WITH NO WASTED MOVEMENTS.
YOUR TECHNIQUES ARE THE EXACT ONES JUBEI-DONO TAUGHT ME.
...AND THAT'S WRONG?
NOT AT ALL.
BUT YOU'VE HIT YOUR CEILING.
WHA...!?
SUU (RAISE)
スゥ

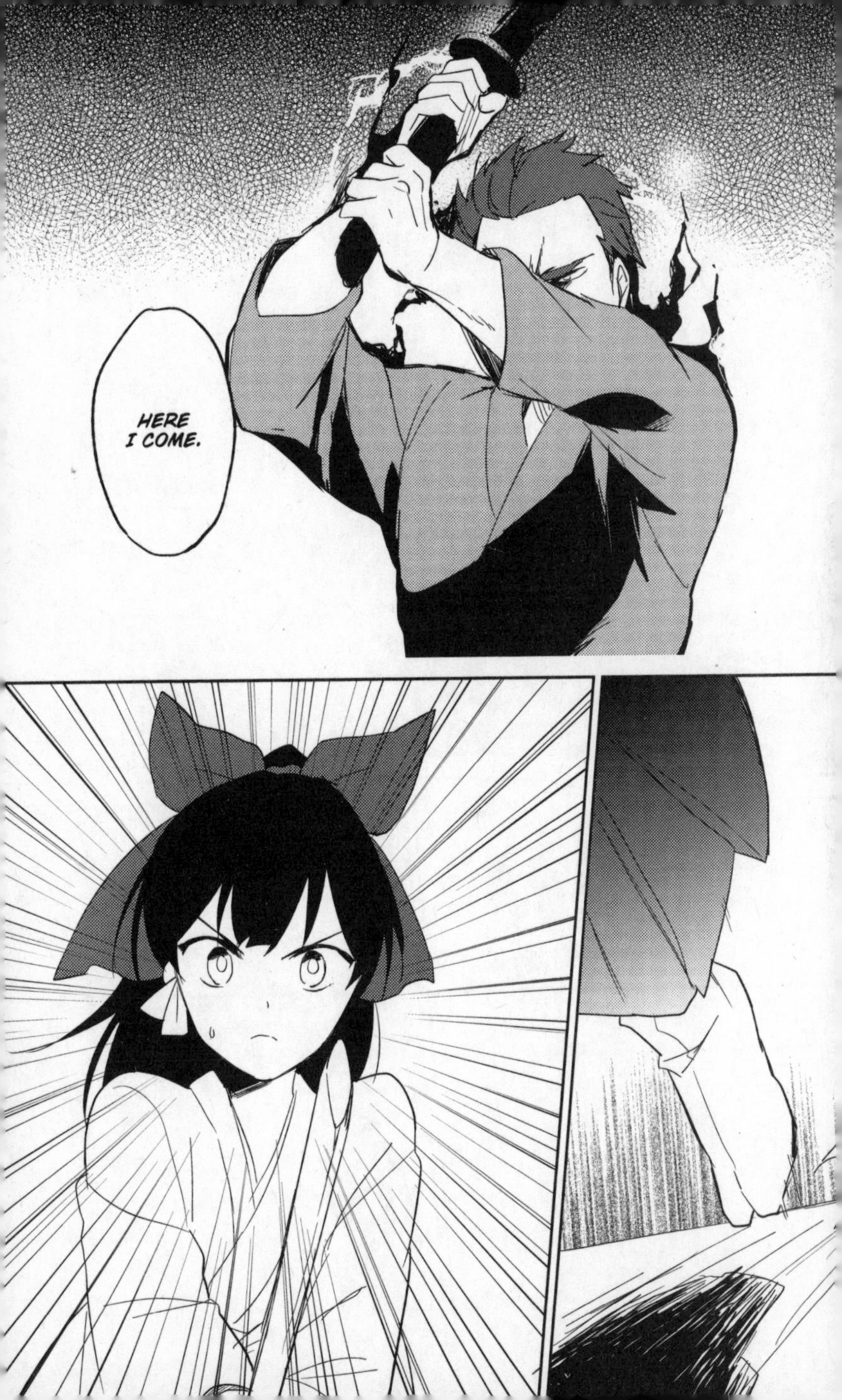
HERE I COME.

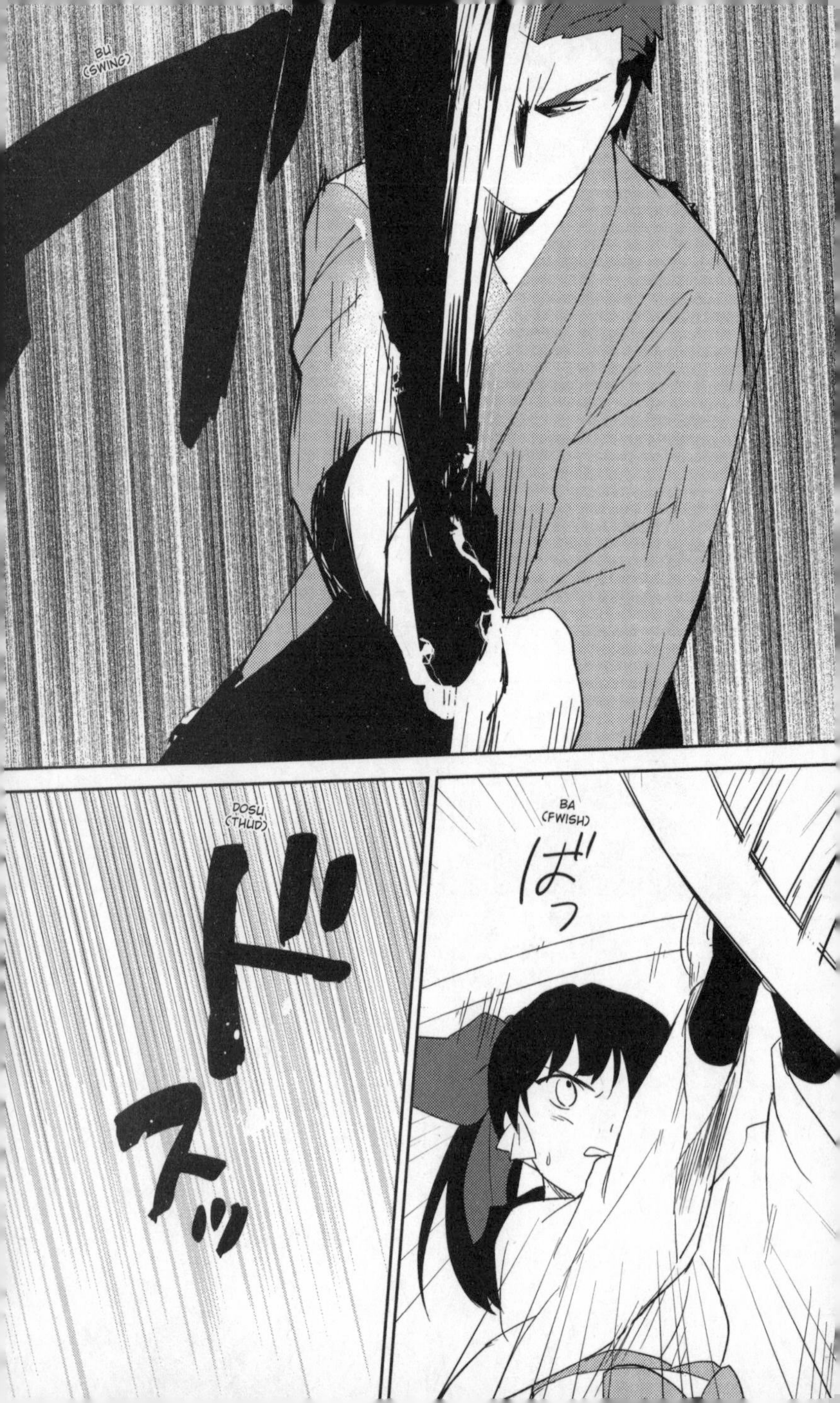
BU
(SWING)
BA
(FWISH)
ばっ
DOSU
(THUD)
ドスッ

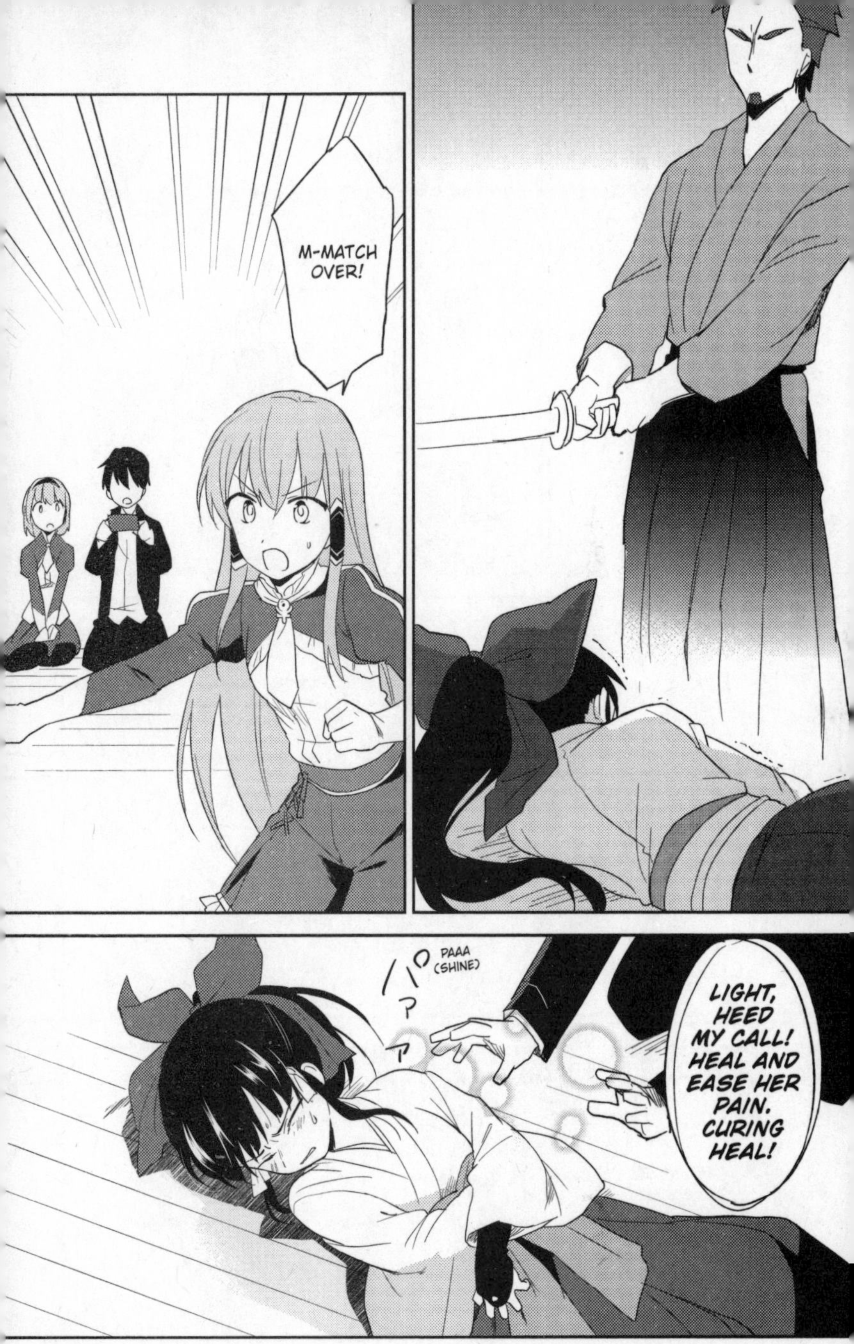
M-MATCH OVER!
LIGHT, HEED MY CALL! HEAL AND EASE HER PAIN. CURING HEAL!
パァァ
PAAA (SHINE)

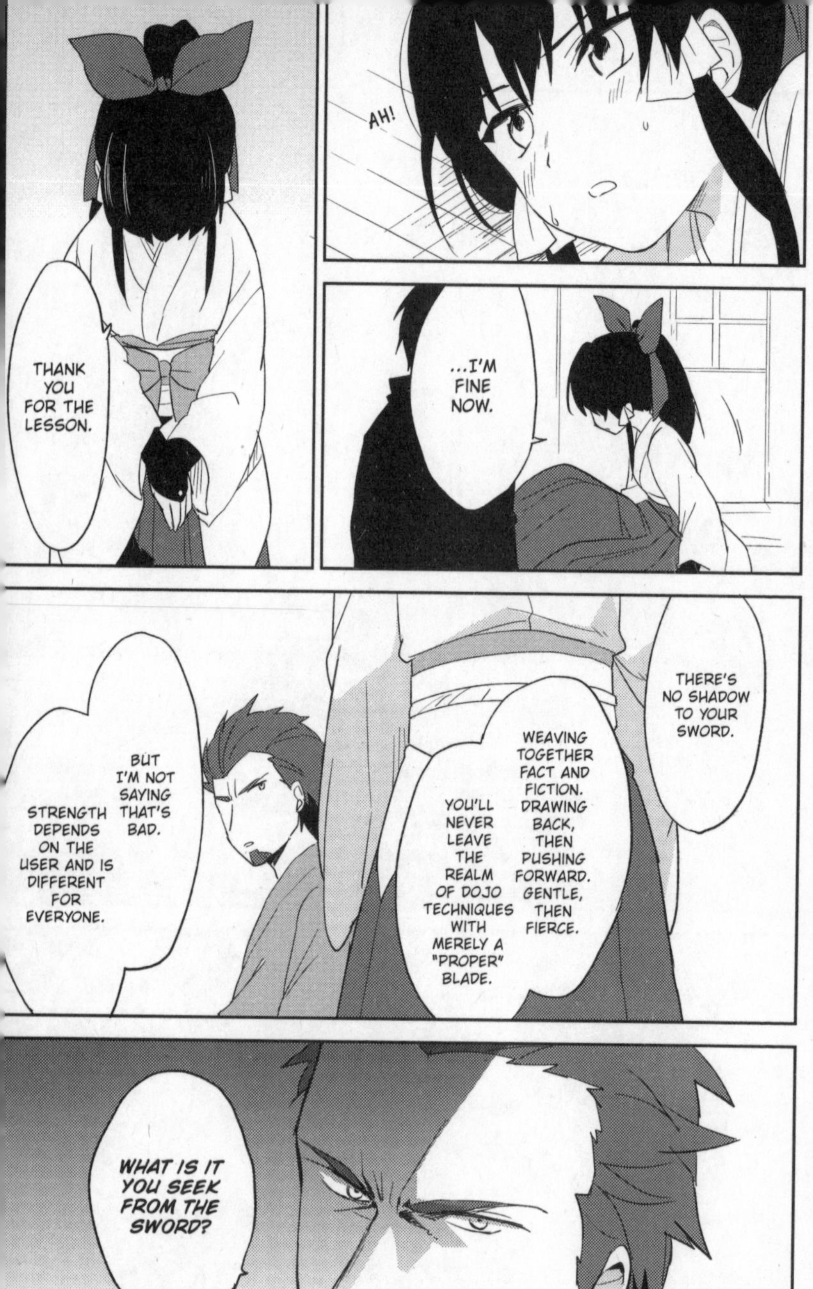
AH!
...I'M FINE NOW.
THANK YOU FOR THE LESSON.
THERE'S NO SHADOW TO YOUR SWORD.
WEAVING TOGETHER FACT AND FICTION. DRAWING BACK, THEN PUSHING FORWARD. GENTLE, THEN FIERCE.
YOU'LL NEVER LEAVE THE REALM OF DOJO TECHNIQUES WITH MERELY A "PROPER" BLADE.
BUT I'M NOT SAYING THAT'S BAD.
STRENGTH DEPENDS ON THE USER AND IS DIFFERENT FOR EVERYONE.
*WHAT IS IT YOU SEEK FROM THE SWORD?*

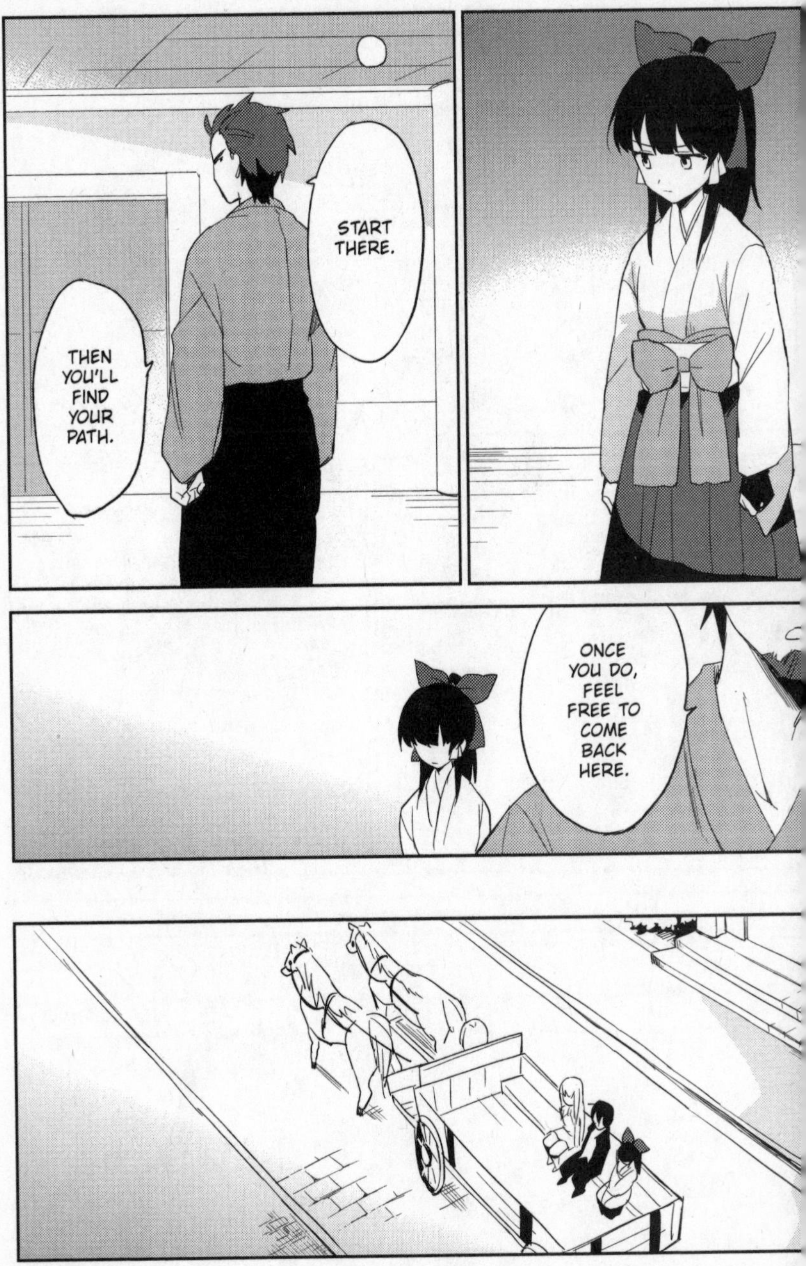
START THERE.
THEN YOU'LL FIND YOUR PATH.
ONCE YOU DO, FEEL FREE TO COME BACK HERE.

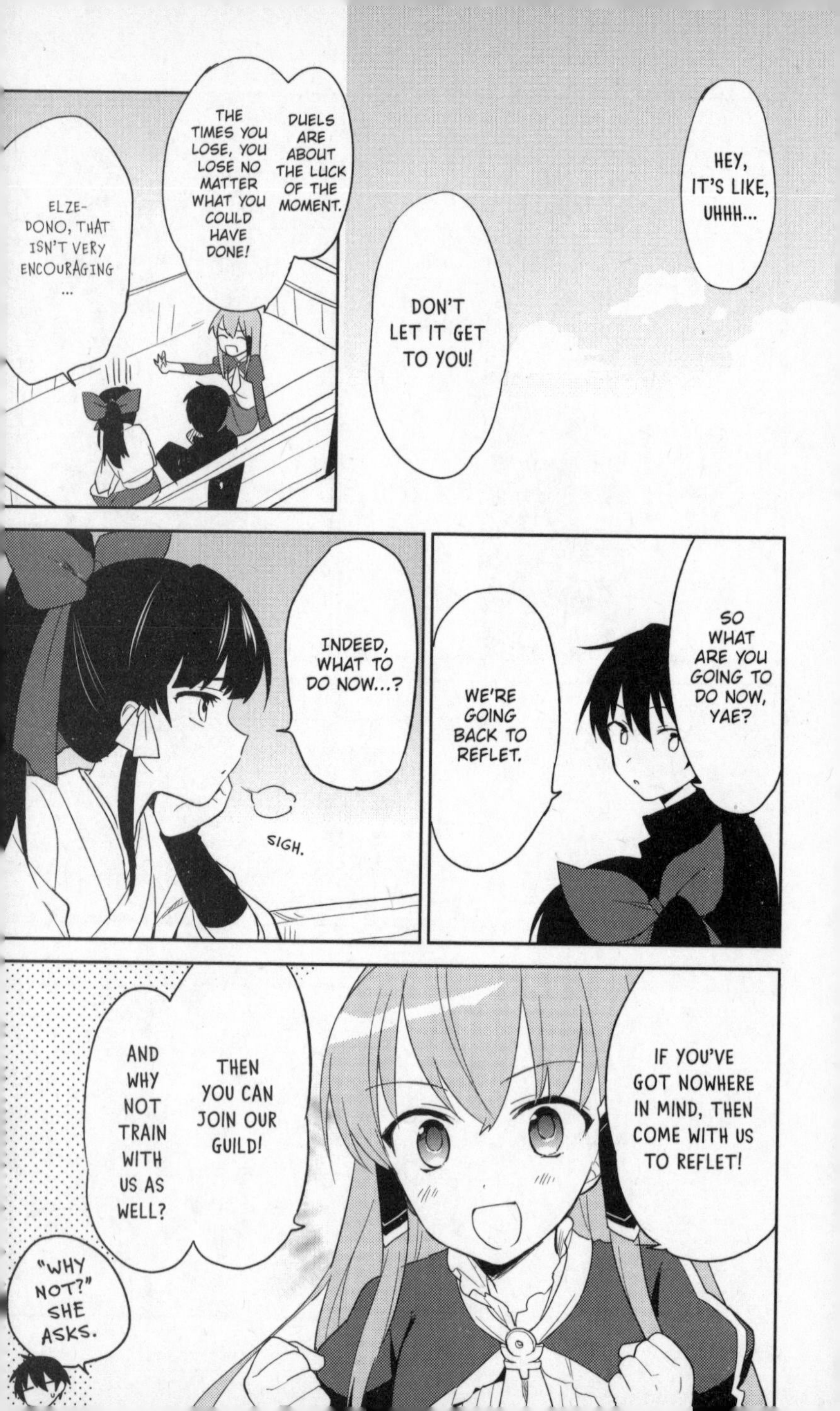

HEY, IT'S LIKE, UHHH...
DON'T LET IT GET TO YOU!
DUELS ARE ABOUT THE LUCK OF THE MOMENT.
THE TIMES YOU LOSE, YOU LOSE NO MATTER WHAT YOU COULD HAVE DONE!
ELZE-DONO, THAT ISN'T VERY ENCOURAGING...
SO WHAT ARE YOU GOING TO DO NOW, YAE?
WE'RE GOING BACK TO REFLET.
INDEED, WHAT TO DO NOW...?
SIGH.
IF YOU'VE GOT NOWHERE IN MIND, THEN COME WITH US TO REFLET!
THEN YOU CAN JOIN OUR GUILD!
AND WHY NOT TRAIN WITH US AS WELL?
"WHY NOT?" SHE ASKS.

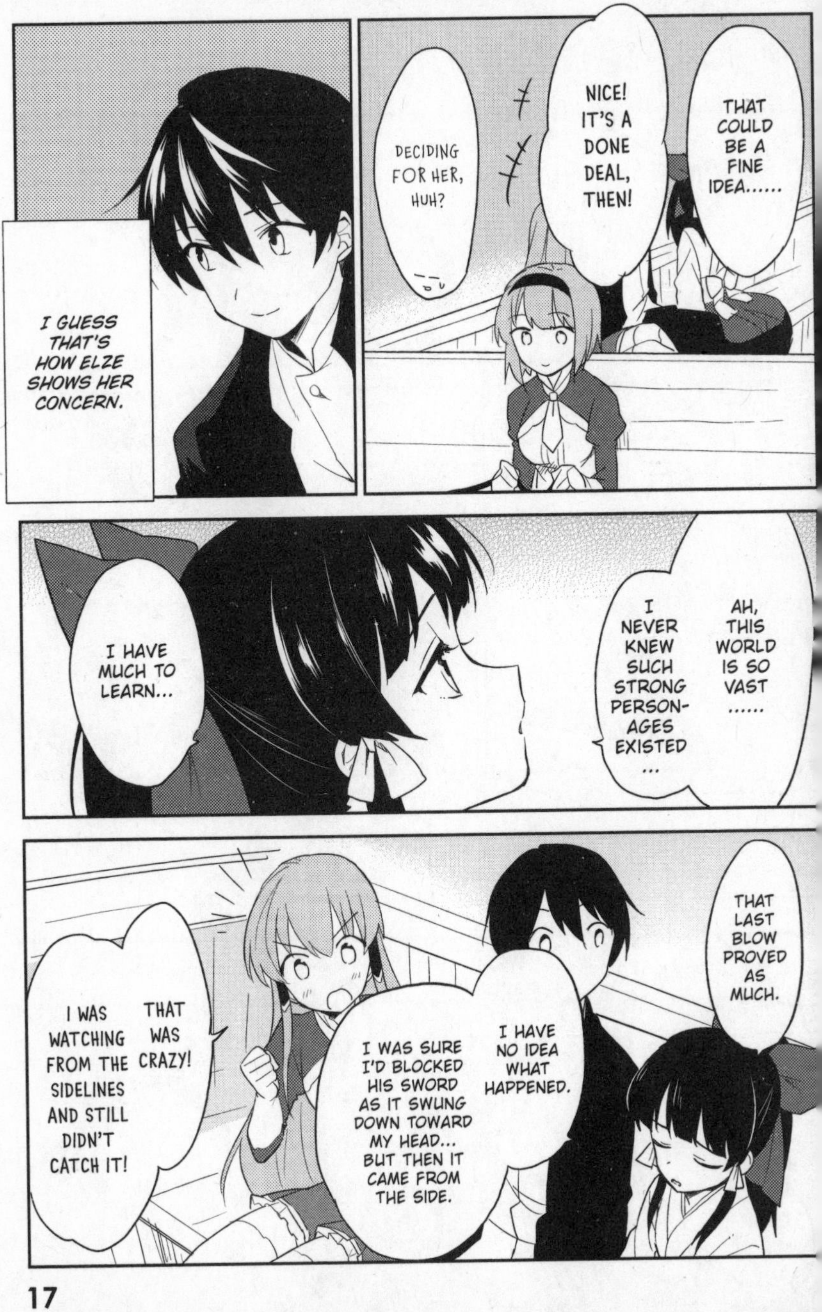
THAT COULD BE A FINE IDEA......
NICE! IT'S A DONE DEAL, THEN!
DECIDING FOR HER, HUH?
I GUESS THAT'S HOW ELZE SHOWS HER CONCERN.
AH, THIS WORLD IS SO VAST......
I NEVER KNEW SUCH STRONG PERSON-AGES EXISTED...
I HAVE MUCH TO LEARN...
THAT LAST BLOW PROVED AS MUCH.
I HAVE NO IDEA WHAT HAPPENED.
I WAS SURE I'D BLOCKED HIS SWORD AS IT SWUNG DOWN TOWARD MY HEAD... BUT THEN IT CAME FROM THE SIDE.
THAT WAS CRAZY!
I WAS WATCHING FROM THE SIDELINES AND STILL DIDN'T CATCH IT!

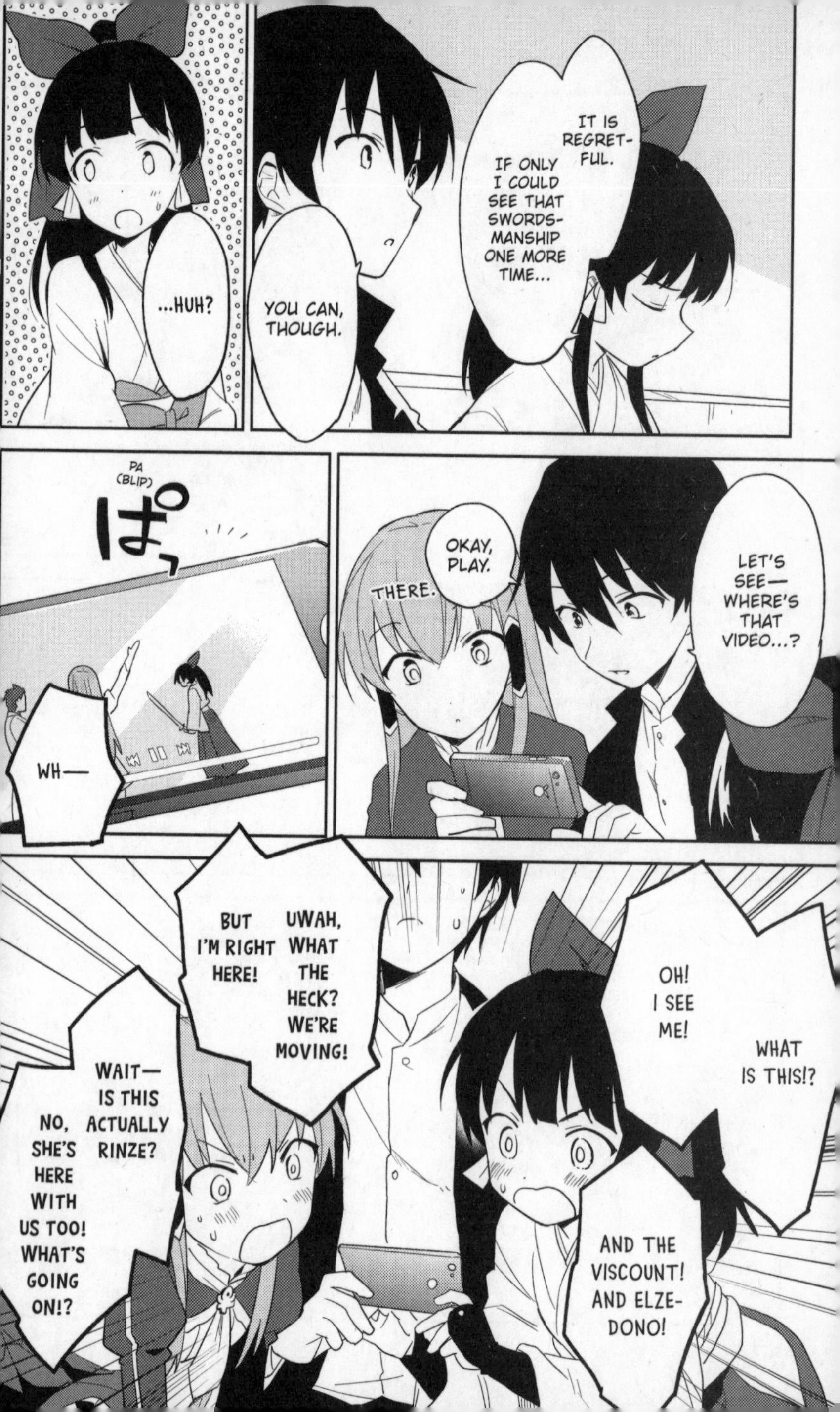
IT IS REGRETFUL.
IF ONLY I COULD SEE THAT SWORDSMANSHIP ONE MORE TIME...
YOU CAN, THOUGH.
...HUH?
LET'S SEE— WHERE'S THAT VIDEO...?
OKAY, PLAY.
THERE.
PA (BLIP)
ぱっ
WH—
OH! I SEE ME!
WHAT IS THIS!?
AND THE VISCOUNT! AND ELZE-DONO!
UWAH, WHAT THE HECK? WE'RE MOVING!
BUT I'M RIGHT HERE!
WAIT— IS THIS ACTUALLY RINZE?
NO, SHE'S HERE WITH US TOO! WHAT'S GOING ON!?

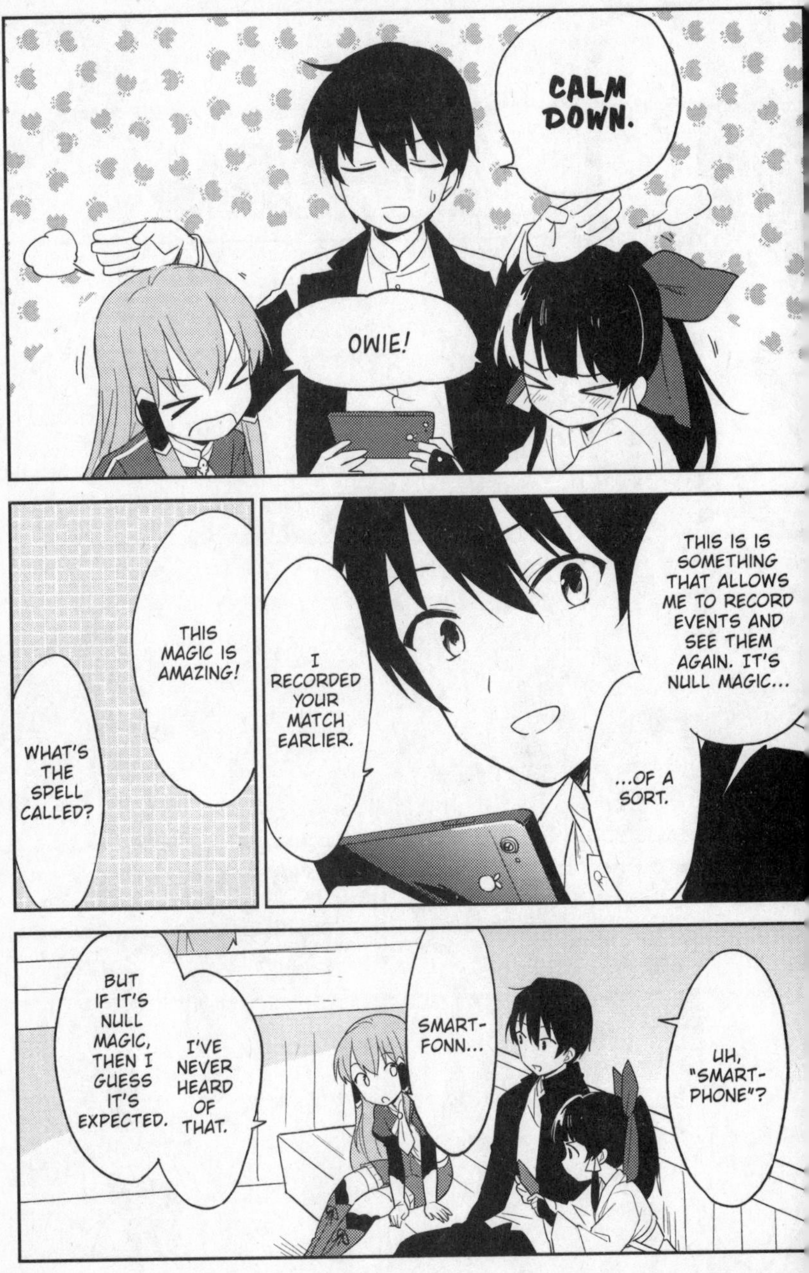
CALM DOWN.
OWIE!
THIS IS IS SOMETHING THAT ALLOWS ME TO RECORD EVENTS AND SEE THEM AGAIN. IT'S NULL MAGIC...
...OF A SORT.
I RECORDED YOUR MATCH EARLIER.
THIS MAGIC IS AMAZING!
WHAT'S THE SPELL CALLED?
UH, "SMART-PHONE"?
SMART-FONN...
I'VE NEVER HEARD OF THAT.
BUT IF IT'S NULL MAGIC, THEN I GUESS IT'S EXPECTED.

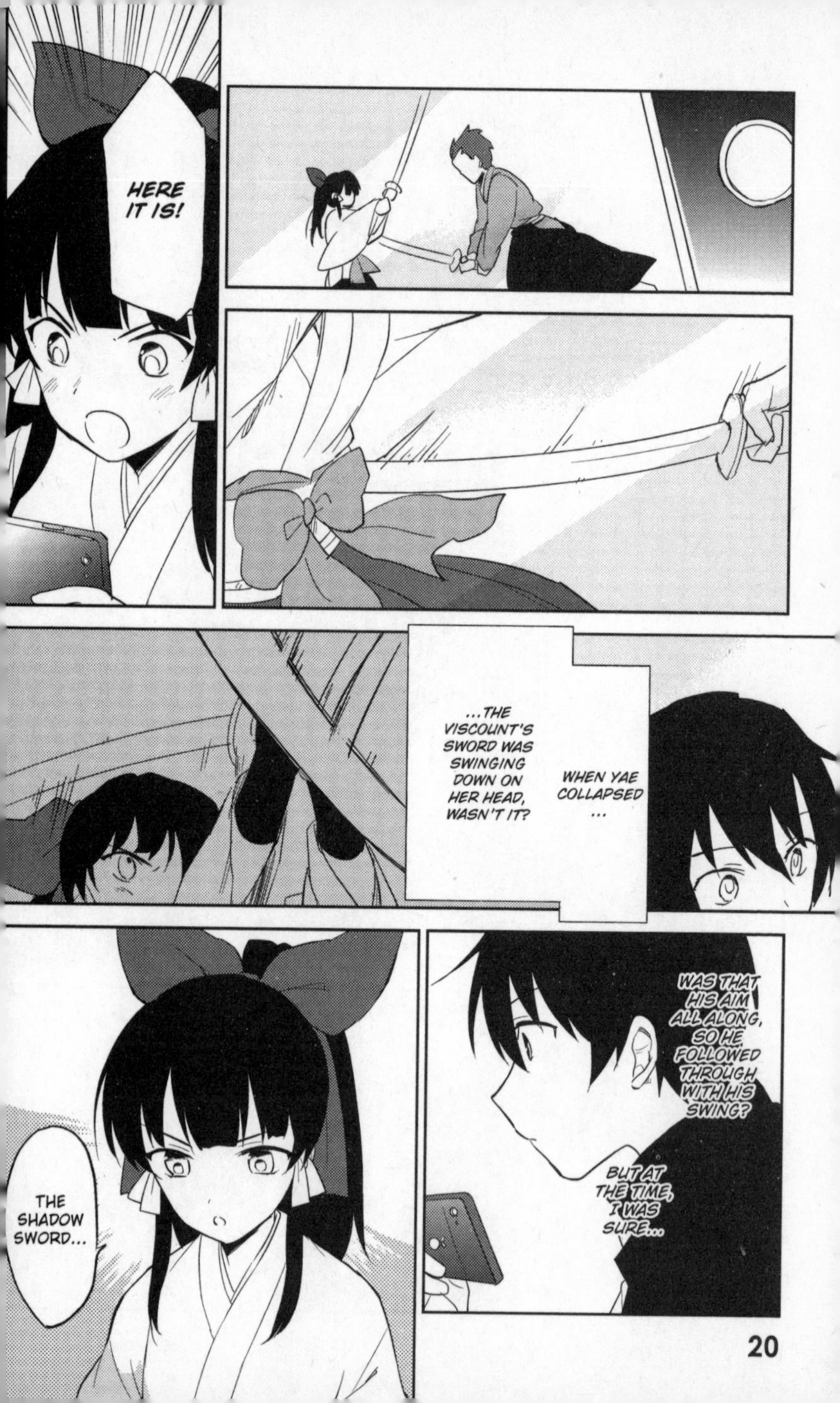
HERE IT IS!
WHEN YAE COLLAPSED ...
...THE VISCOUNT'S SWORD WAS SWINGING DOWN ON HER HEAD, WASN'T IT?
WAS THAT HIS AIM ALL ALONG, SO HE FOLLOWED THROUGH WITH HIS SWING?
BUT AT THE TIME, I WAS SURE...
THE SHADOW SWORD...

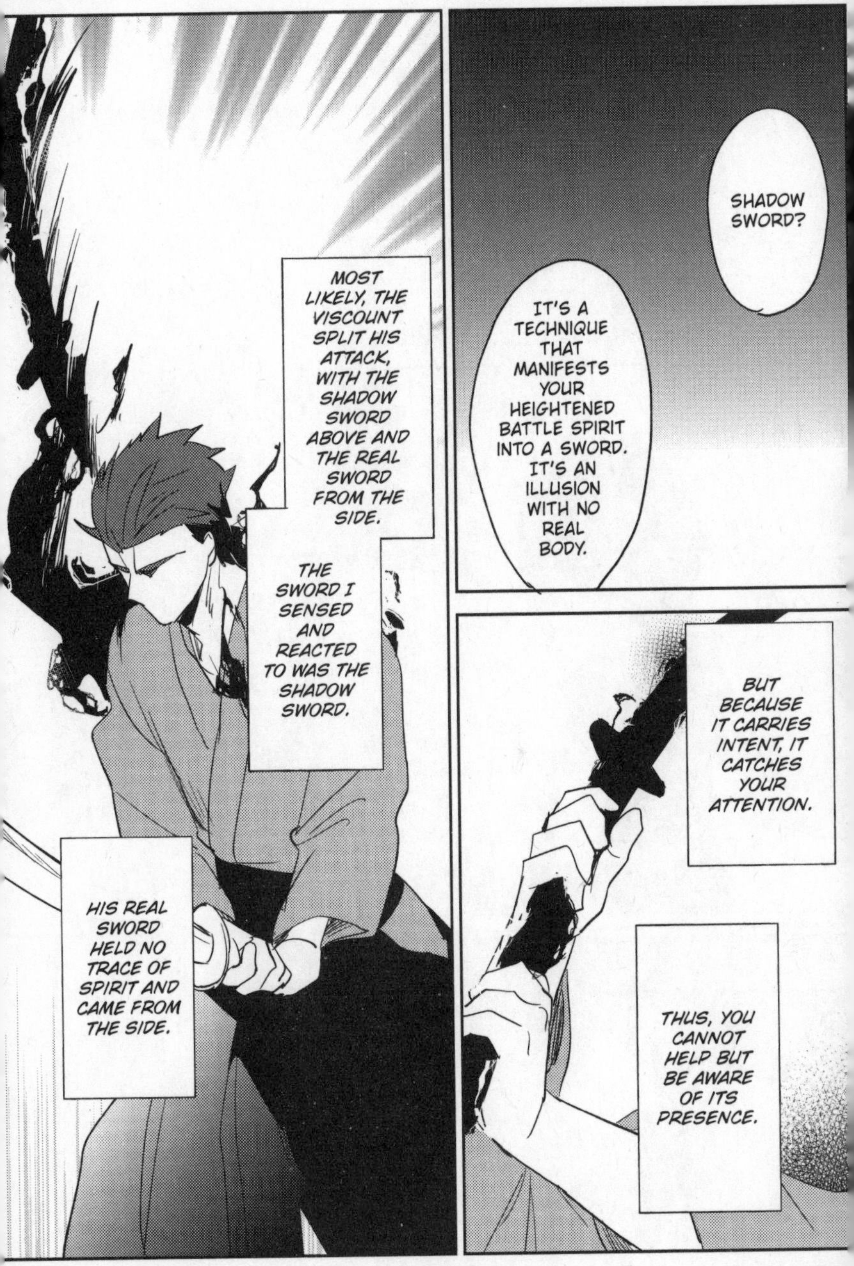
SHADOW SWORD?
IT'S A TECHNIQUE THAT MANIFESTS YOUR HEIGHTENED BATTLE SPIRIT INTO A SWORD. IT'S AN ILLUSION WITH NO REAL BODY.
BUT BECAUSE IT CARRIES INTENT, IT CATCHES YOUR ATTENTION.
THUS, YOU CANNOT HELP BUT BE AWARE OF ITS PRESENCE.
MOST LIKELY, THE VISCOUNT SPLIT HIS ATTACK, WITH THE SHADOW SWORD ABOVE AND THE REAL SWORD FROM THE SIDE.
THE SWORD I SENSED AND REACTED TO WAS THE SHADOW SWORD.
HIS REAL SWORD HELD NO TRACE OF SPIRIT AND CAME FROM THE SIDE.

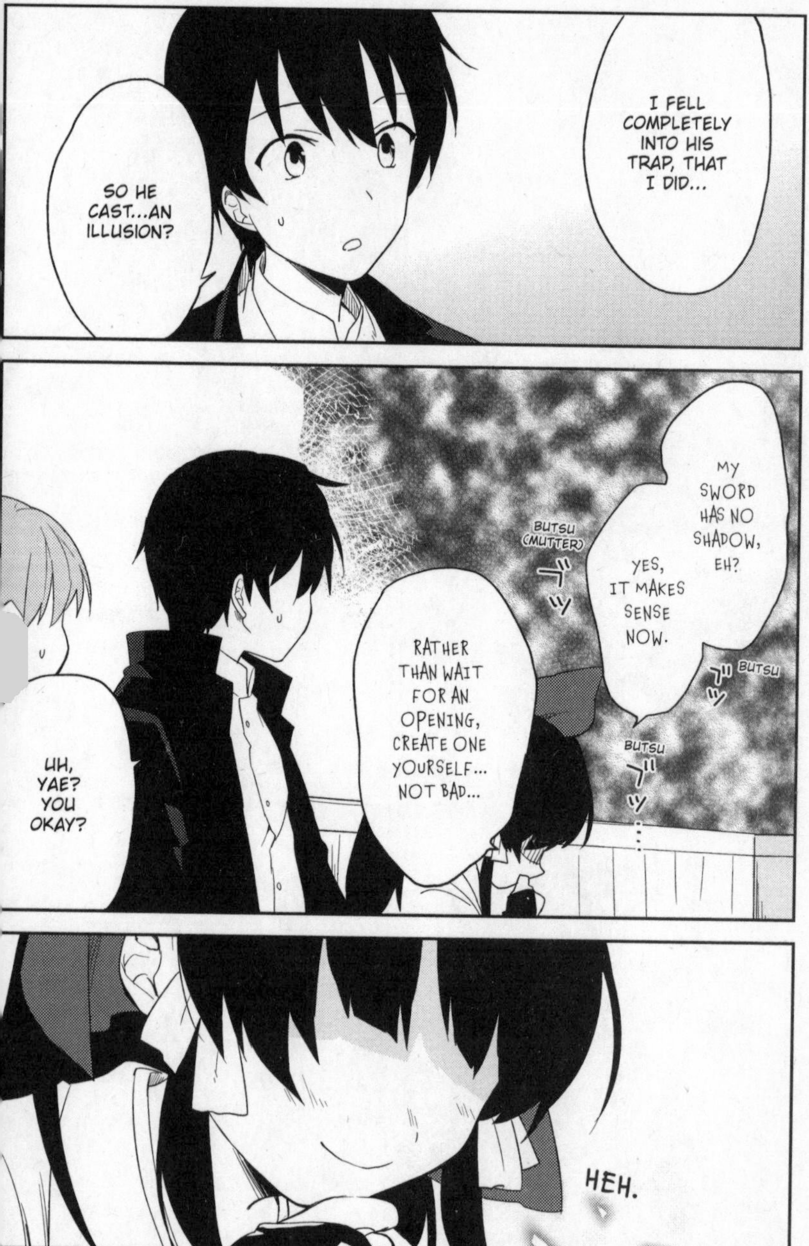
I FELL COMPLETELY INTO HIS TRAP, THAT I DID...
SO HE CAST...AN ILLUSION?
MY SWORD HAS NO SHADOW, EH?
BUTSU
YES, IT MAKES SENSE NOW.
BUTSU (MUTTER)
BUTSU
RATHER THAN WAIT FOR AN OPENING, CREATE ONE YOURSELF... NOT BAD...
UH, YAE? YOU OKAY?
HEH.

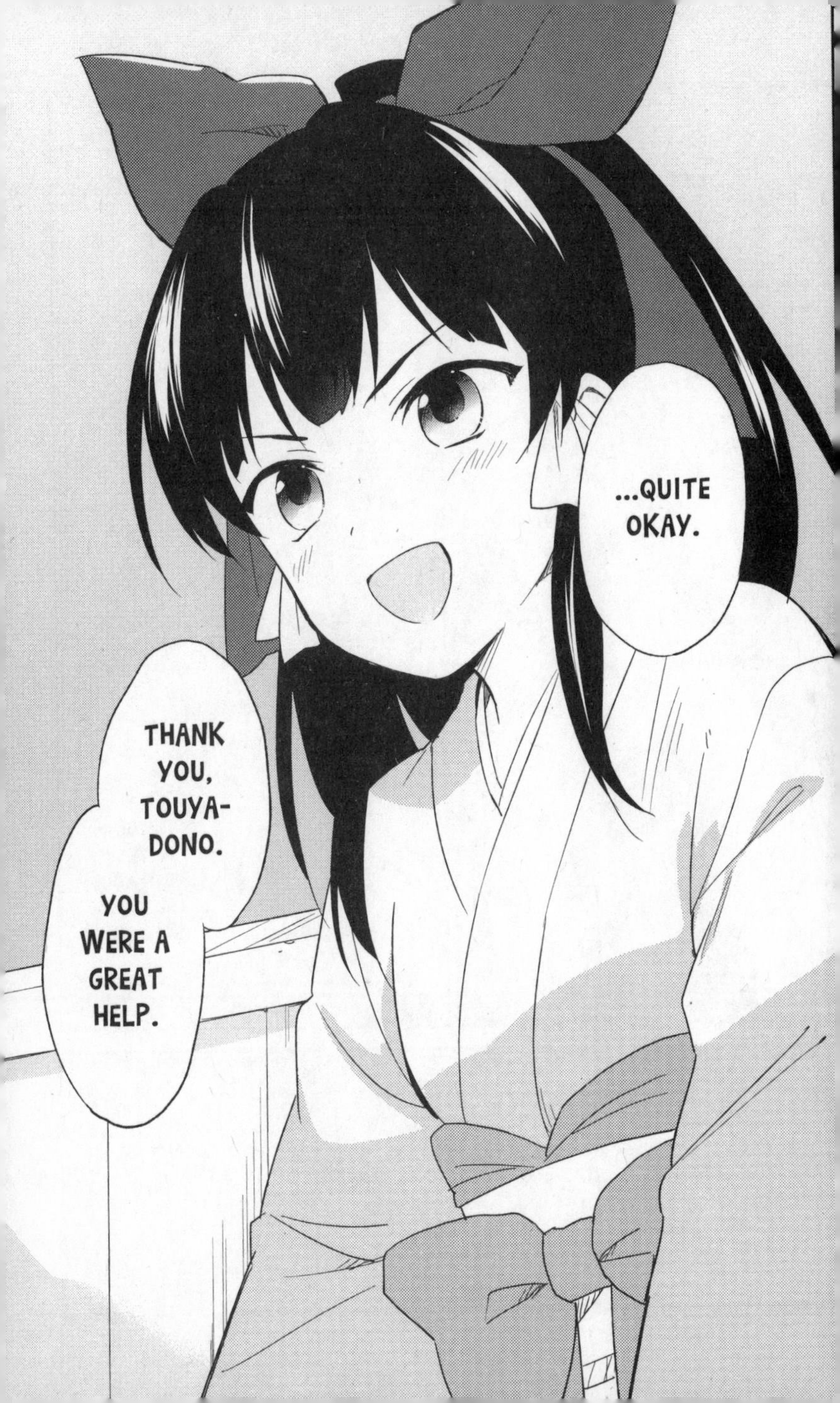
...QUITE OKAY.
THANK YOU, TOUYA-DONO.
YOU WERE A GREAT HELP.

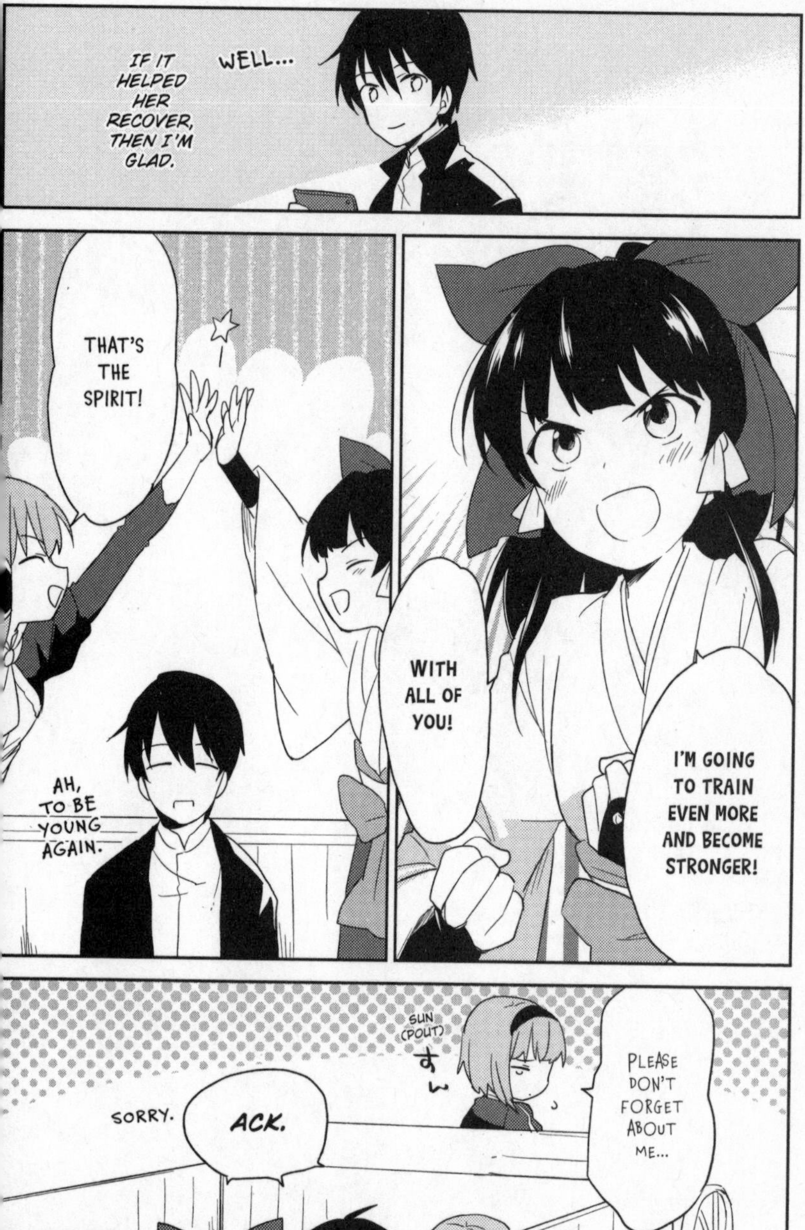
WELL...
IF IT HELPED HER RECOVER, THEN I'M GLAD.
I'M GOING TO TRAIN EVEN MORE AND BECOME STRONGER!
WITH ALL OF YOU!
THAT'S THE SPIRIT!
AH, TO BE YOUNG AGAIN.
PLEASE DON'T FORGET ABOUT ME...
SUN (POUT)
すん
ACK.
SORRY.
EPISODE: 05 »END

In Another World With
My Smartphone

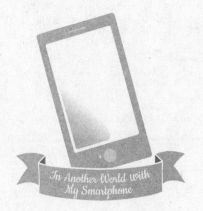

In Another World with My Smartphone

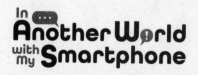

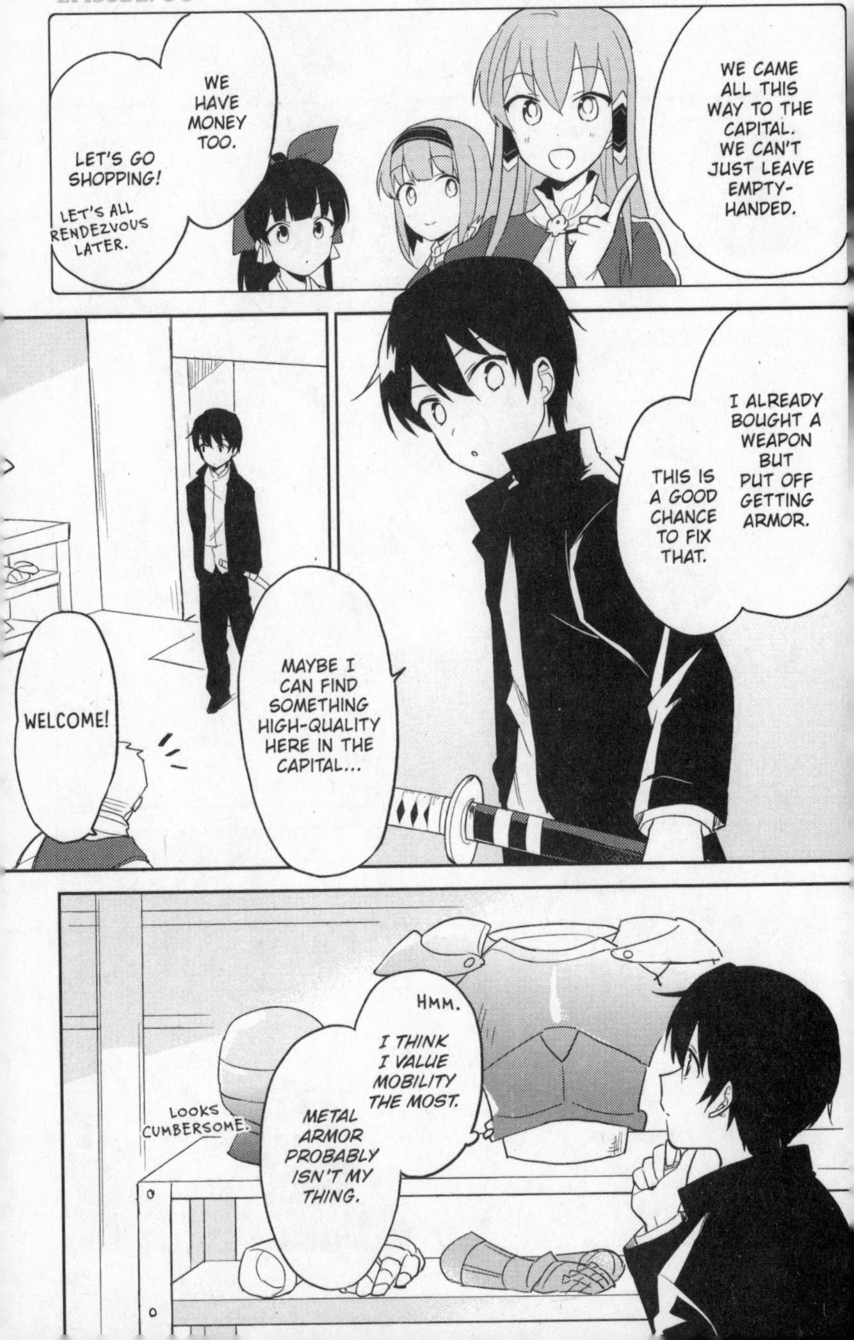
WE CAME ALL THIS WAY TO THE CAPITAL. WE CAN'T JUST LEAVE EMPTY-HANDED.
WE HAVE MONEY TOO.
LET'S GO SHOPPING!
LET'S ALL RENDEZVOUS LATER.
I ALREADY BOUGHT A WEAPON BUT PUT OFF GETTING ARMOR.
THIS IS A GOOD CHANCE TO FIX THAT.
MAYBE I CAN FIND SOMETHING HIGH-QUALITY HERE IN THE CAPITAL...
WELCOME!
HMM.
I THINK I VALUE MOBILITY THE MOST.
METAL ARMOR PROBABLY ISN'T MY THING.
LOOKS CUMBERSOME.

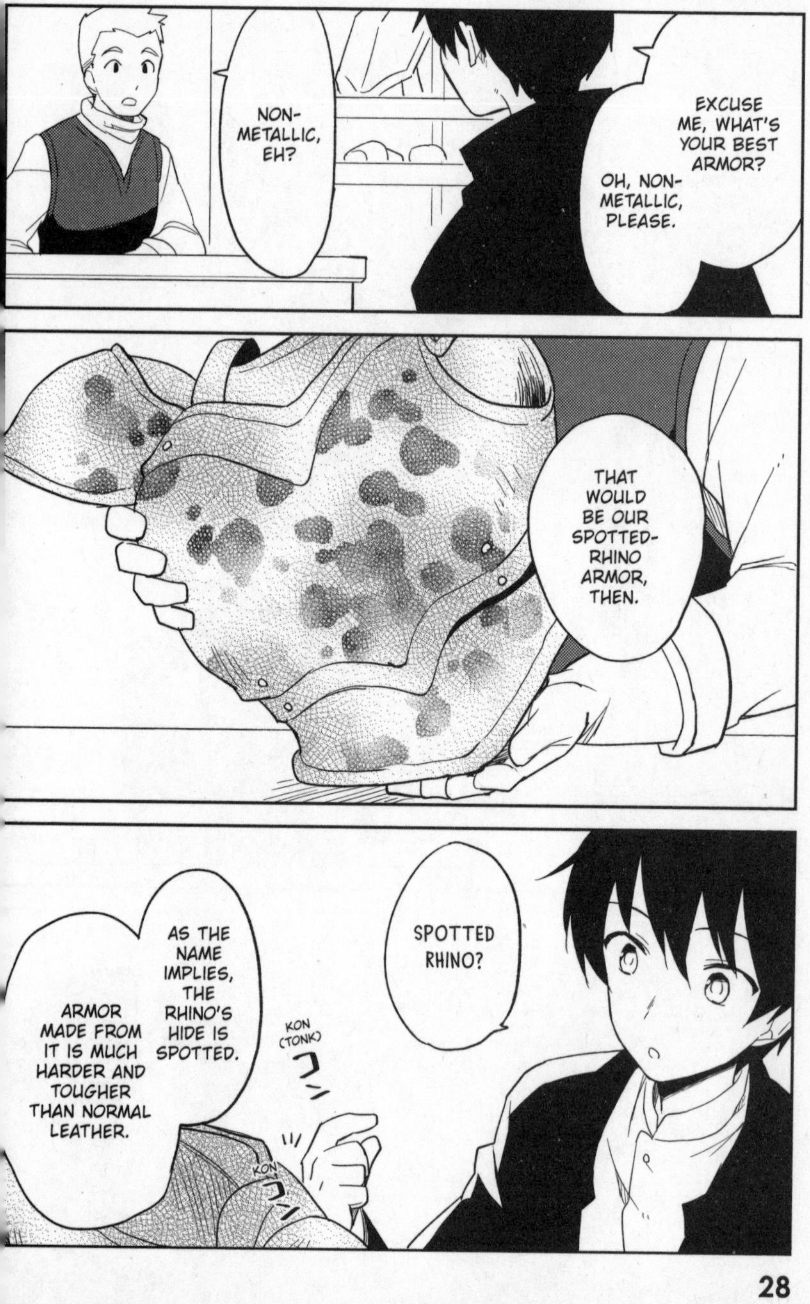
EXCUSE ME, WHAT'S YOUR BEST ARMOR?
OH, NON-METALLIC, PLEASE.
NON-METALLIC, EH?
THAT WOULD BE OUR SPOTTED-RHINO ARMOR, THEN.
SPOTTED RHINO?
AS THE NAME IMPLIES, THE RHINO'S HIDE IS SPOTTED.
KON (TONK)
ARMOR MADE FROM IT IS MUCH HARDER AND TOUGHER THAN NORMAL LEATHER.
KON

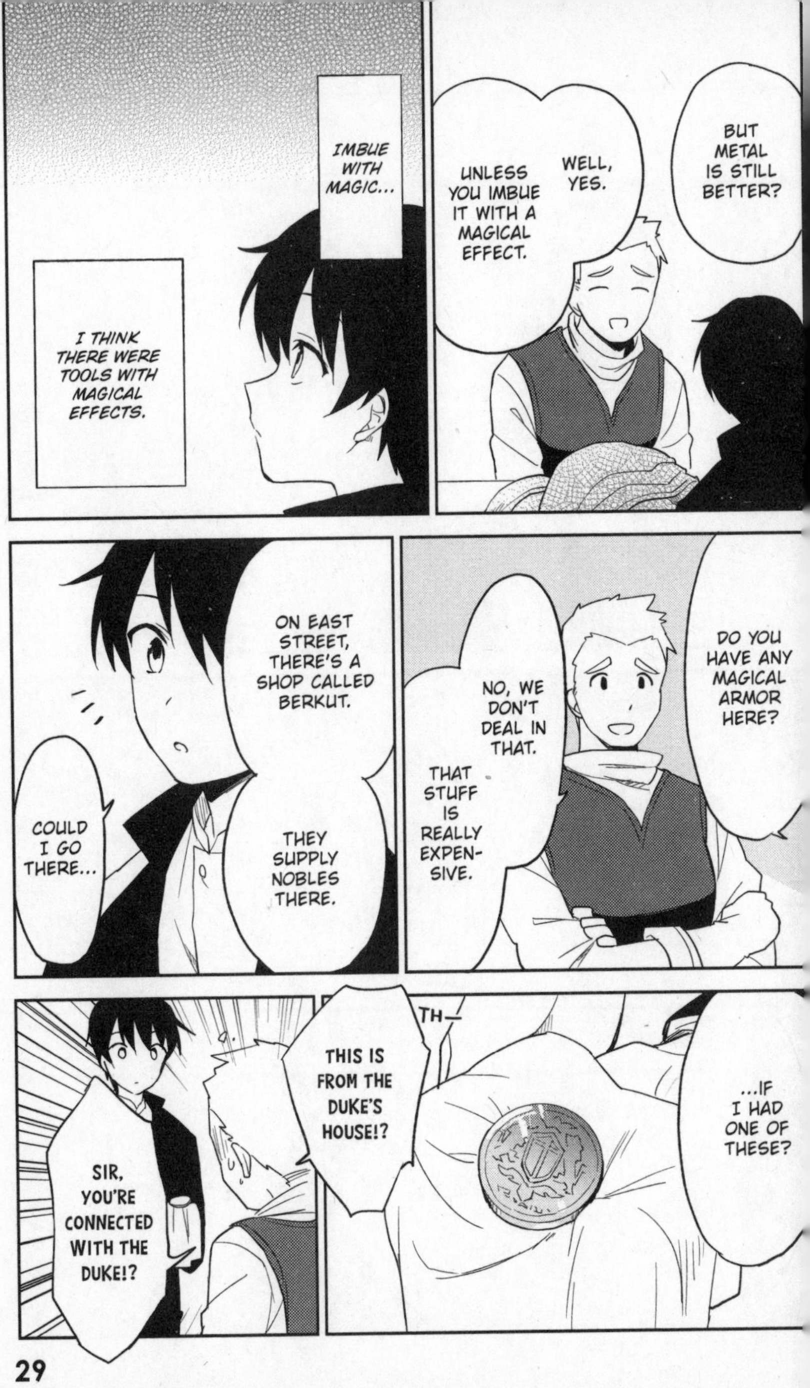
BUT METAL IS STILL BETTER?
WELL, YES.
UNLESS YOU IMBUE IT WITH A MAGICAL EFFECT.
IMBUE WITH MAGIC...
I THINK THERE WERE TOOLS WITH MAGICAL EFFECTS.
DO YOU HAVE ANY MAGICAL ARMOR HERE?
NO, WE DON'T DEAL IN THAT.
THAT STUFF IS REALLY EXPEN-SIVE.
ON EAST STREET, THERE'S A SHOP CALLED BERKUT.
THEY SUPPLY NOBLES THERE.
COULD I GO THERE...
...IF I HAD ONE OF THESE?
TH—
THIS IS FROM THE DUKE'S HOUSE!?
SIR, YOU'RE CONNECTED WITH THE DUKE!?

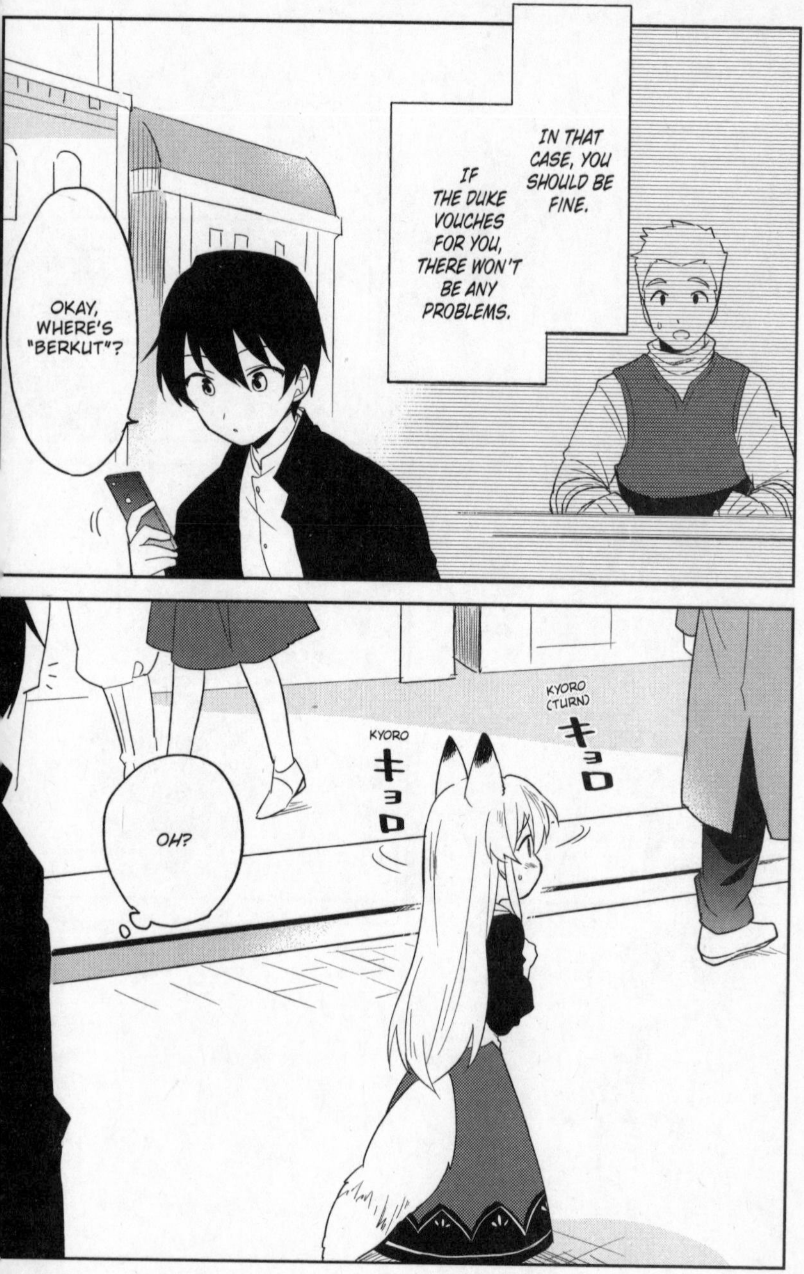
IN THAT CASE, YOU SHOULD BE FINE.
IF THE DUKE VOUCHES FOR YOU, THERE WON'T BE ANY PROBLEMS.
OKAY, WHERE'S "BERKUT"?
KYORO (TURN)
キョロ
KYORO
キョロ
OH?

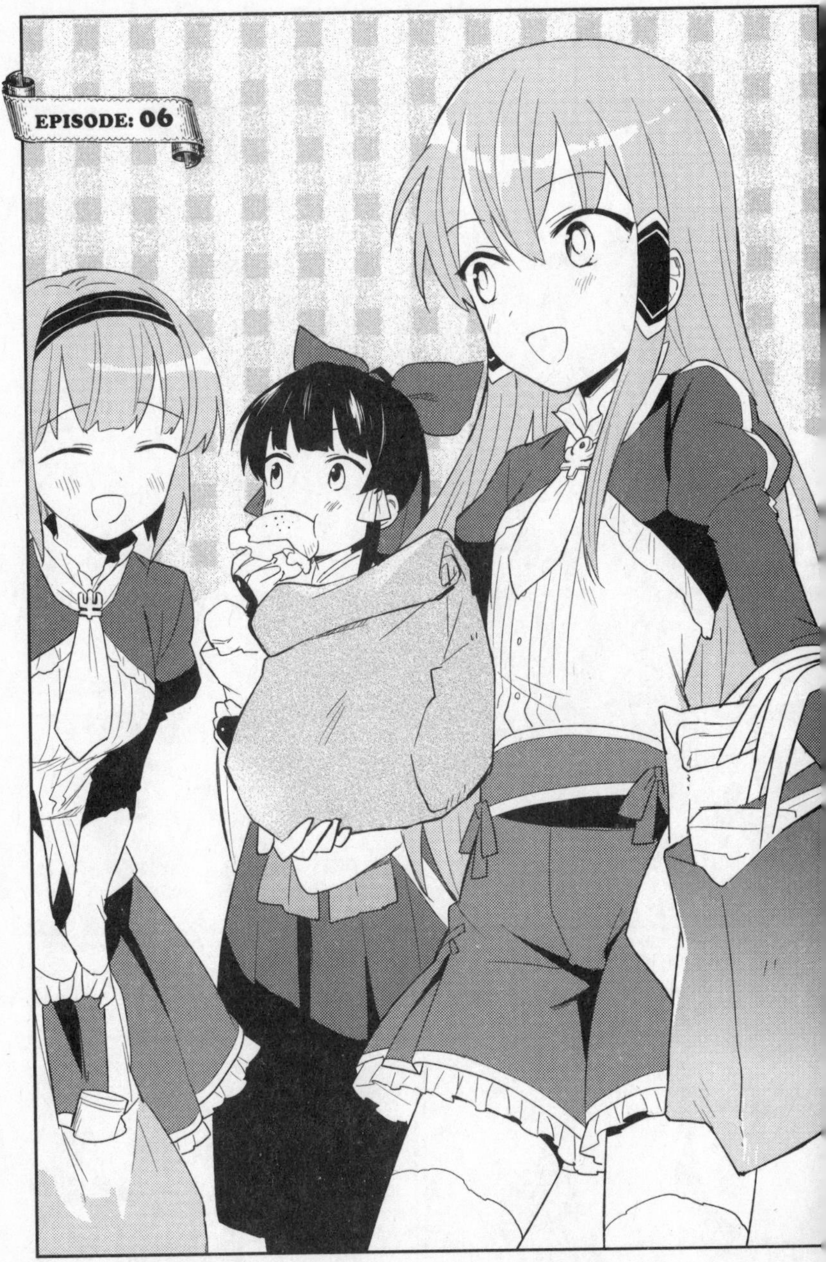
EPISODE: 06

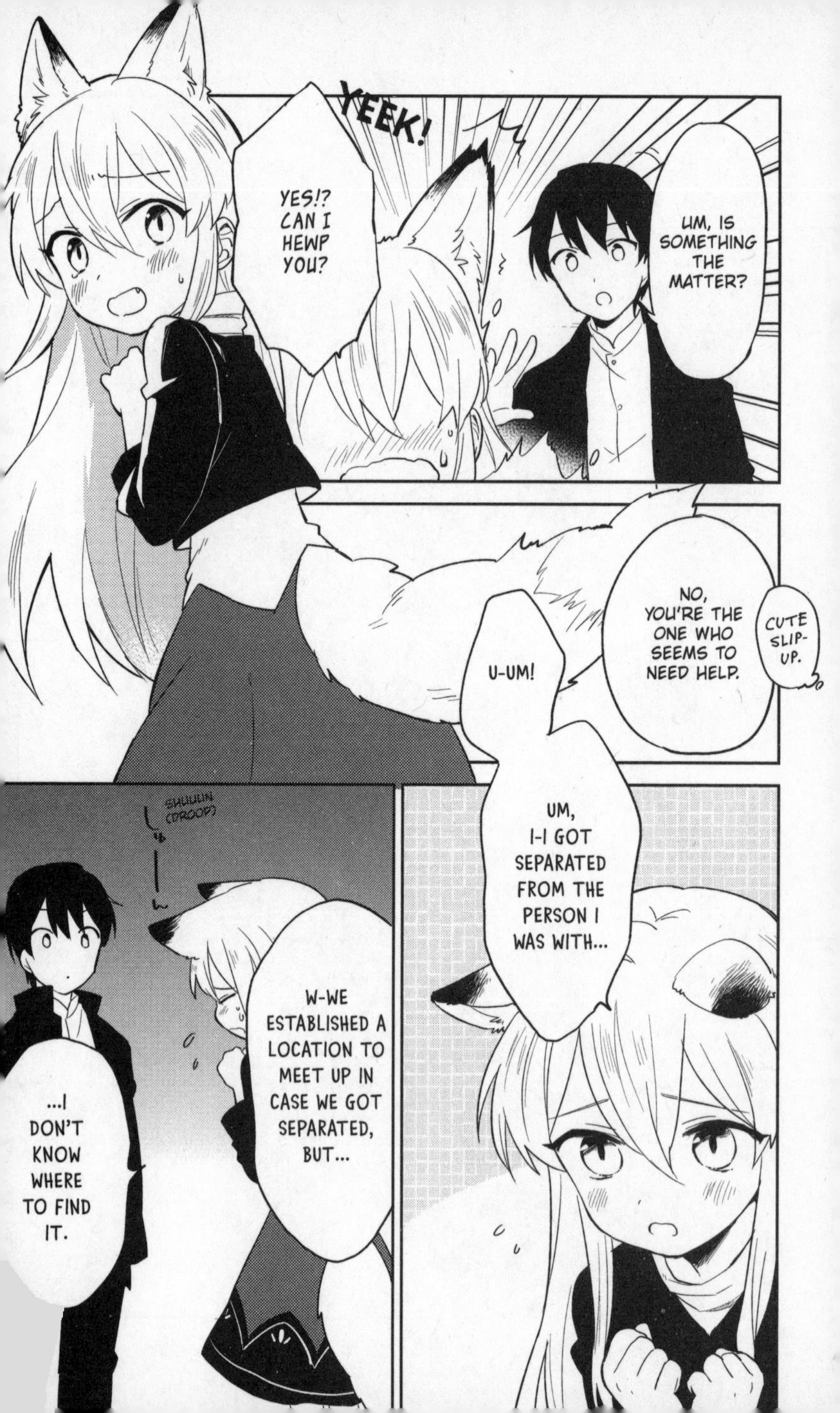
UM, IS SOMETHING THE MATTER?
YEEK!
YES!? CAN I HEWP YOU?
NO, YOU'RE THE ONE WHO SEEMS TO NEED HELP.
CUTE SLIP-UP.
U-UM!
UM, I-I GOT SEPARATED FROM THE PERSON I WAS WITH...
SHUUUN (DROOP)
W-WE ESTABLISHED A LOCATION TO MEET UP IN CASE WE GOT SEPARATED, BUT...
...I DON'T KNOW WHERE TO FIND IT.

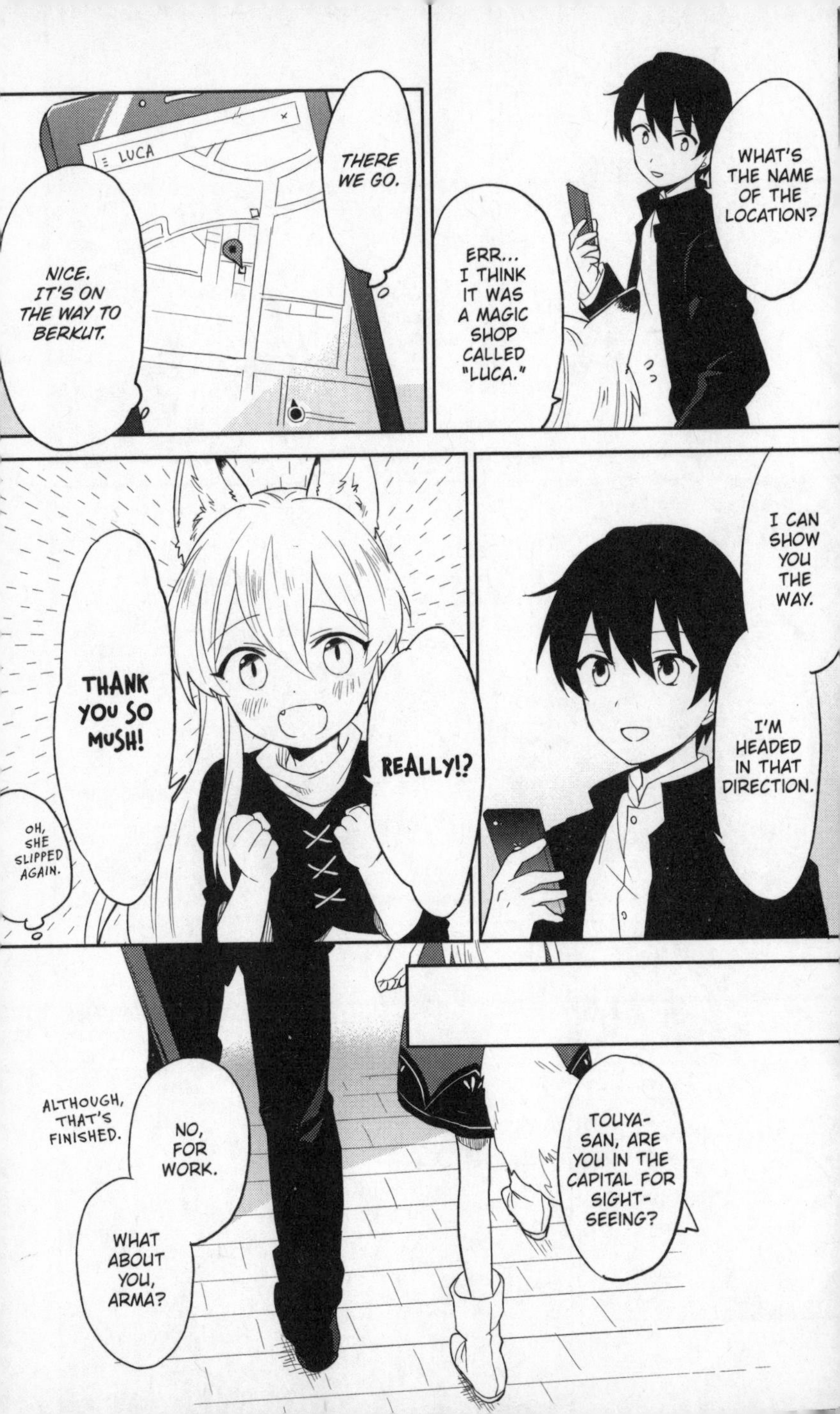
WHAT'S THE NAME OF THE LOCATION?
ERR... I THINK IT WAS A MAGIC SHOP CALLED "LUCA."
LUCA
THERE WE GO.
NICE. IT'S ON THE WAY TO BERKUT.
I CAN SHOW YOU THE WAY.
I'M HEADED IN THAT DIRECTION.
REALLY!?
THANK YOU SO MUSH!
OH, SHE SLIPPED AGAIN.
TOUYA-SAN, ARE YOU IN THE CAPITAL FOR SIGHT-SEEING?
NO, FOR WORK.
ALTHOUGH, THAT'S FINISHED.
WHAT ABOUT YOU, ARMA?

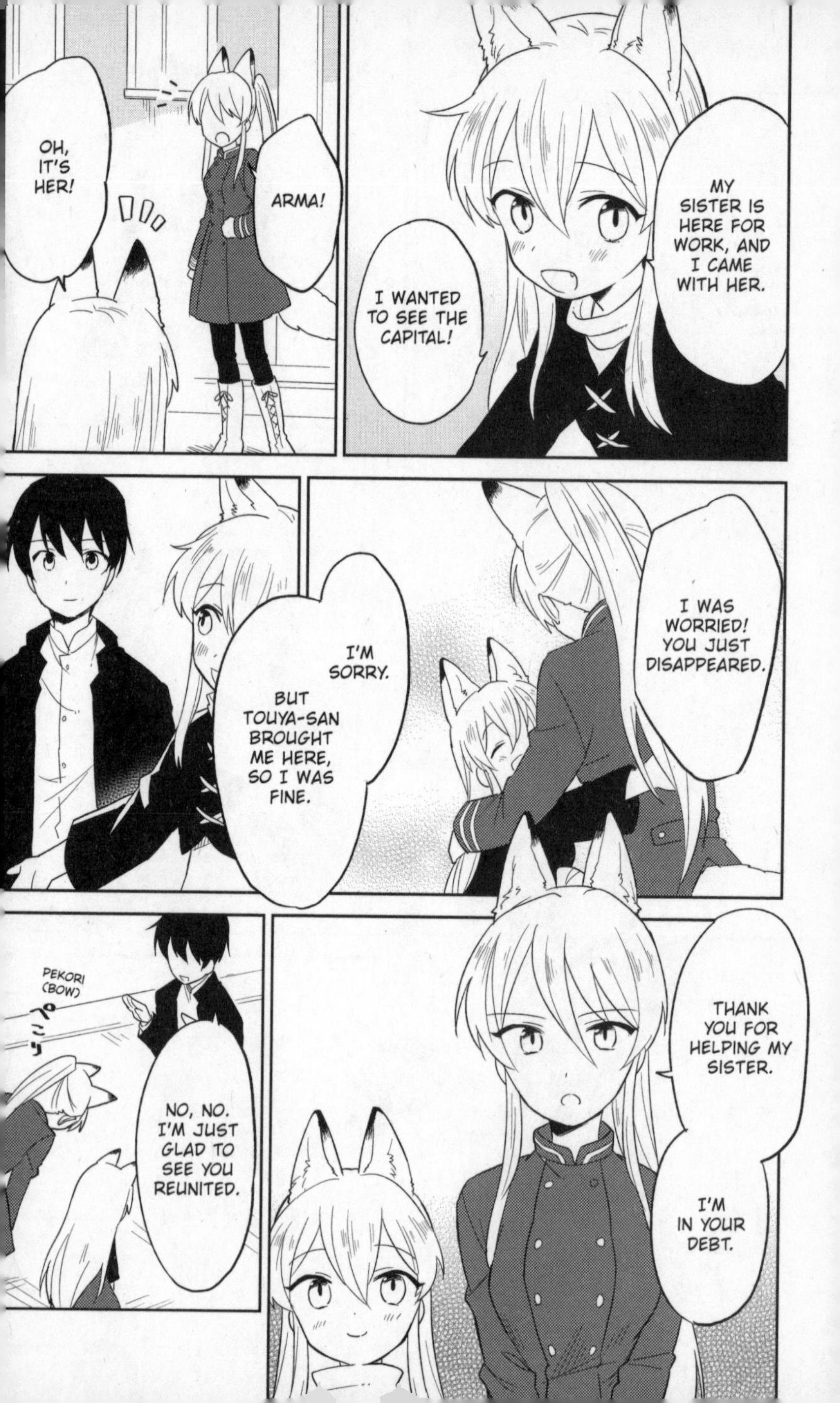
MY SISTER IS HERE FOR WORK, AND I CAME WITH HER.
I WANTED TO SEE THE CAPITAL!
ARMA!
OH, IT'S HER!
I WAS WORRIED! YOU JUST DISAPPEARED.
I'M SORRY.
BUT TOUYA-SAN BROUGHT ME HERE, SO I WAS FINE.
THANK YOU FOR HELPING MY SISTER.
I'M IN YOUR DEBT.
PEKORI (BOW)
NO, NO. I'M JUST GLAD TO SEE YOU REUNITED.

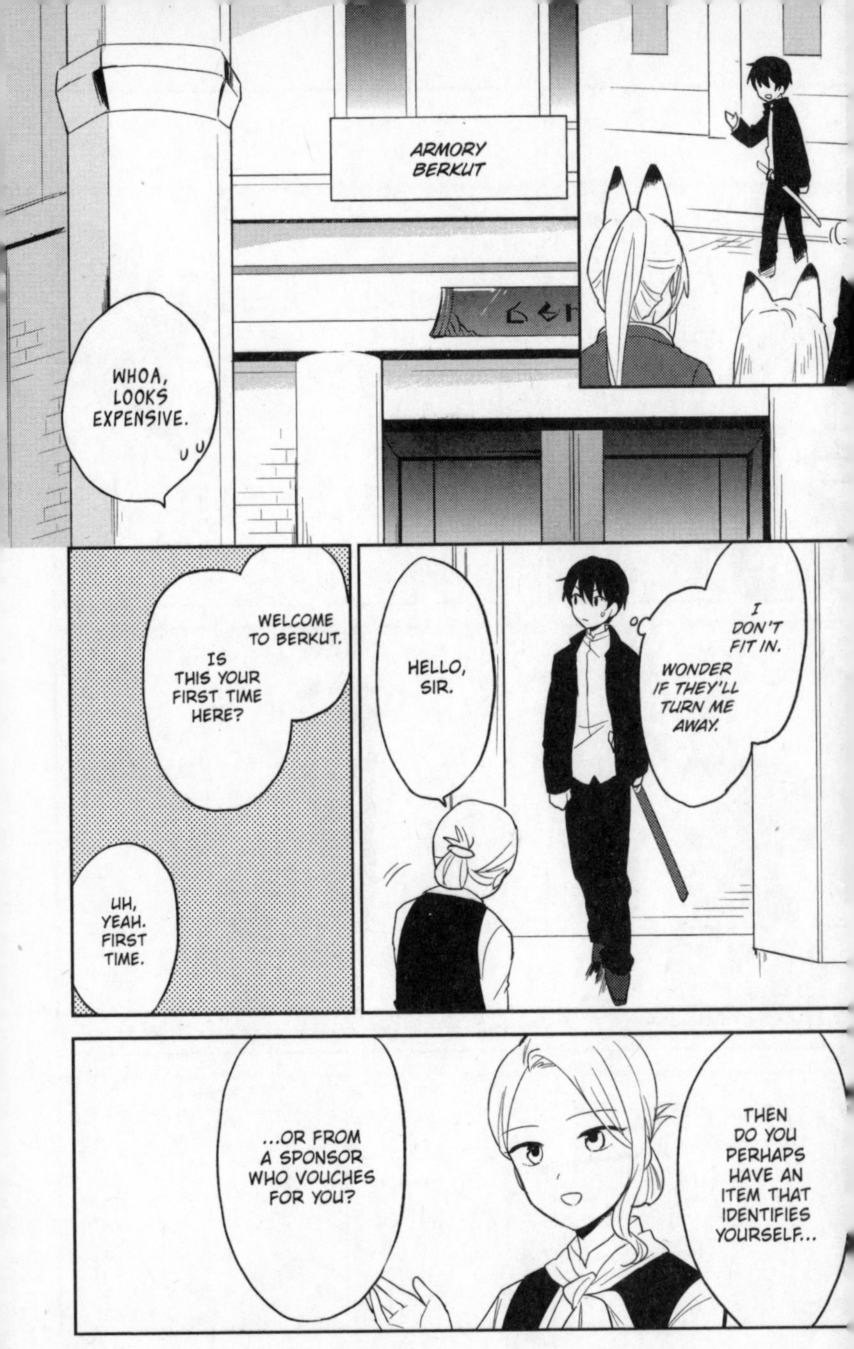
ARMORY BERKUT
WHOA, LOOKS EXPENSIVE.
I DON'T FIT IN.
WONDER IF THEY'LL TURN ME AWAY.
HELLO, SIR.
WELCOME TO BERKUT.
IS THIS YOUR FIRST TIME HERE?
UH, YEAH. FIRST TIME.
THEN DO YOU PERHAPS HAVE AN ITEM THAT IDENTIFIES YOURSELF...
...OR FROM A SPONSOR WHO VOUCHES FOR YOU?

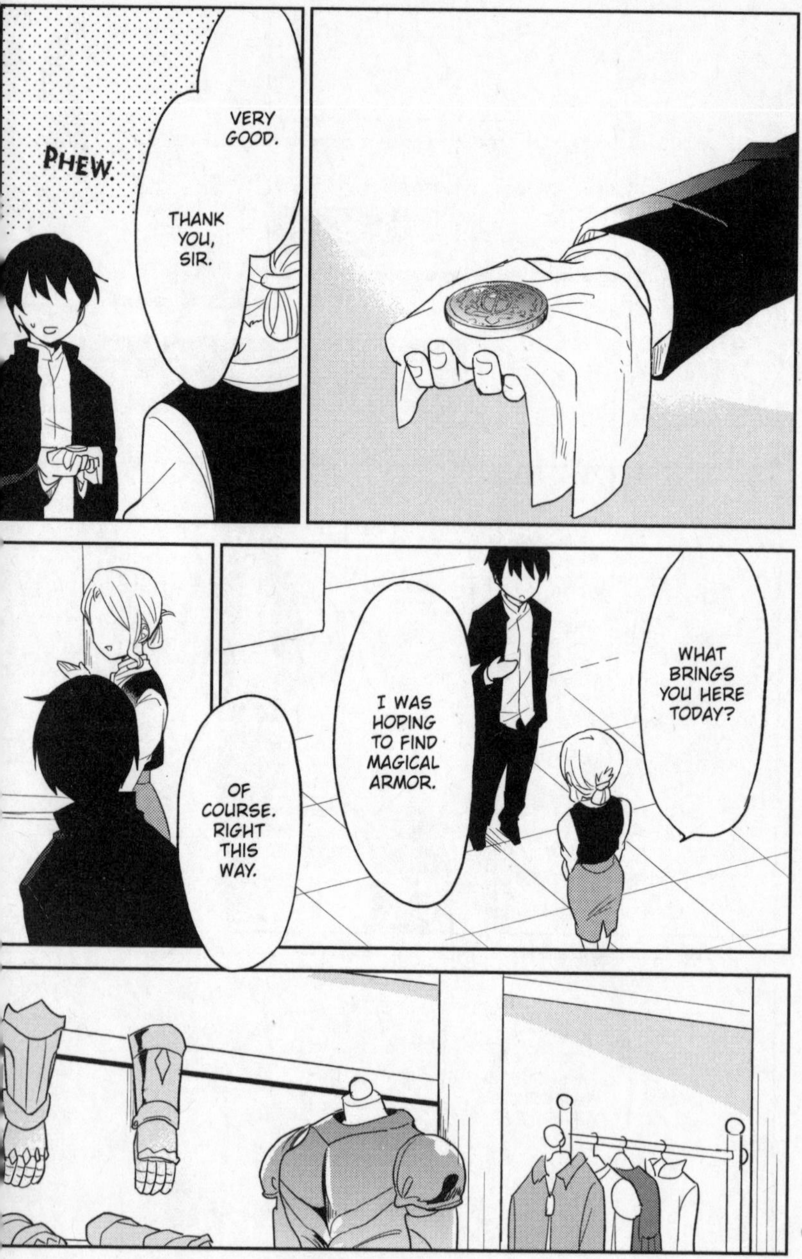
VERY GOOD.
THANK YOU, SIR.
PHEW.
WHAT BRINGS YOU HERE TODAY?
I WAS HOPING TO FIND MAGICAL ARMOR.
OF COURSE. RIGHT THIS WAY.

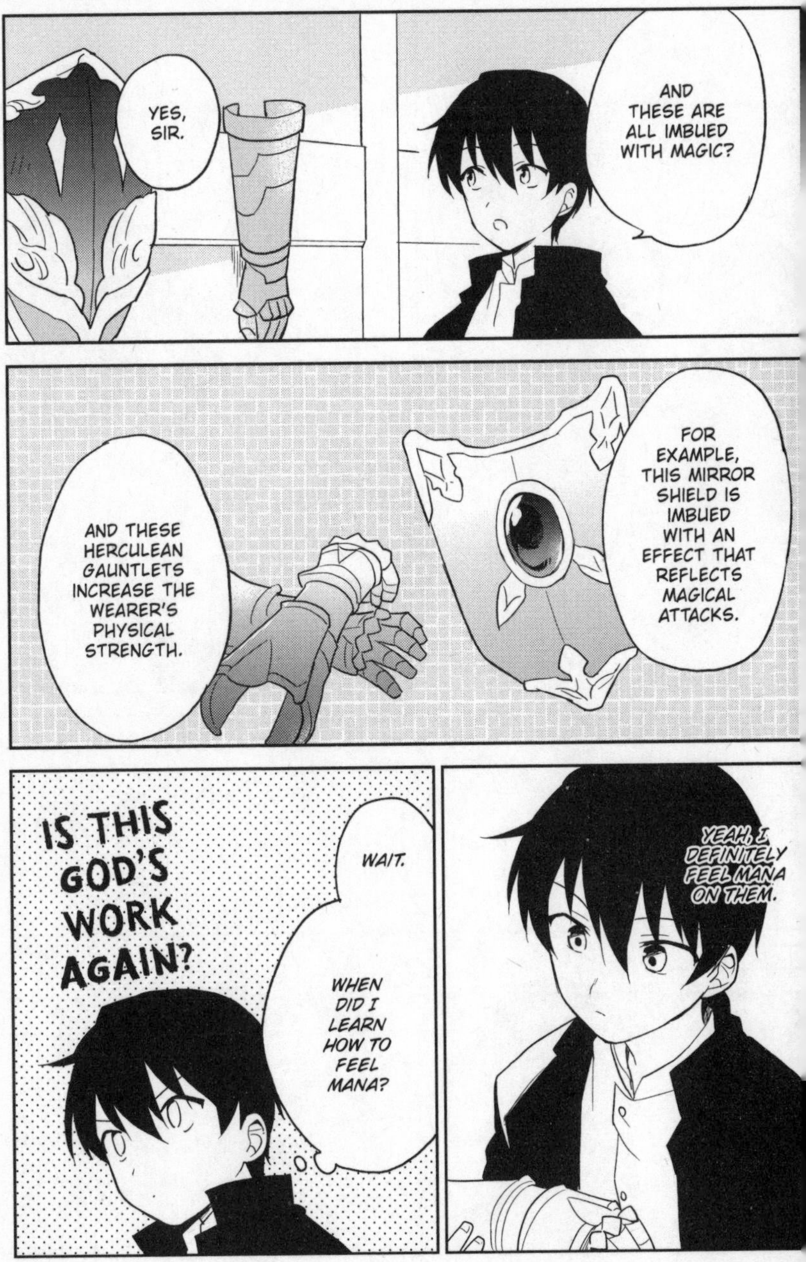
AND THESE ARE ALL IMBUED WITH MAGIC?
YES, SIR.
FOR EXAMPLE, THIS MIRROR SHIELD IS IMBUED WITH AN EFFECT THAT REFLECTS MAGICAL ATTACKS.
AND THESE HERCULEAN GAUNTLETS INCREASE THE WEARER'S PHYSICAL STRENGTH.
YEAH, I DEFINITELY FEEL MANA ON THEM.
WAIT.
WHEN DID I LEARN HOW TO FEEL MANA?
IS THIS GOD'S WORK AGAIN?

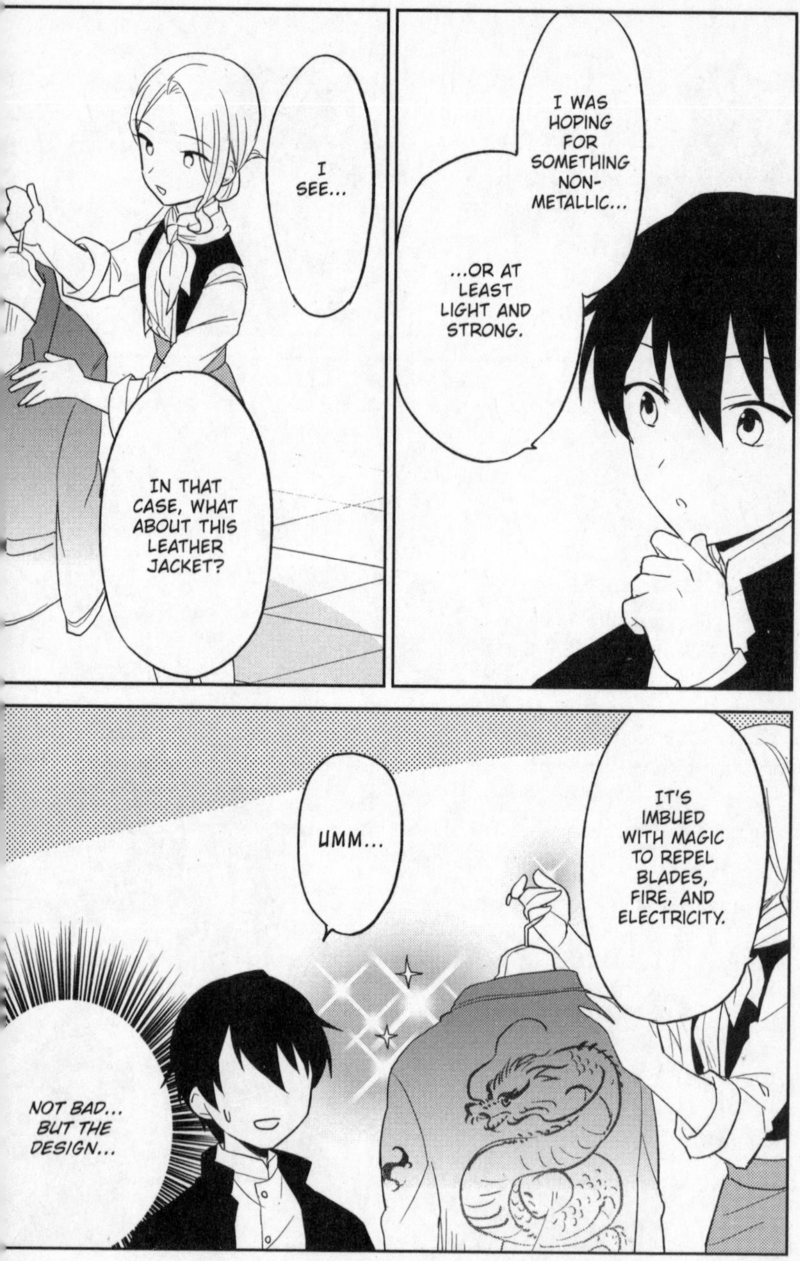
I WAS HOPING FOR SOMETHING NON-METALLIC...
...OR AT LEAST LIGHT AND STRONG.
I SEE...
IN THAT CASE, WHAT ABOUT THIS LEATHER JACKET?
IT'S IMBUED WITH MAGIC TO REPEL BLADES, FIRE, AND ELECTRICITY.
UMM...
NOT BAD... BUT THE DESIGN...

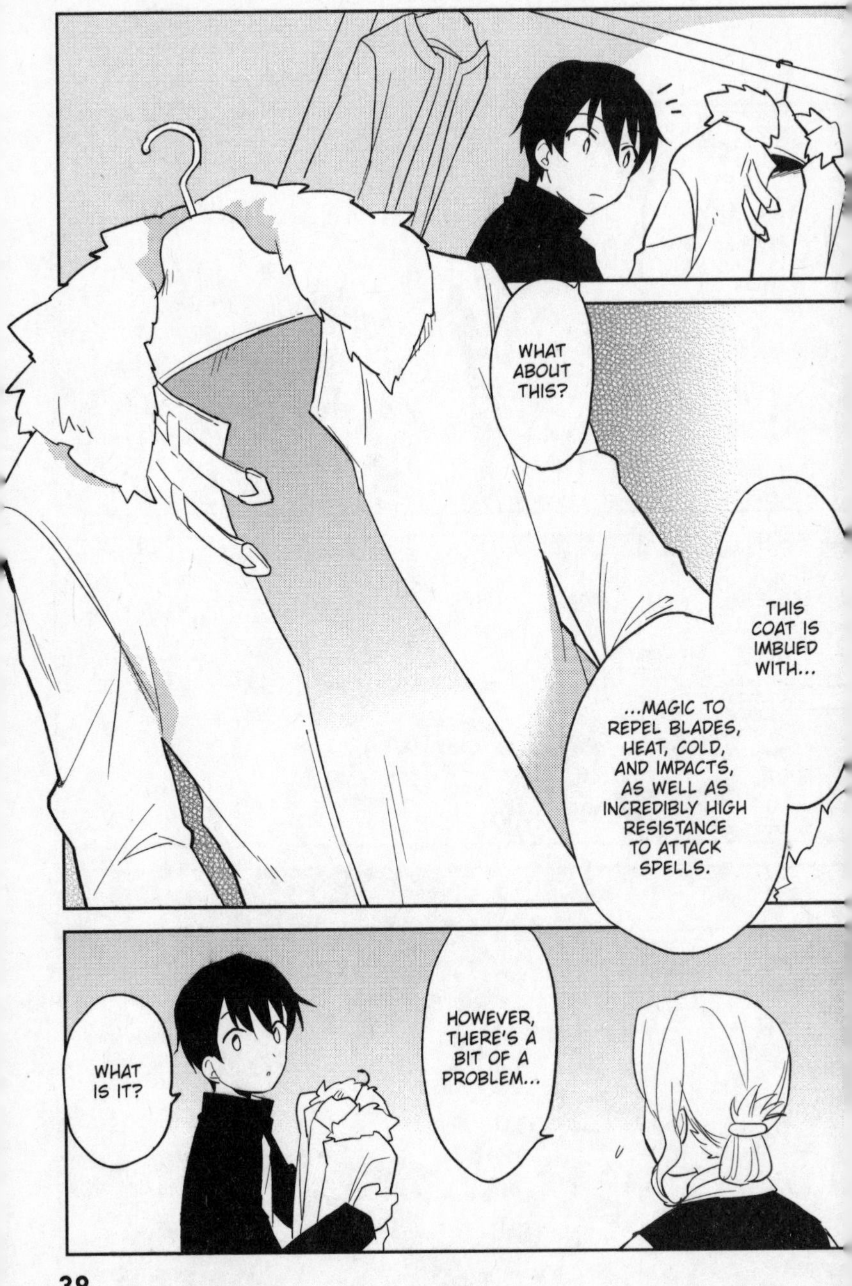
WHAT ABOUT THIS?
THIS COAT IS IMBUED WITH...
...MAGIC TO REPEL BLADES, HEAT, COLD, AND IMPACTS, AS WELL AS INCREDIBLY HIGH RESISTANCE TO ATTACK SPELLS.
HOWEVER, THERE'S A BIT OF A PROBLEM...
WHAT IS IT?

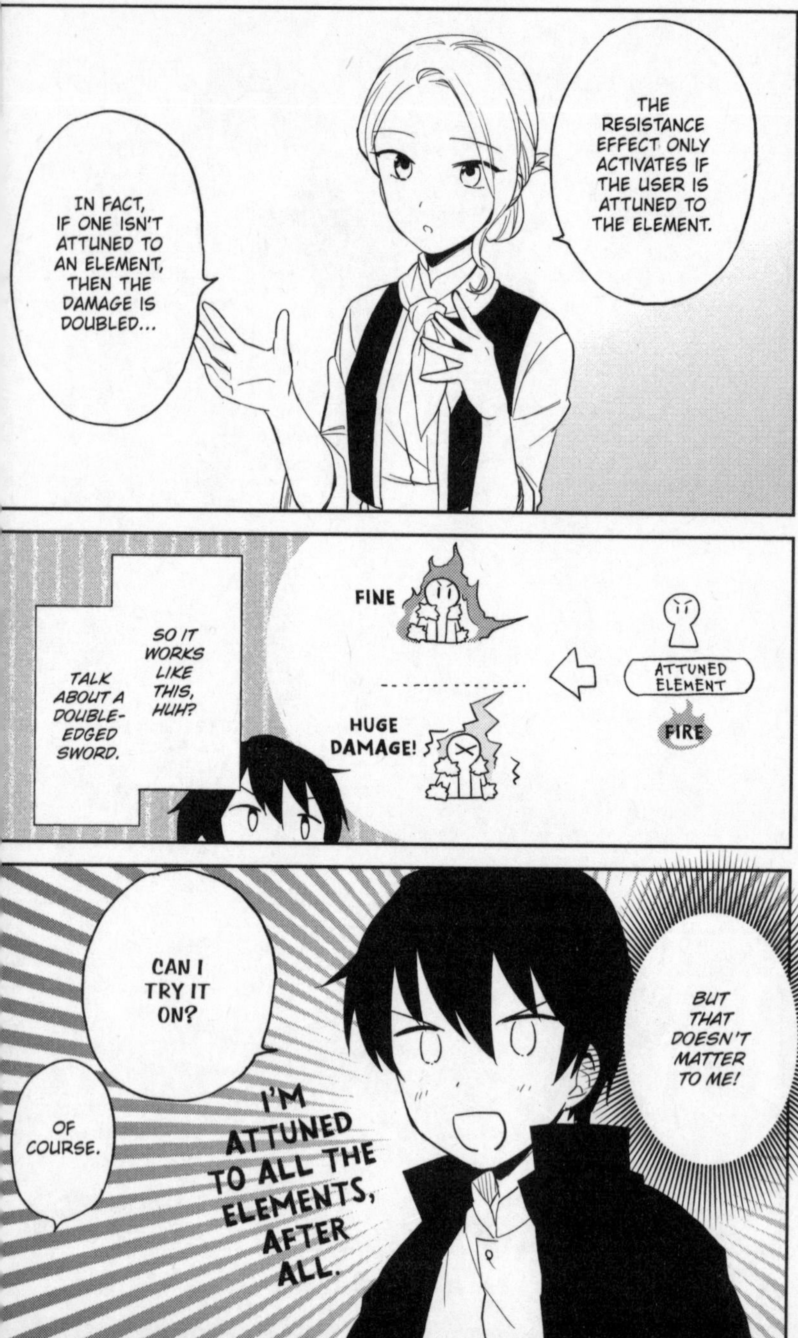
THE RESISTANCE EFFECT ONLY ACTIVATES IF THE USER IS ATTUNED TO THE ELEMENT.
IN FACT, IF ONE ISN'T ATTUNED TO AN ELEMENT, THEN THE DAMAGE IS DOUBLED...
ATTUNED ELEMENT
FIRE
FINE
HUGE DAMAGE!
SO IT WORKS LIKE THIS, HUH?
TALK ABOUT A DOUBLE-EDGED SWORD.
BUT THAT DOESN'T MATTER TO ME!
I'M ATTUNED TO ALL THE ELEMENTS, AFTER ALL.
CAN I TRY IT ON?
OF COURSE.

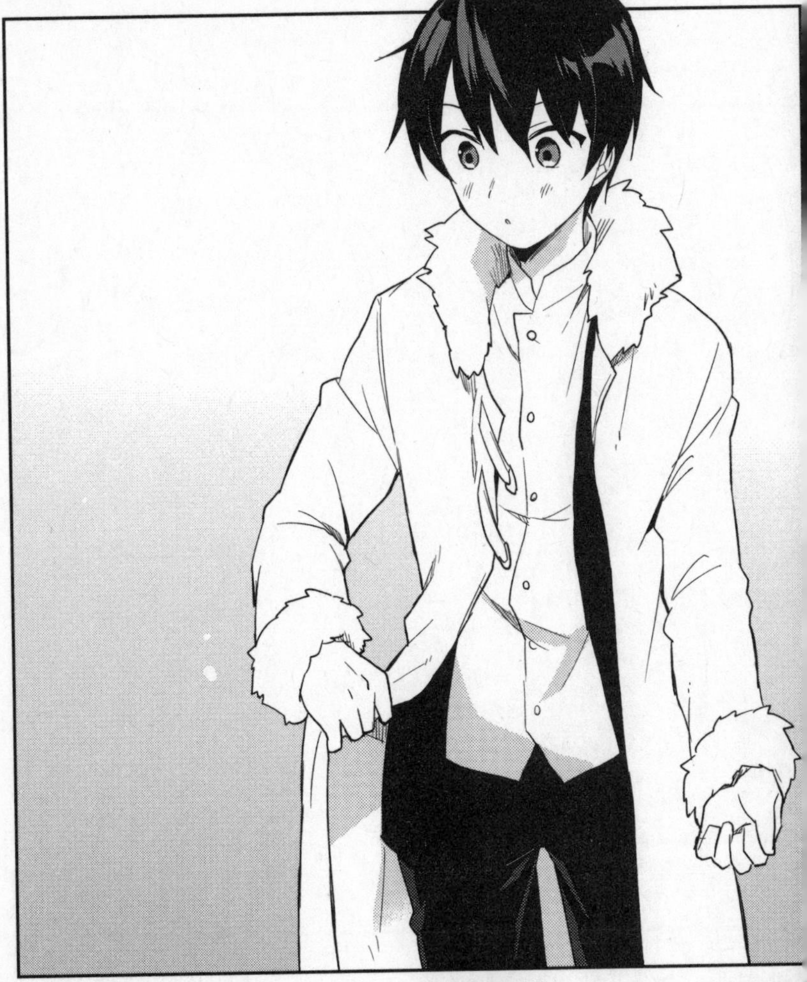

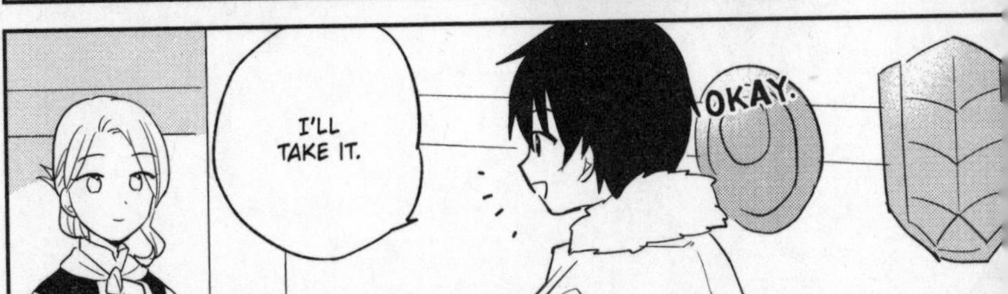
OKAY.
I'LL TAKE IT.

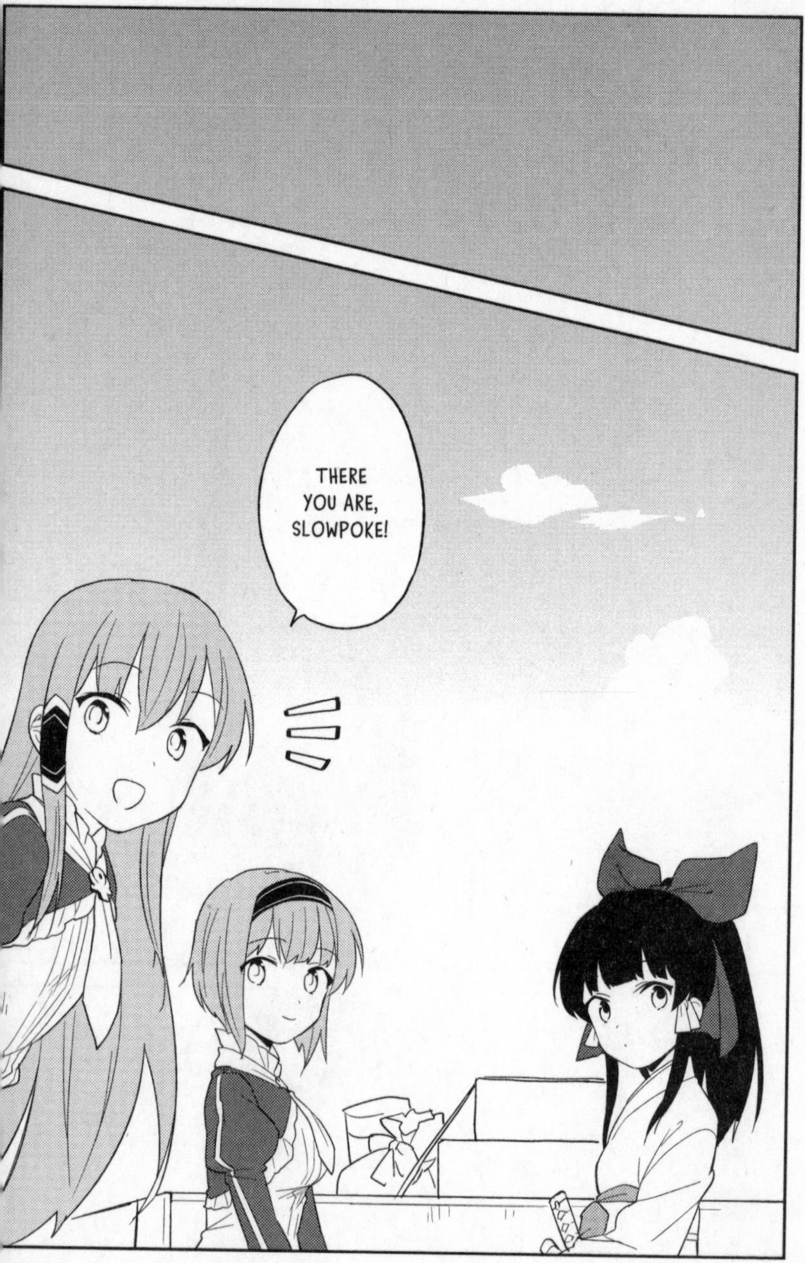
THERE YOU ARE, SLOWPOKE!

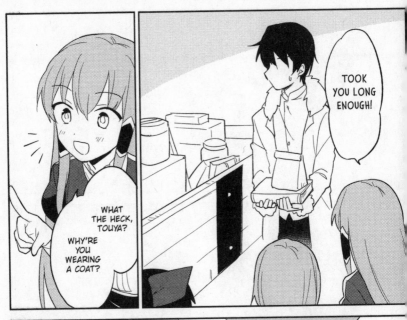

TOOK YOU LONG ENOUGH!
WHAT THE HECK, TOUYA?
WHY'RE YOU WEARING A COAT?
OH, THIS IS A MAGICAL COAT.
IT RESISTS ALL ELEMENTAL SPELLS.
AS WELL AS BLADES, IMPACTS, HEAT, AND COLD.
ALL ELEMENTS? THAT'S AMAZING.
HOW MUCH DID IT COST?

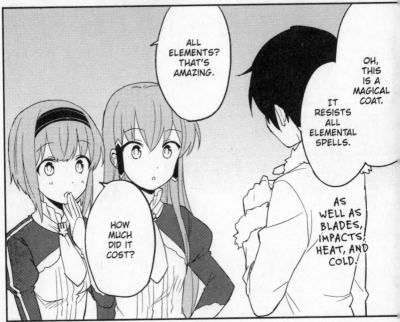

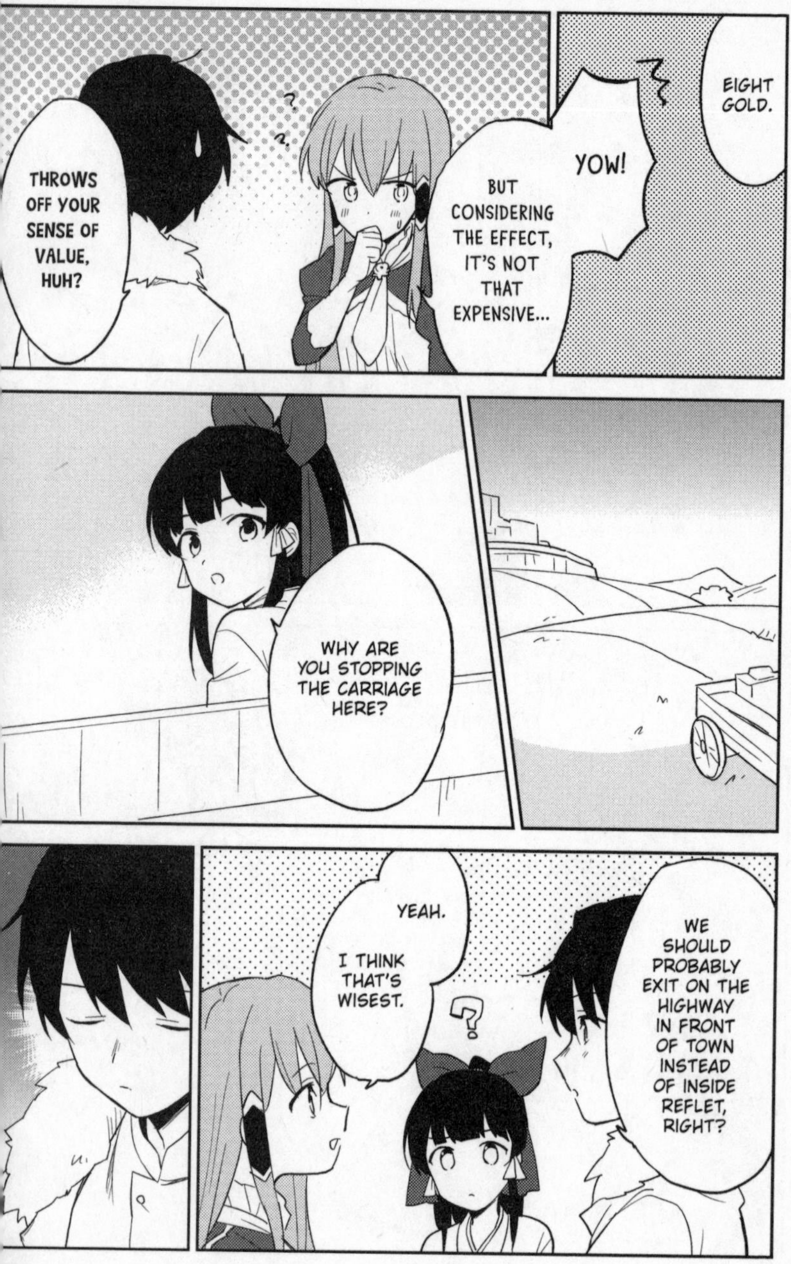
EIGHT GOLD.
YOW!
BUT CONSIDERING THE EFFECT, IT'S NOT THAT EXPENSIVE...
THROWS OFF YOUR SENSE OF VALUE, HUH?
WHY ARE YOU STOPPING THE CARRIAGE HERE?
WE SHOULD PROBABLY EXIT ON THE HIGHWAY IN FRONT OF TOWN INSTEAD OF INSIDE REFLET, RIGHT?
YEAH.
I THINK THAT'S WISEST.

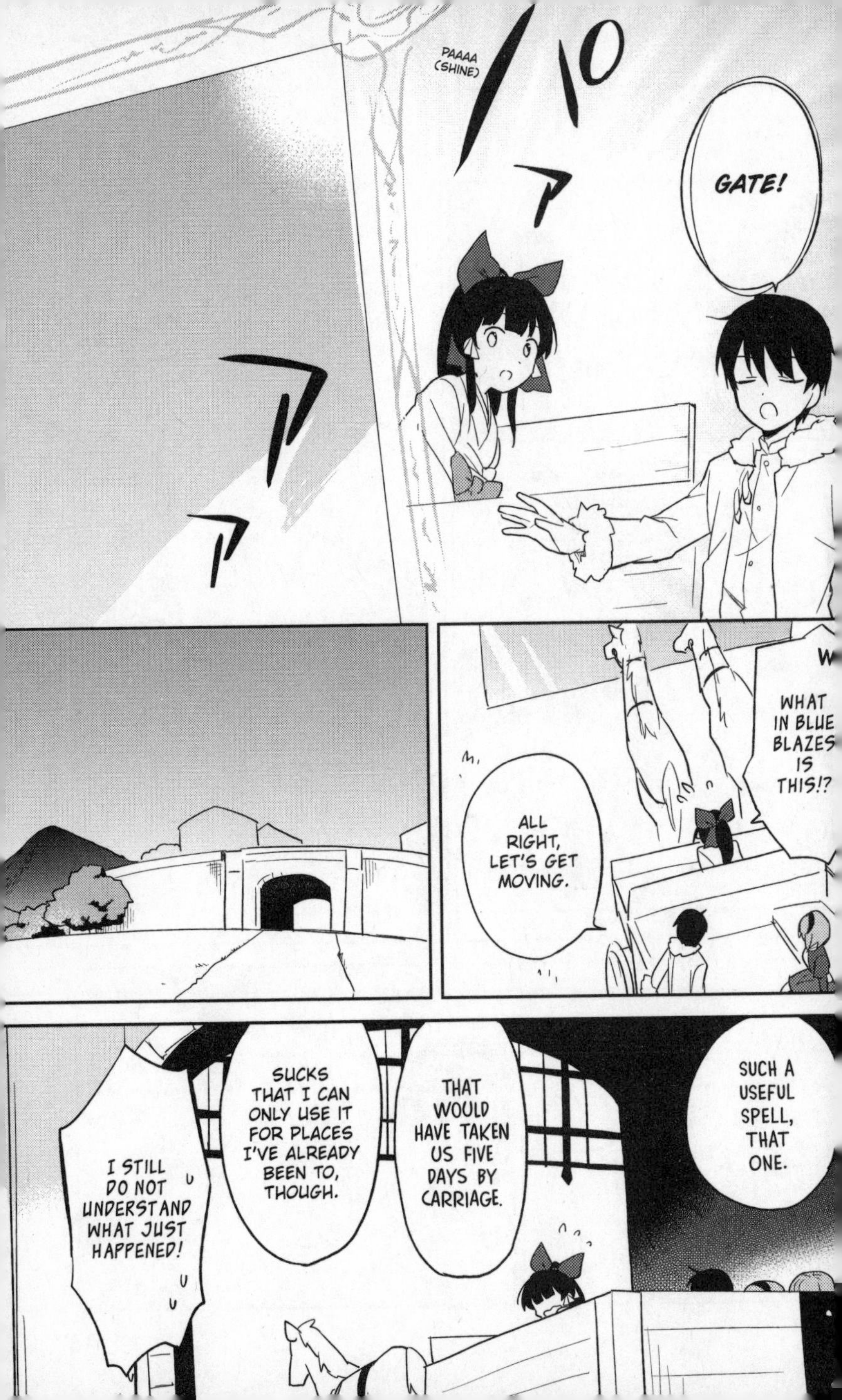
GATE!
PAAAA (SHINE)
WHAT IN BLUE BLAZES IS THIS!?
ALL RIGHT, LET'S GET MOVING.
SUCH A USEFUL SPELL, THAT ONE.
THAT WOULD HAVE TAKEN US FIVE DAYS BY CARRIAGE.
SUCKS THAT I CAN ONLY USE IT FOR PLACES I'VE ALREADY BEEN TO, THOUGH.
I STILL DO NOT UNDERSTAND WHAT JUST HAPPENED!

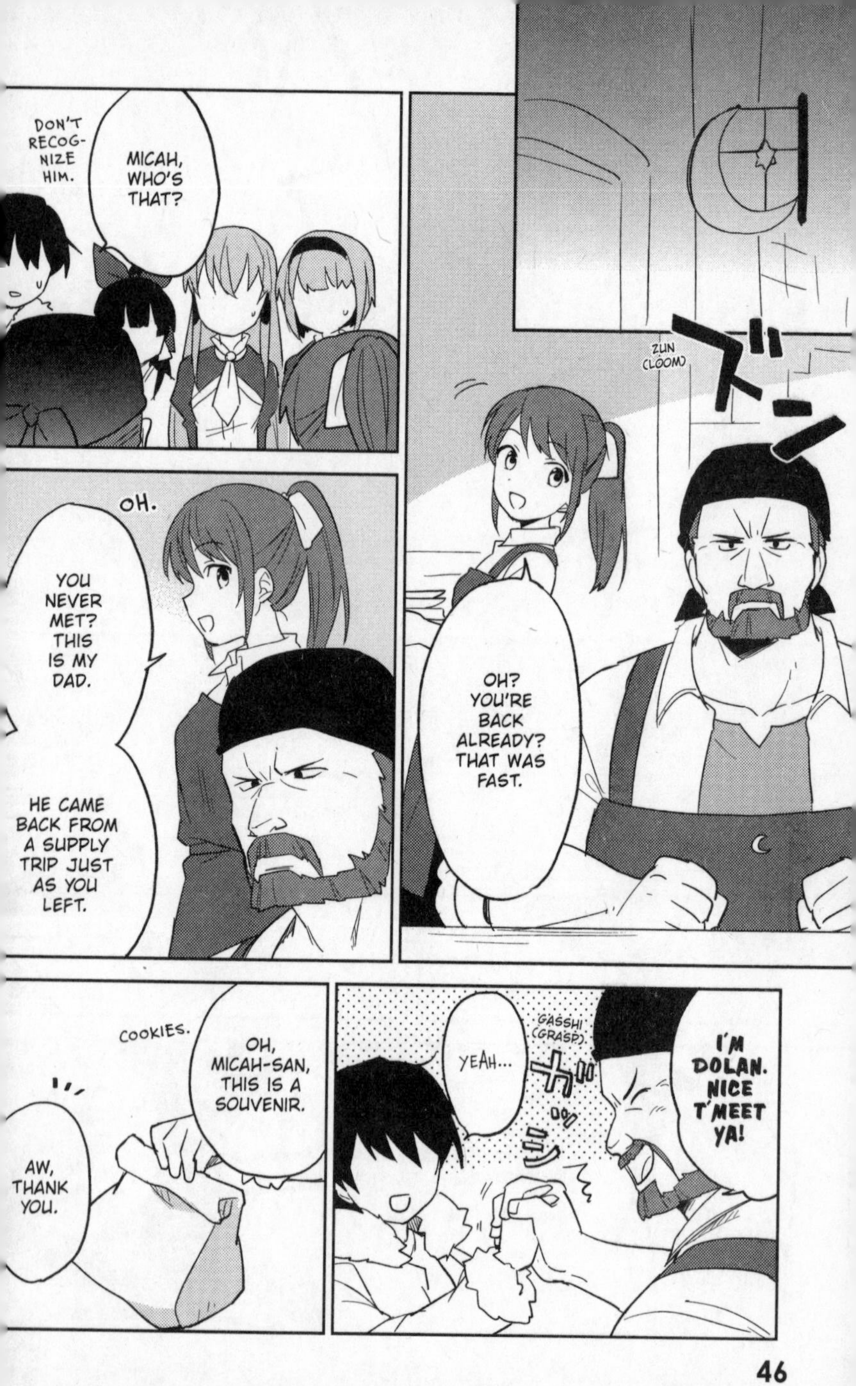
ZUN (LOOM)
OH? YOU'RE BACK ALREADY? THAT WAS FAST.
MICAH, WHO'S THAT?
DON'T RECOG-NIZE HIM.
OH.
YOU NEVER MET? THIS IS MY DAD.
HE CAME BACK FROM A SUPPLY TRIP JUST AS YOU LEFT.
I'M DOLAN. NICE T'MEET YA!
GASSHI (GRASP)
YEAH...
OH, MICAH-SAN, THIS IS A SOUVENIR.
COOKIES.
AW, THANK YOU.

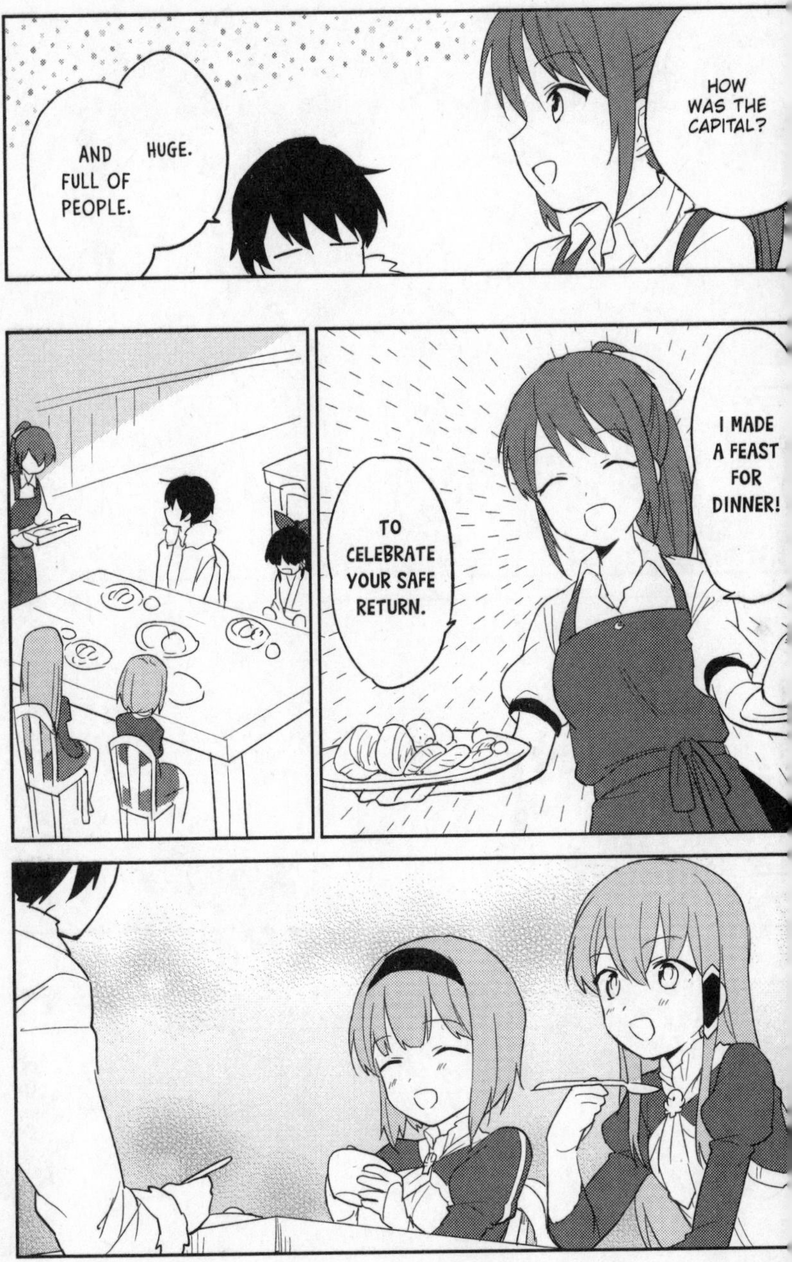
HOW WAS THE CAPITAL?
HUGE.
AND FULL OF PEOPLE.
I MADE A FEAST FOR DINNER!
TO CELEBRATE YOUR SAFE RETURN.

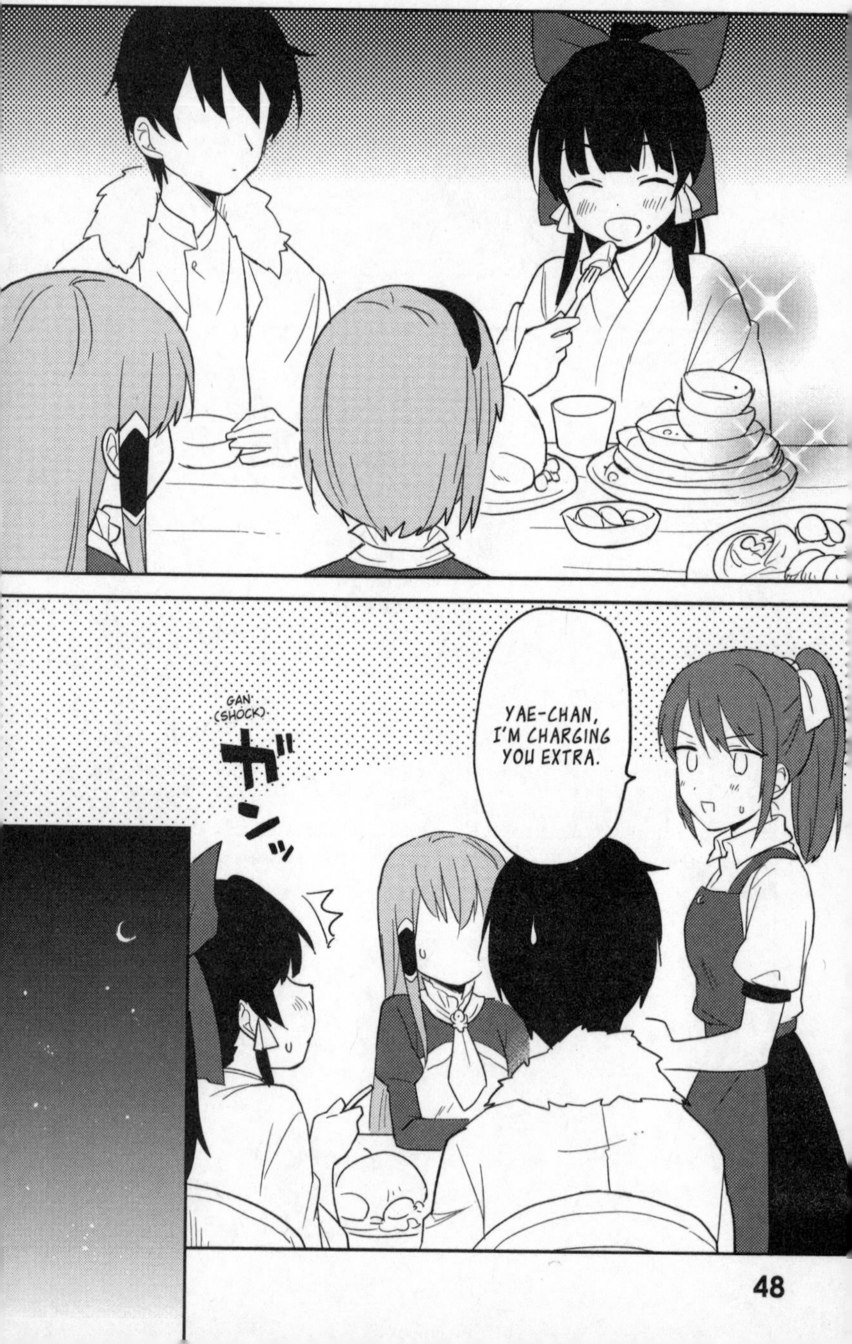
YAE-CHAN, I'M CHARGING YOU EXTRA.
GAN (SHOCK)
ガーンッ

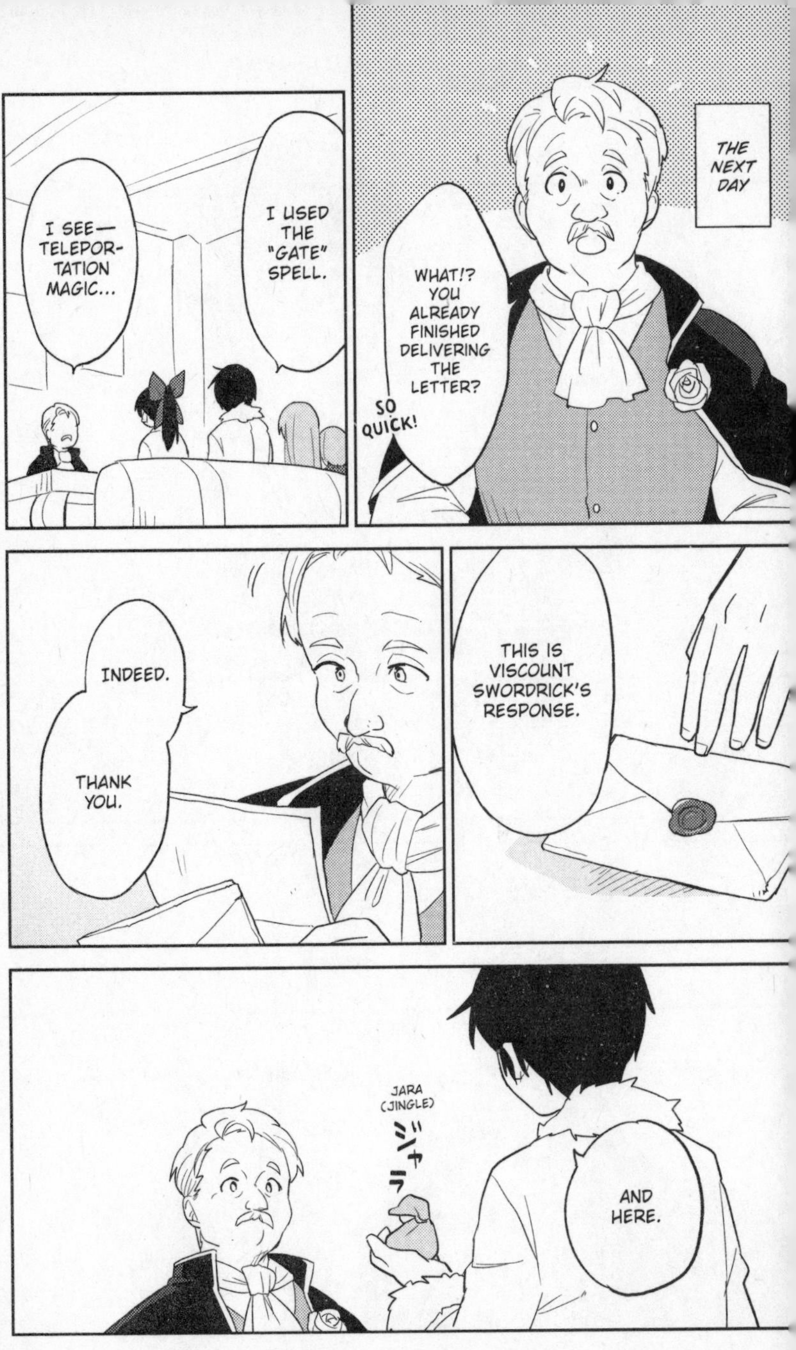

THE NEXT DAY
WHAT!? YOU ALREADY FINISHED DELIVERING THE LETTER?
SO QUICK!
I USED THE "GATE" SPELL.
I SEE— TELEPORTATION MAGIC...
THIS IS VISCOUNT SWORDRICK'S RESPONSE.
INDEED.
THANK YOU.
ジャラ
JARA (JINGLE)
AND HERE.

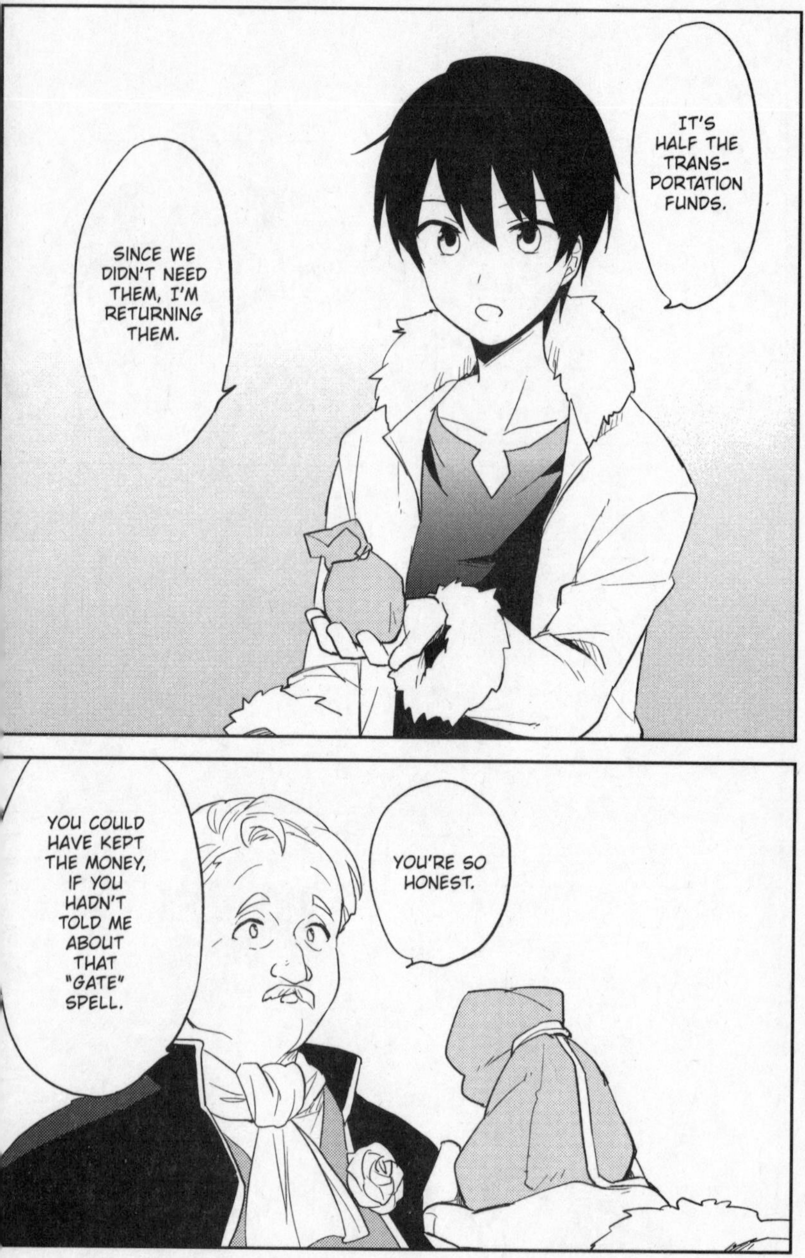
IT'S HALF THE TRANS-PORTATION FUNDS.
SINCE WE DIDN'T NEED THEM, I'M RETURNING THEM.
YOU'RE SO HONEST.
YOU COULD HAVE KEPT THE MONEY, IF YOU HADN'T TOLD ME ABOUT THAT "GATE" SPELL.

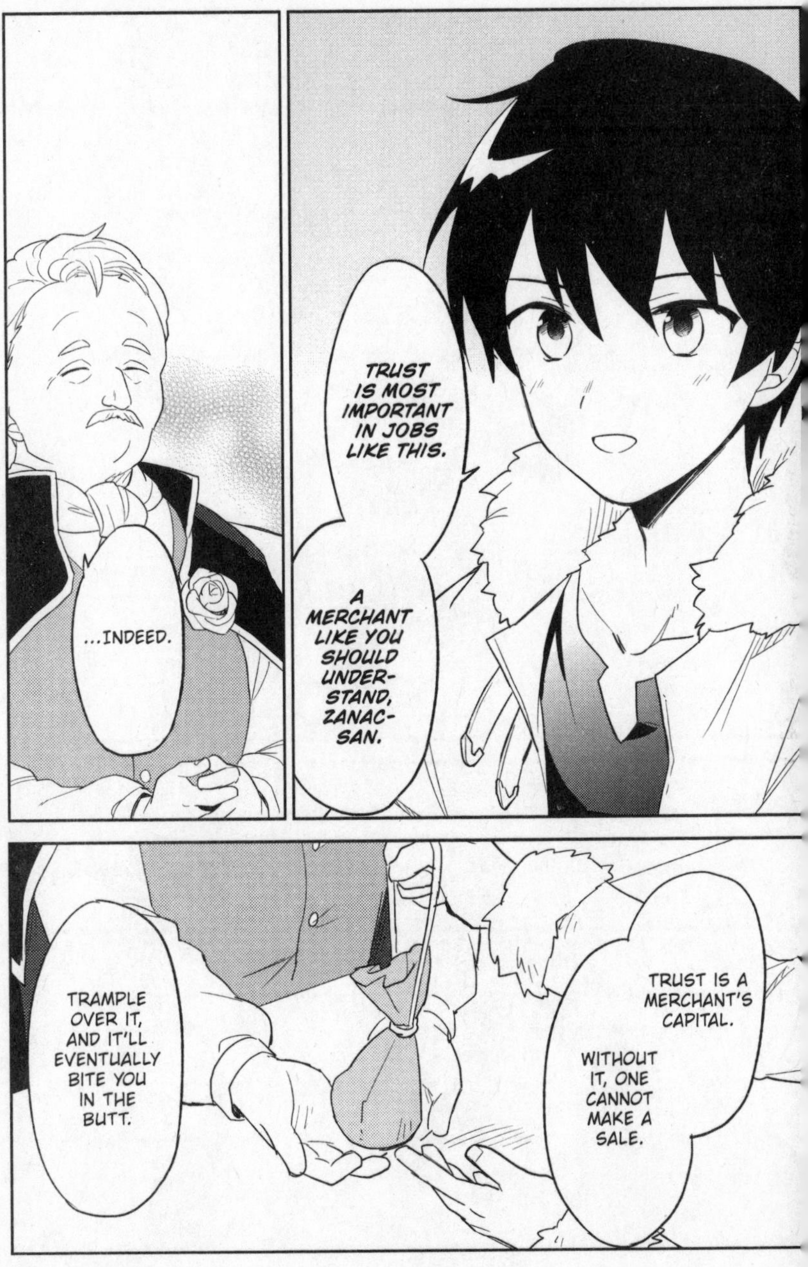
TRUST IS MOST IMPORTANT IN JOBS LIKE THIS.
A MERCHANT LIKE YOU SHOULD UNDER-STAND, ZANAC-SAN.
...INDEED.
TRUST IS A MERCHANT'S CAPITAL.
WITHOUT IT, ONE CANNOT MAKE A SALE.
TRAMPLE OVER IT, AND IT'LL EVENTUALLY BITE YOU IN THE BUTT.

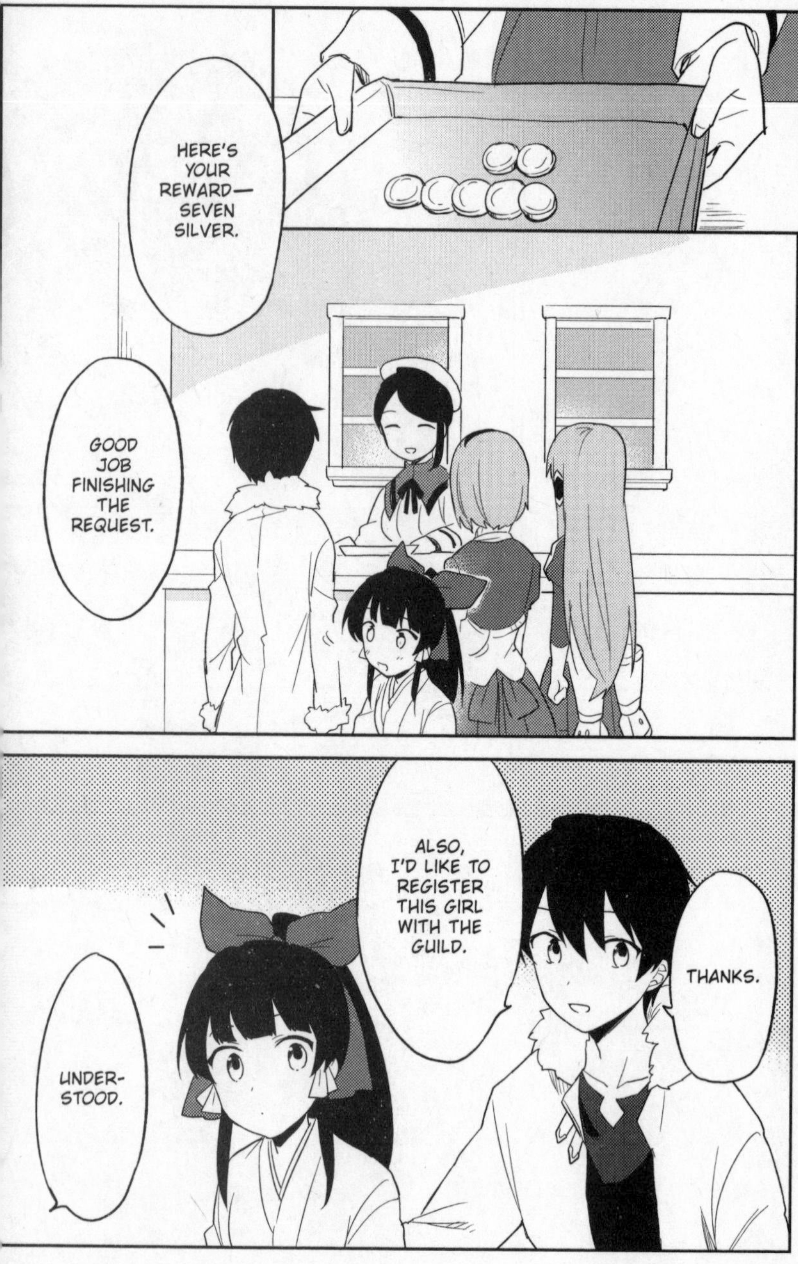
HERE'S YOUR REWARD— SEVEN SILVER.
GOOD JOB FINISHING THE REQUEST.
THANKS.
ALSO, I'D LIKE TO REGISTER THIS GIRL WITH THE GUILD.
UNDER-STOOD.

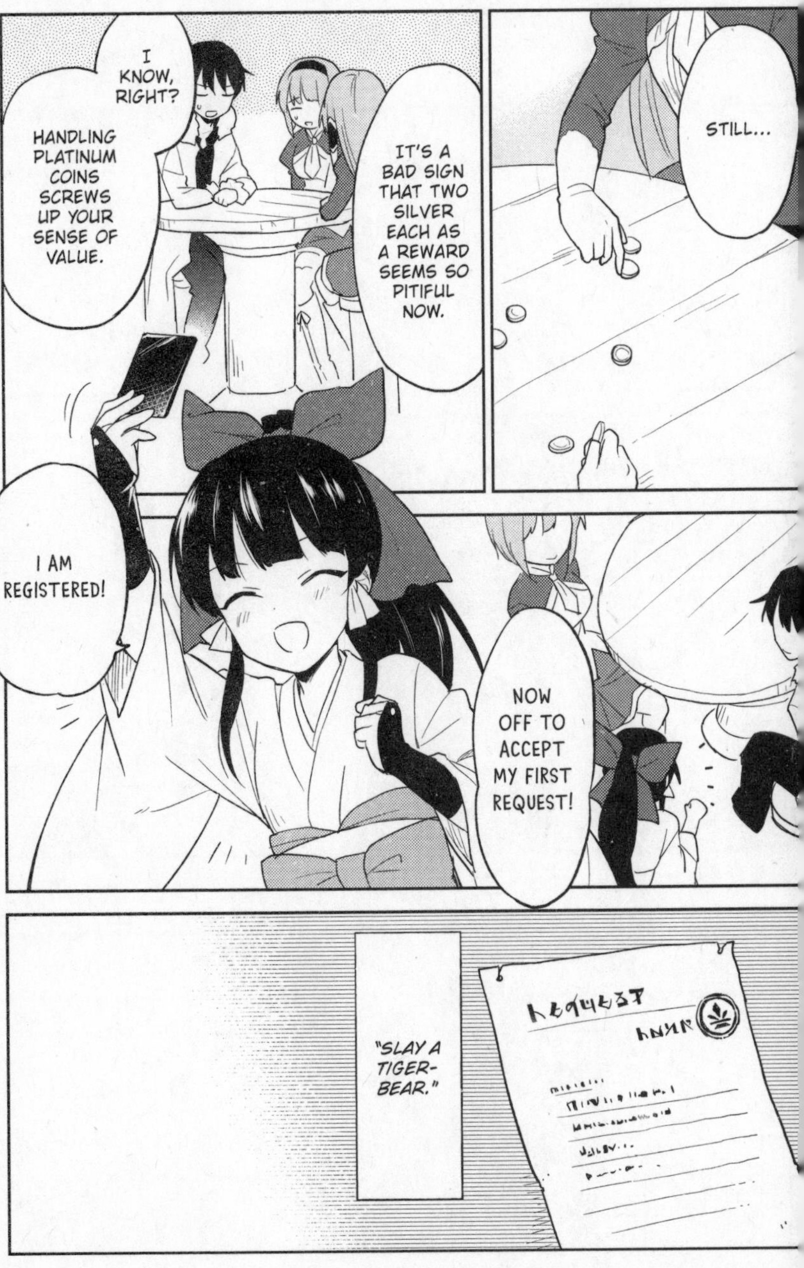

STILL...
IT'S A BAD SIGN THAT TWO SILVER EACH AS A REWARD SEEMS SO PITIFUL NOW.
I KNOW, RIGHT?
HANDLING PLATINUM COINS SCREWS UP YOUR SENSE OF VALUE.
I AM REGISTERED!
NOW OFF TO ACCEPT MY FIRST REQUEST!
"SLAY A TIGER-BEAR."

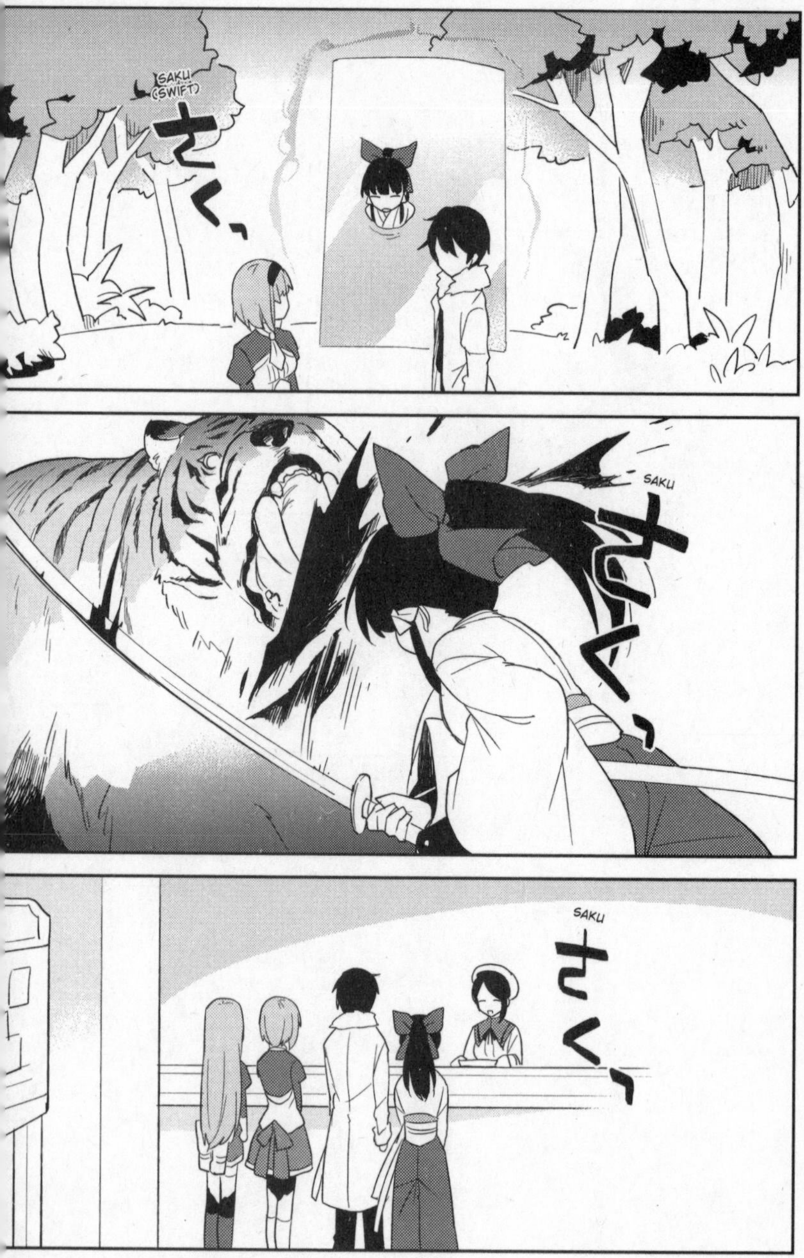
SAKU (SWIFT)
さく、
SAKU
さく、
SAKU
さく、

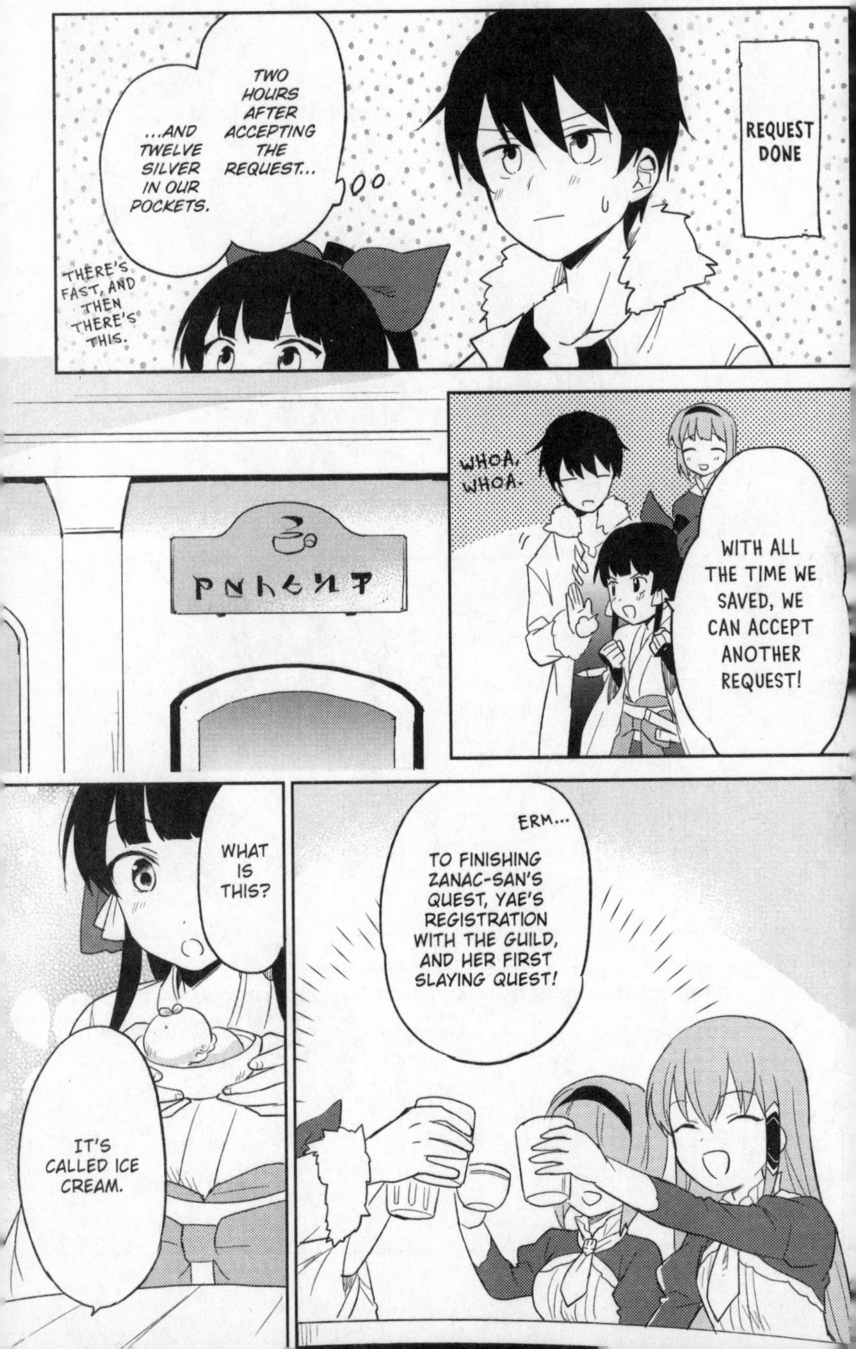
REQUEST DONE
TWO HOURS AFTER ACCEPTING THE REQUEST...
...AND TWELVE SILVER IN OUR POCKETS.
THERE'S FAST, AND THEN THERE'S THIS.
WITH ALL THE TIME WE SAVED, WE CAN ACCEPT ANOTHER REQUEST!
WHOA, WHOA.
ERM...
TO FINISHING ZANAC-SAN'S QUEST, YAE'S REGISTRATION WITH THE GUILD, AND HER FIRST SLAYING QUEST!
WHAT IS THIS?
IT'S CALLED ICE CREAM.

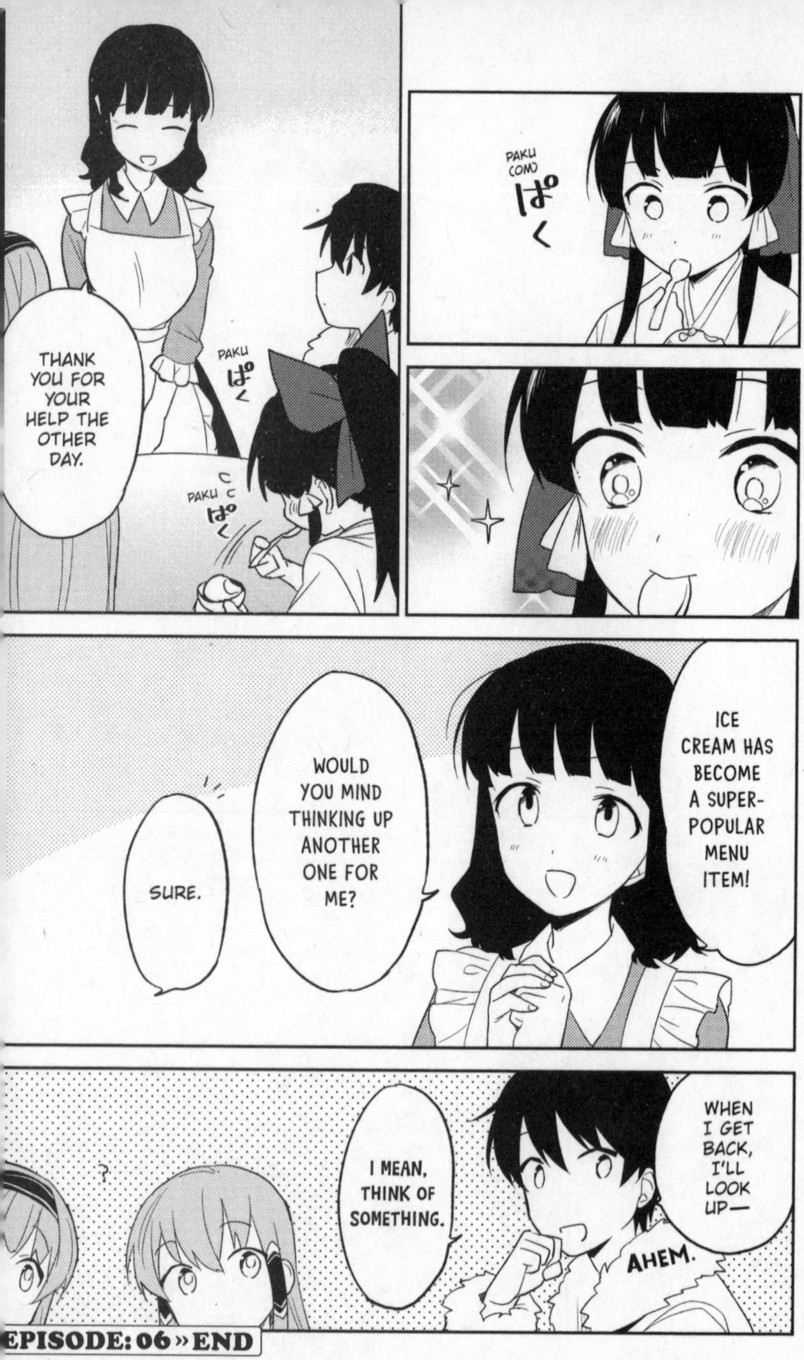
PAKU (OM)
ぱく
THANK YOU FOR YOUR HELP THE OTHER DAY.
PAKU
ぱく
PAKU
ぱく
ICE CREAM HAS BECOME A SUPER-POPULAR MENU ITEM!
WOULD YOU MIND THINKING UP ANOTHER ONE FOR ME?
SURE.
WHEN I GET BACK, I'LL LOOK UP—
AHEM.
I MEAN, THINK OF SOMETHING.
?
EPISODE: 06 » END

In Another World with
My Smartphone

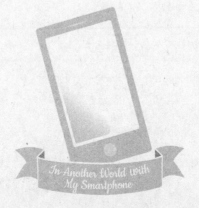

In Another World with My Smartphone

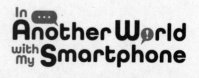

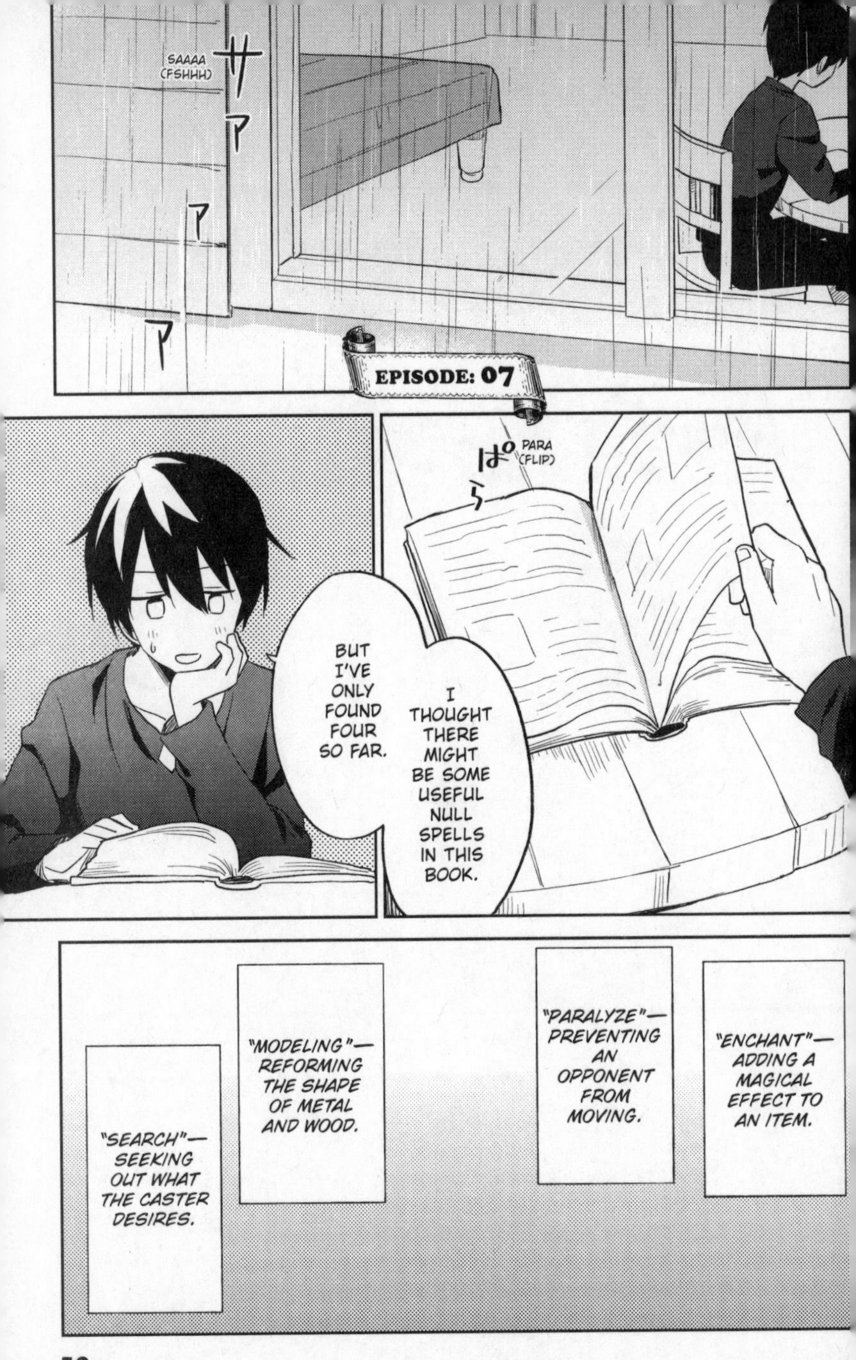
サァァァ
SAAAA (FSHHH)
EPISODE: 07
ぱら
PARA (FLIP)
I THOUGHT THERE MIGHT BE SOME USEFUL NULL SPELLS IN THIS BOOK.
BUT I'VE ONLY FOUND FOUR SO FAR.
"ENCHANT"—ADDING A MAGICAL EFFECT TO AN ITEM.
"PARALYZE"—PREVENTING AN OPPONENT FROM MOVING.
"MODELING"—REFORMING THE SHAPE OF METAL AND WOOD.
"SEARCH"—SEEKING OUT WHAT THE CASTER DESIRES.

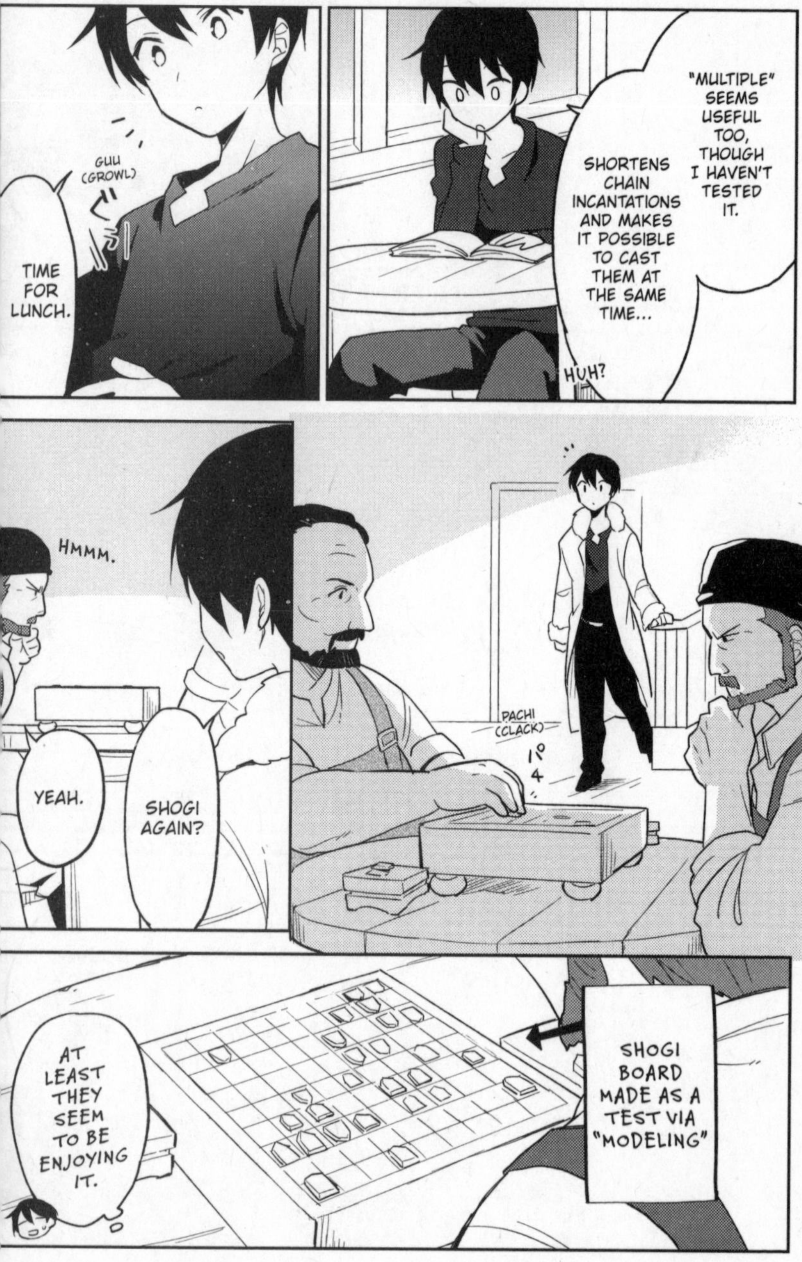
SHORTENS CHAIN INCANTATIONS AND MAKES IT POSSIBLE TO CAST THEM AT THE SAME TIME...
"MULTIPLE" SEEMS USEFUL TOO, THOUGH I HAVEN'T TESTED IT.
HUH?
GUU (GROWL)
TIME FOR LUNCH.
PACHI (CLACK)
HMMM.
SHOGI AGAIN?
YEAH.
SHOGI BOARD MADE AS A TEST VIA "MODELING"
AT LEAST THEY SEEM TO BE ENJOYING IT.

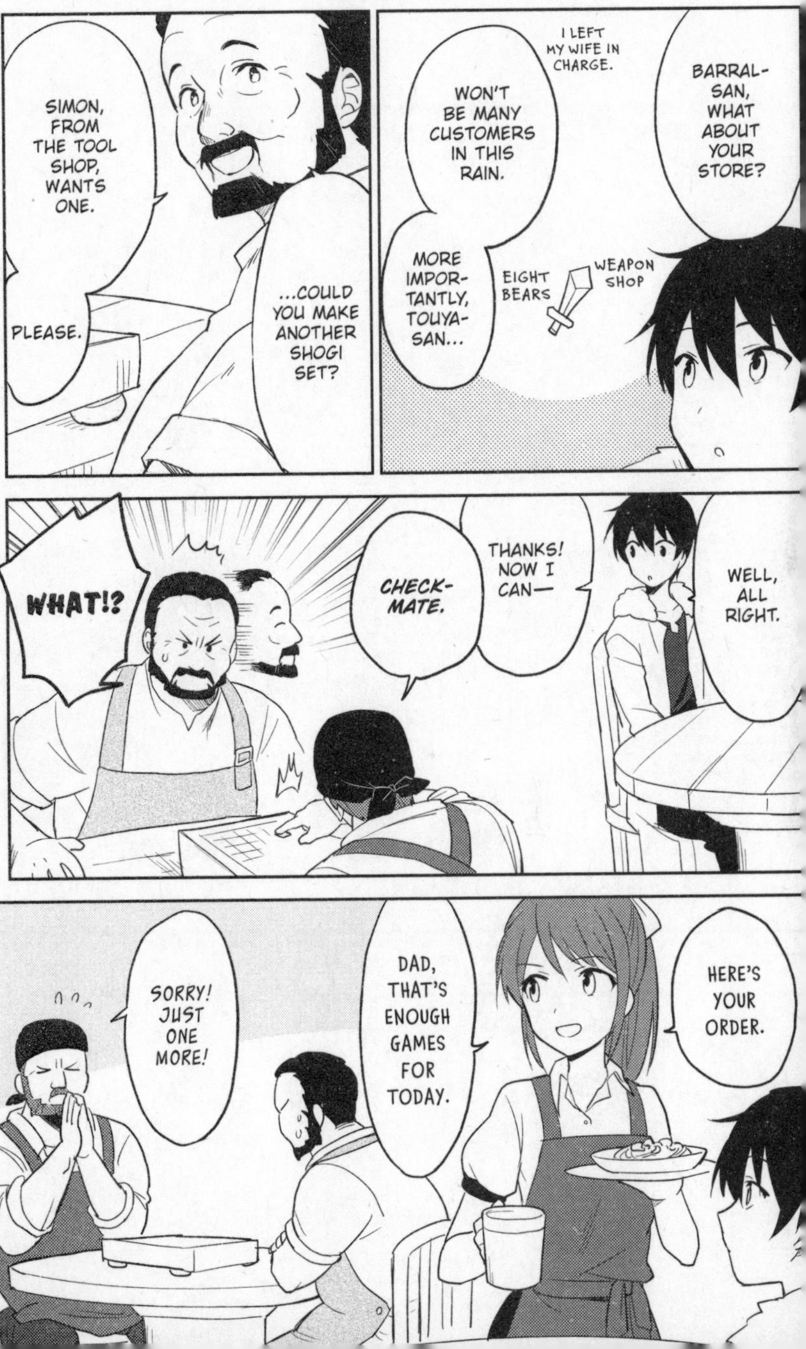
BARRAL-SAN, WHAT ABOUT YOUR STORE?
I LEFT MY WIFE IN CHARGE.
WON'T BE MANY CUSTOMERS IN THIS RAIN.
WEAPON SHOP
EIGHT BEARS
MORE IMPORTANTLY, TOUYA-SAN...
...COULD YOU MAKE ANOTHER SHOGI SET?
SIMON, FROM THE TOOL SHOP, WANTS ONE.
PLEASE.
WELL, ALL RIGHT.
THANKS! NOW I CAN—
*CHECK-MATE.*
WHAT!?
HERE'S YOUR ORDER.
DAD, THAT'S ENOUGH GAMES FOR TODAY.
SORRY! JUST ONE MORE!

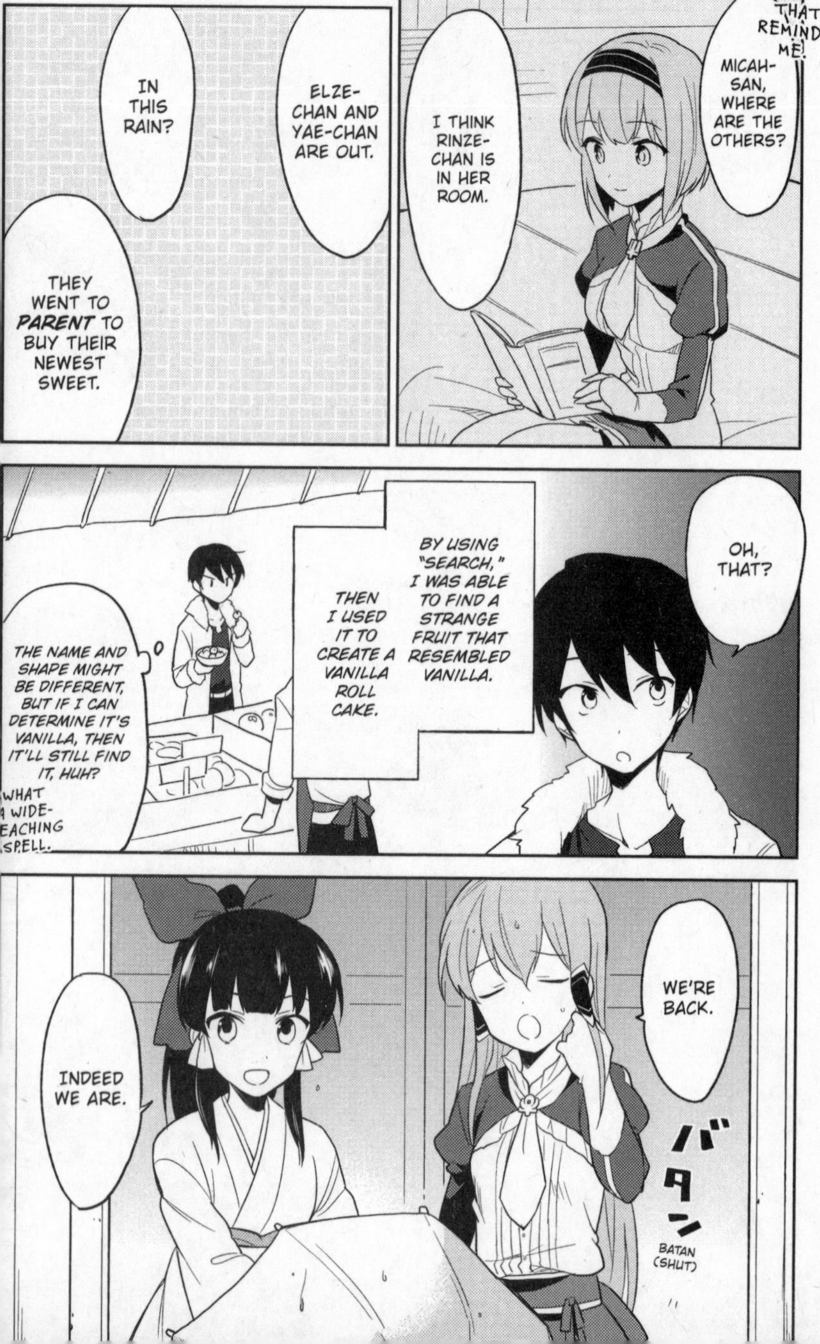
THAT REMINDS ME!
MICAH-SAN, WHERE ARE THE OTHERS?
I THINK RINZE-CHAN IS IN HER ROOM.
ELZE-CHAN AND YAE-CHAN ARE OUT.
IN THIS RAIN?
THEY WENT TO *PARENT* TO BUY THEIR NEWEST SWEET.
OH, THAT?
BY USING "SEARCH," I WAS ABLE TO FIND A STRANGE FRUIT THAT RESEMBLED VANILLA.
THEN I USED IT TO CREATE A VANILLA ROLL CAKE.
THE NAME AND SHAPE MIGHT BE DIFFERENT, BUT IF I CAN DETERMINE IT'S VANILLA, THEN IT'LL STILL FIND IT, HUH?
WHAT A WIDE-EACHING SPELL.
WE'RE BACK.
バタン
BATAN (SHUT)
INDEED WE ARE.

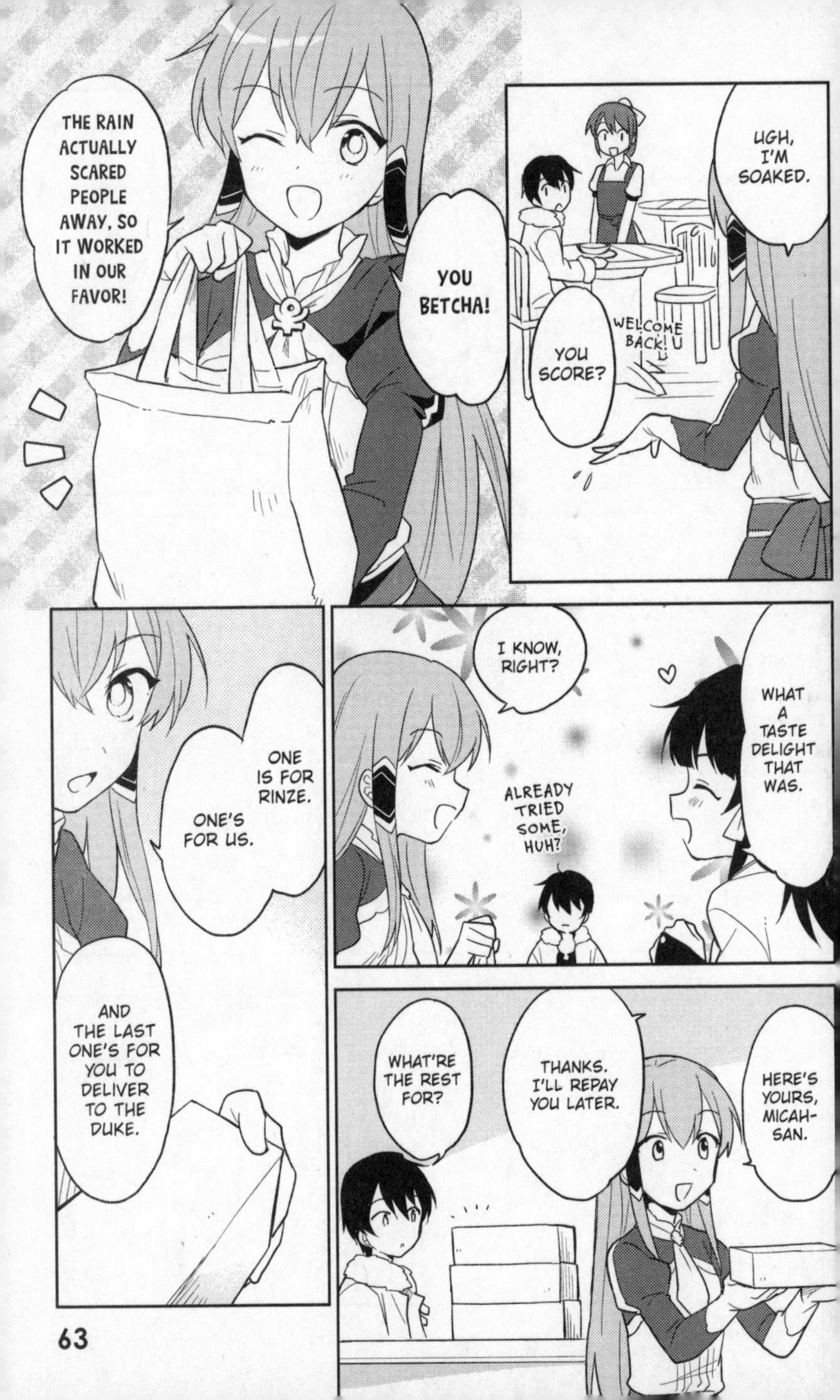
UGH, I'M SOAKED.
WELCOME BACK!
YOU SCORE?
YOU BETCHA!
THE RAIN ACTUALLY SCARED PEOPLE AWAY, SO IT WORKED IN OUR FAVOR!
WHAT A TASTE DELIGHT THAT WAS.
ALREADY TRIED SOME, HUH?
I KNOW, RIGHT?
HERE'S YOURS, MICAH-SAN.
THANKS. I'LL REPAY YOU LATER.
WHAT'RE THE REST FOR?
ONE IS FOR RINZE.
ONE'S FOR US.
AND THE LAST ONE'S FOR YOU TO DELIVER TO THE DUKE.

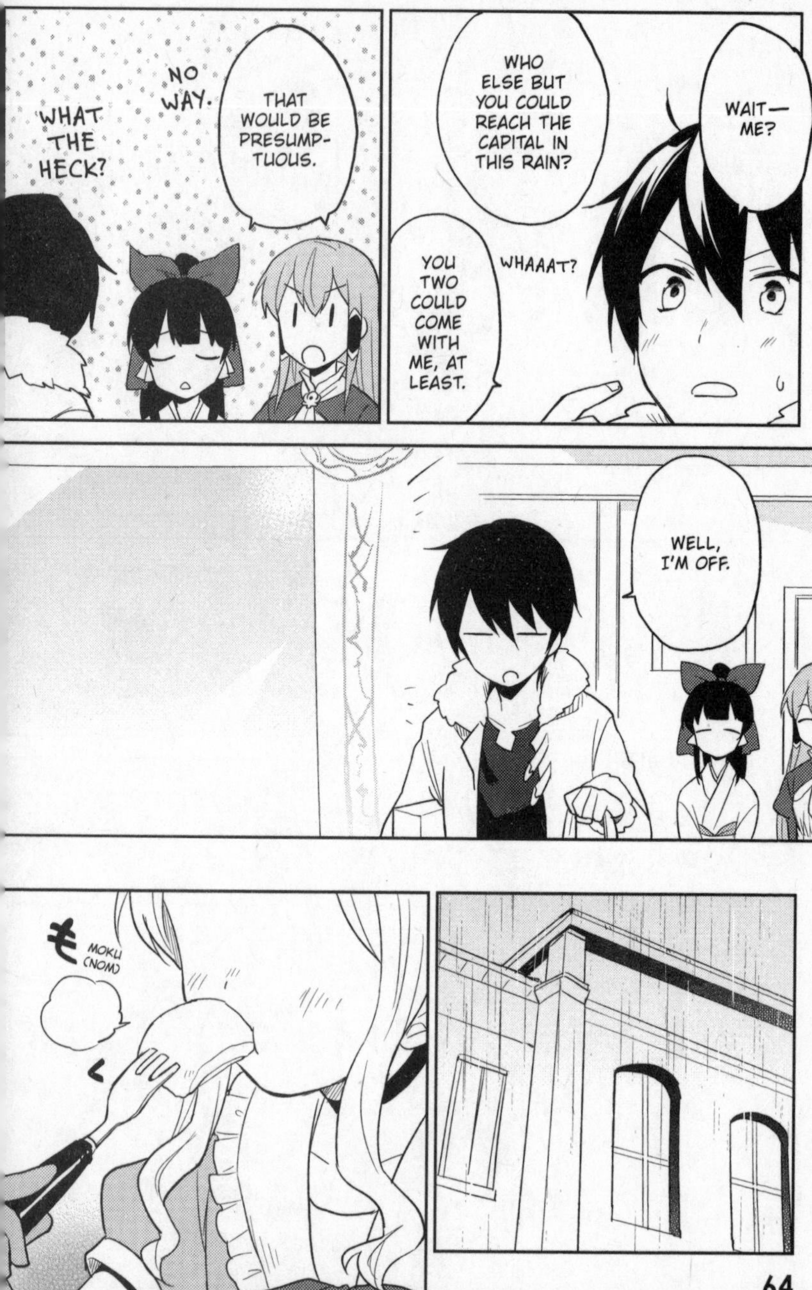
WAIT— ME?
WHO ELSE BUT YOU COULD REACH THE CAPITAL IN THIS RAIN?
WHAAAT?
YOU TWO COULD COME WITH ME, AT LEAST.
THAT WOULD BE PRESUMPTUOUS.
NO WAY.
WHAT THE HECK?
WELL, I'M OFF.
も
MOKU (NOM)

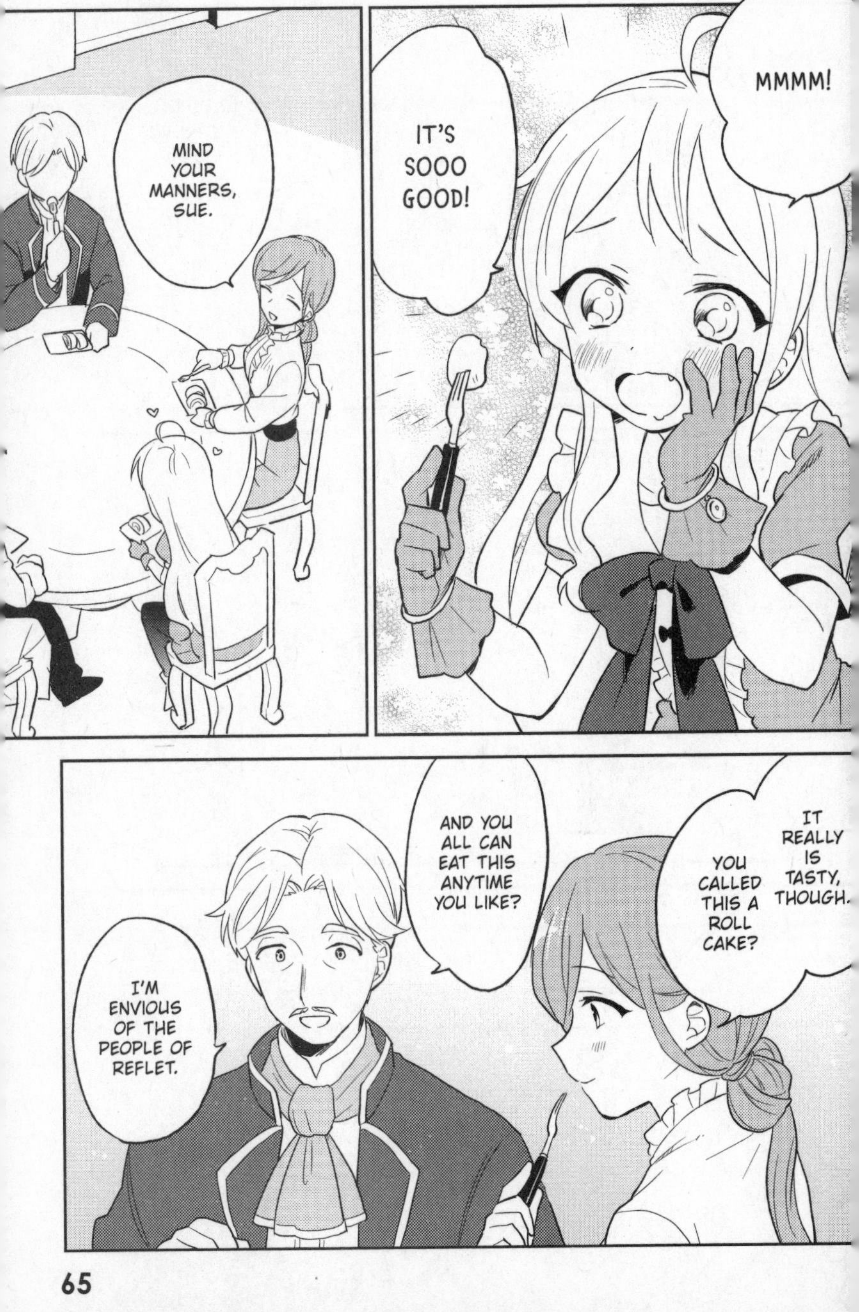
MMMM!
IT'S SOOO GOOD!
MIND YOUR MANNERS, SUE.
IT REALLY IS TASTY, THOUGH.
YOU CALLED THIS A ROLL CAKE?
AND YOU ALL CAN EAT THIS ANYTIME YOU LIKE?
I'M ENVIOUS OF THE PEOPLE OF REFLET.

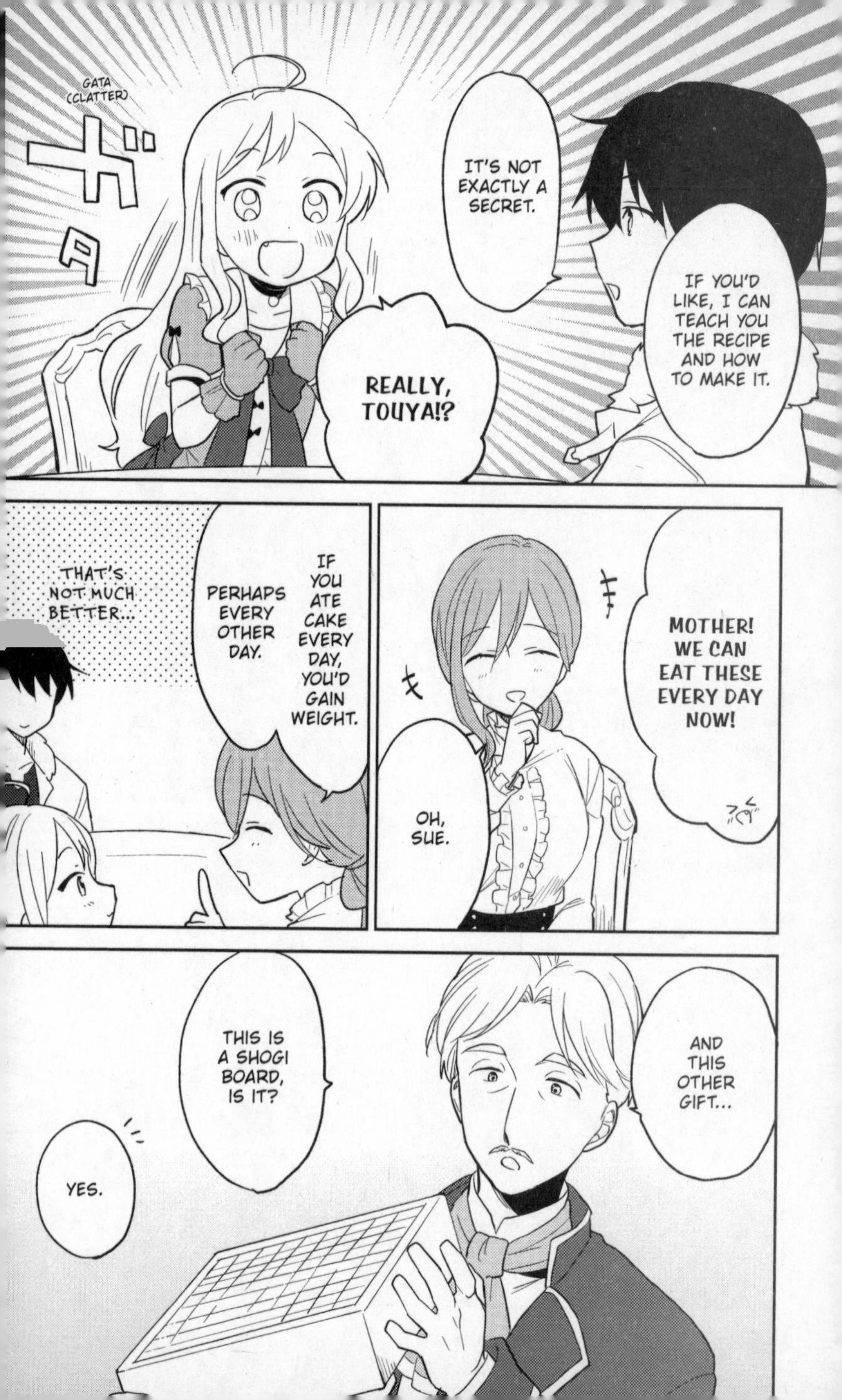
IT'S NOT EXACTLY A SECRET.
IF YOU'D LIKE, I CAN TEACH YOU THE RECIPE AND HOW TO MAKE IT.
GATA (CLATTER)
REALLY, TOUYA!?
MOTHER! WE CAN EAT THESE EVERY DAY NOW!
OH, SUE.
IF YOU ATE CAKE EVERY DAY, YOU'D GAIN WEIGHT.
PERHAPS EVERY OTHER DAY.
THAT'S NOT MUCH BETTER...
AND THIS OTHER GIFT...
THIS IS A SHOGI BOARD, IS IT?
YES.

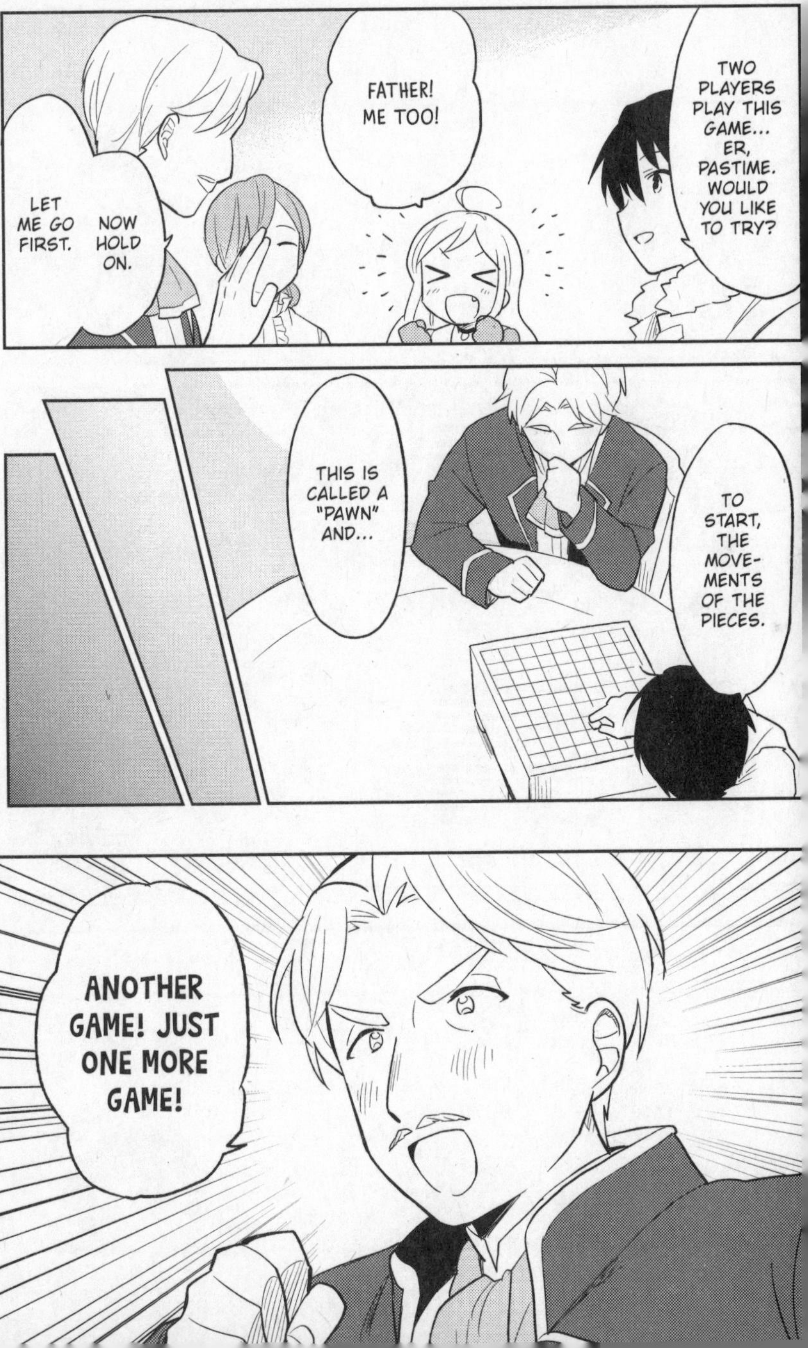
TWO PLAYERS PLAY THIS GAME... ER, PASTIME. WOULD YOU LIKE TO TRY?
FATHER! ME TOO!
NOW HOLD ON.
LET ME GO FIRST.
TO START, THE MOVEMENTS OF THE PIECES.
THIS IS CALLED A "PAWN" AND...
ANOTHER GAME! JUST ONE MORE GAME!

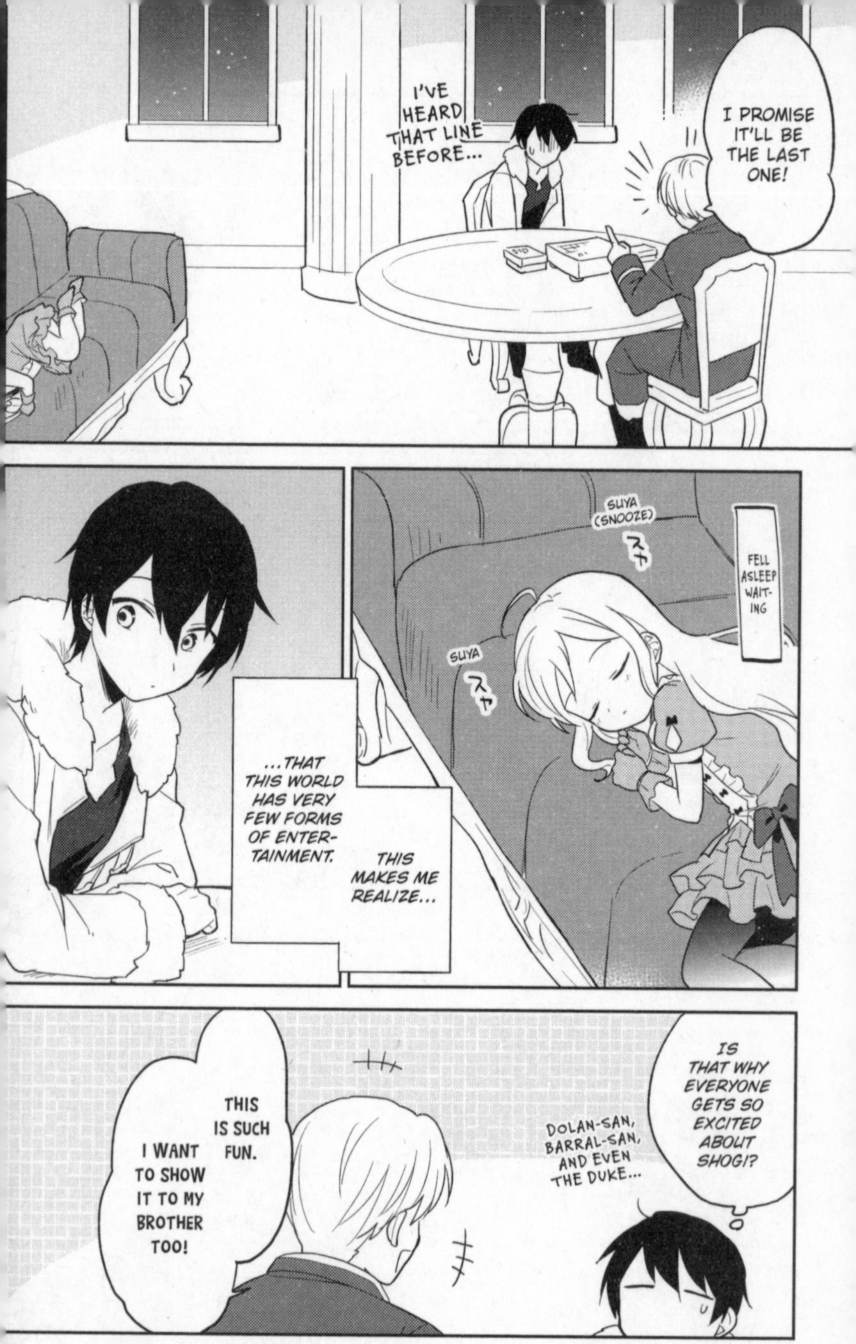
I PROMISE IT'LL BE THE LAST ONE!
I'VE HEARD THAT LINE BEFORE...
SUYA (SNOOZE)
スヤ
FELL ASLEEP WAITING
SUYA
スヤ
THIS MAKES ME REALIZE...
...THAT THIS WORLD HAS VERY FEW FORMS OF ENTERTAINMENT.
IS THAT WHY EVERYONE GETS SO EXCITED ABOUT SHOGI?
DOLAN-SAN, BARRAL-SAN, AND EVEN THE DUKE...
THIS IS SUCH FUN.
I WANT TO SHOW IT TO MY BROTHER TOO!

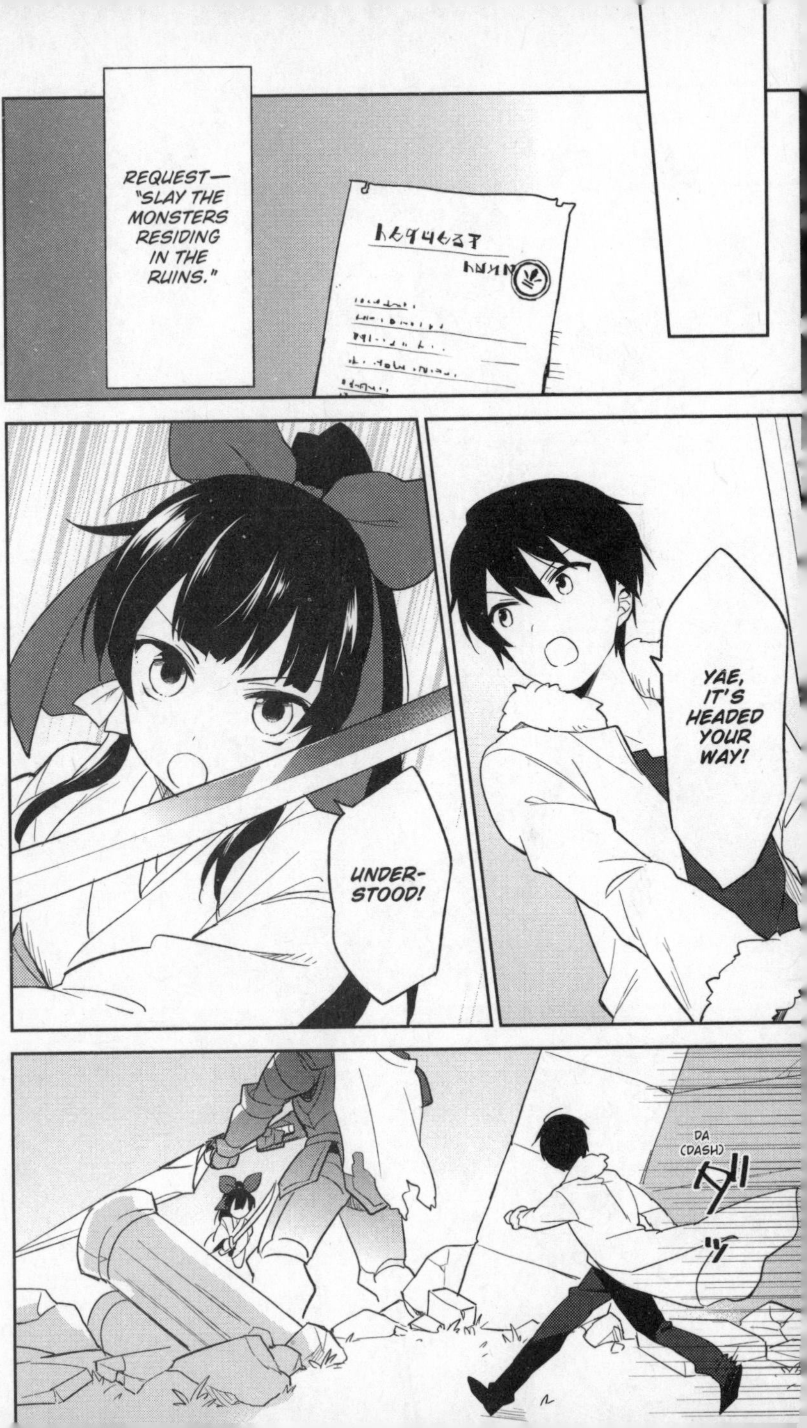
REQUEST— "SLAY THE MONSTERS RESIDING IN THE RUINS."
YAE, IT'S HEADED YOUR WAY!
UNDER-STOOD!
DA (DASH)

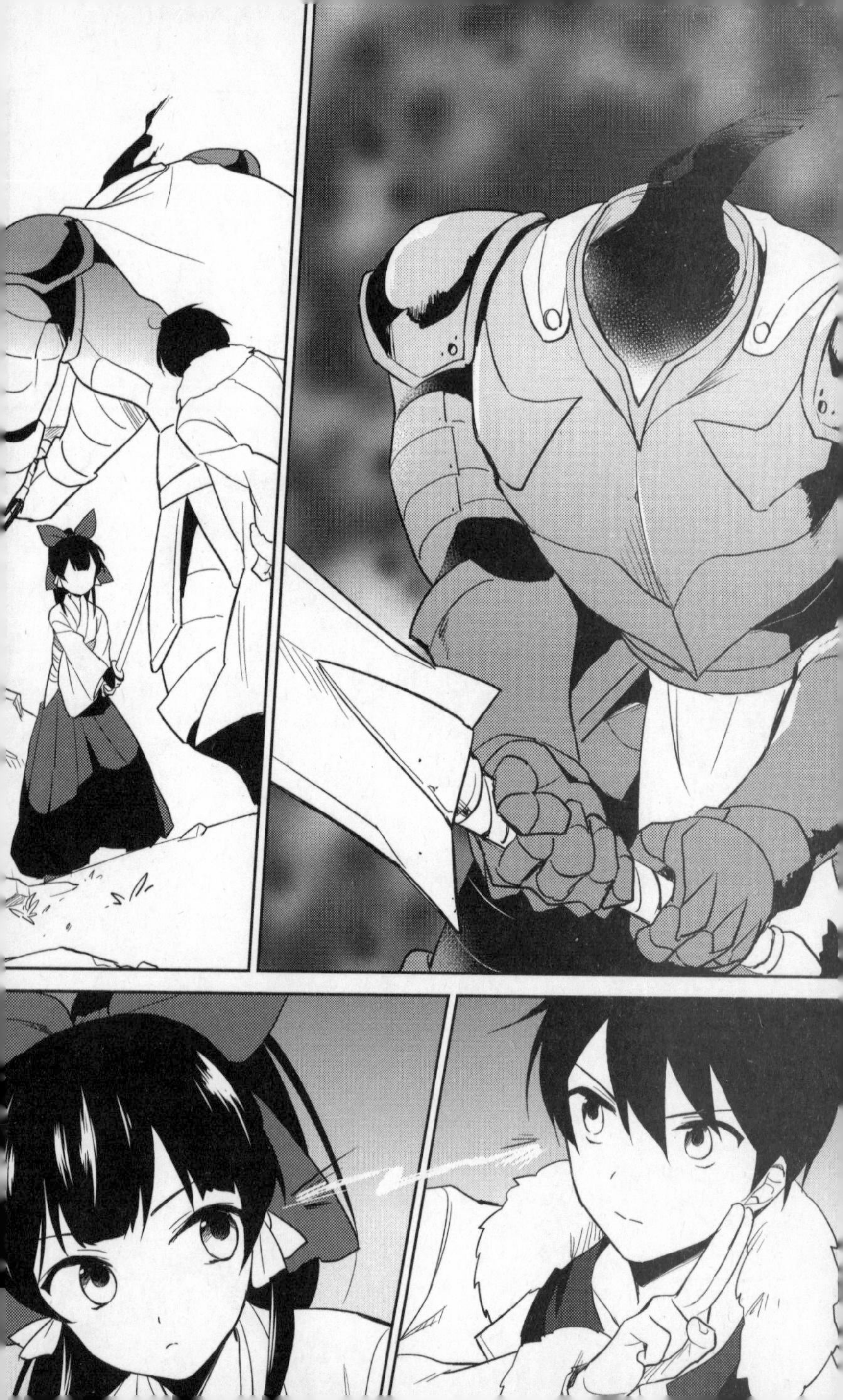

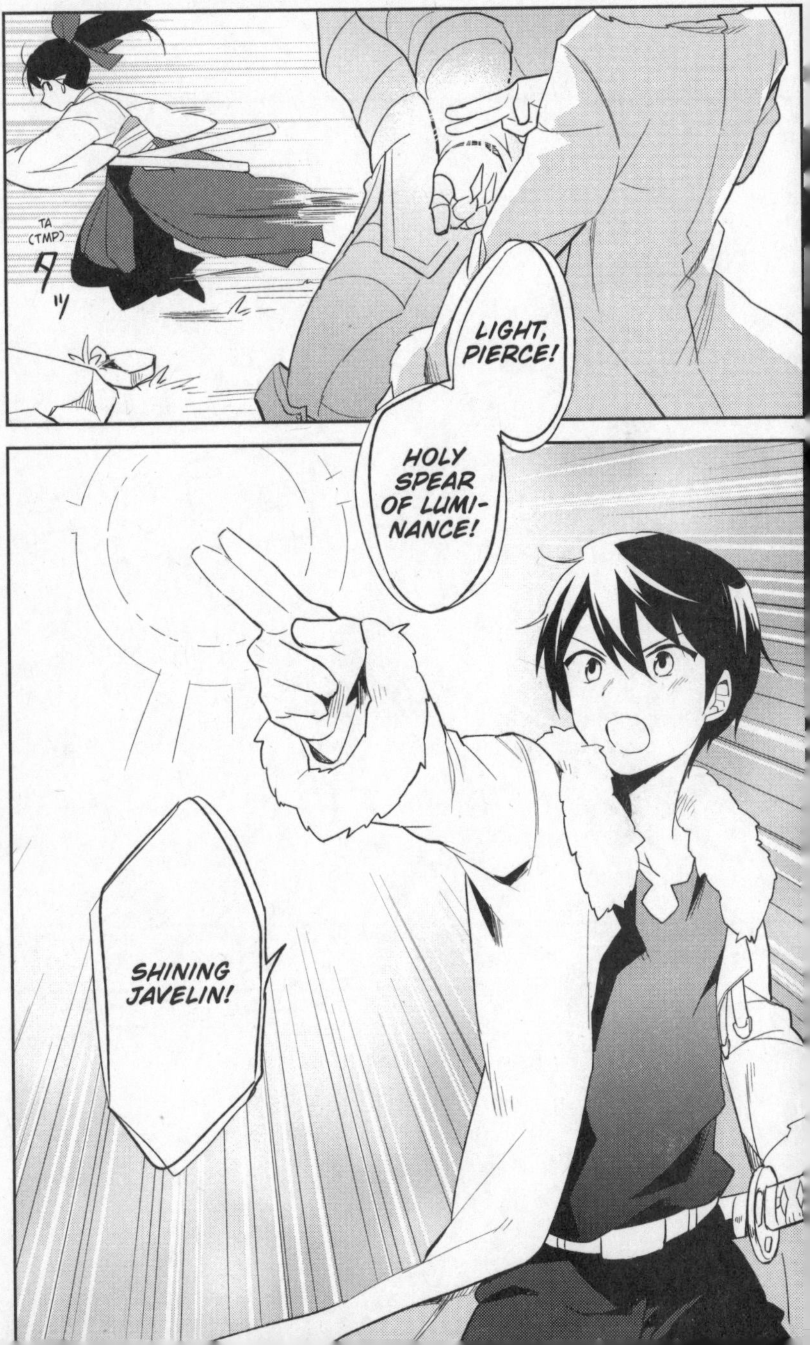
LIGHT, PIERCE!
TA (TMP)
タッ
HOLY SPEAR OF LUMI-NANCE!
SHINING JAVELIN!

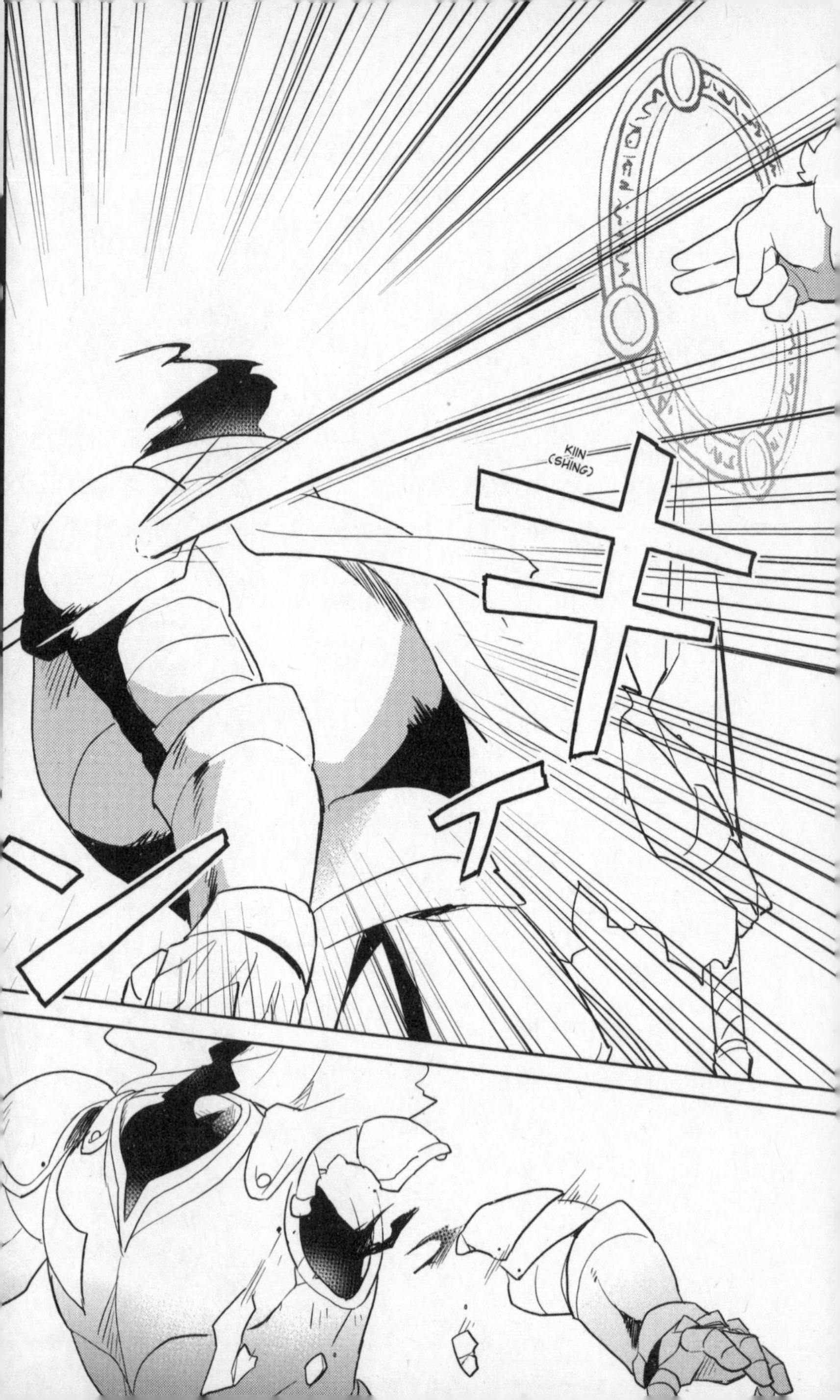
KIIN (SHING)

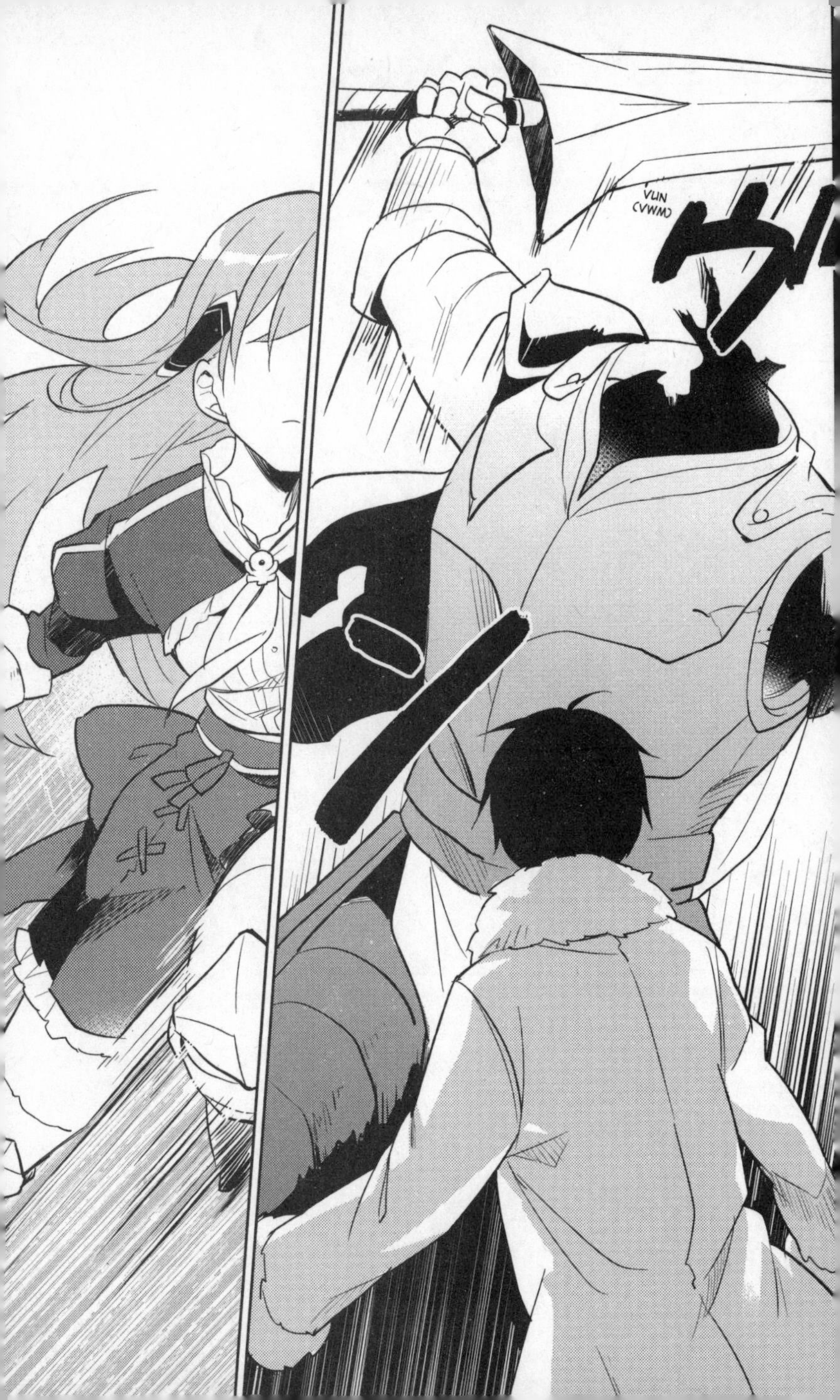
VUN
(VWM)

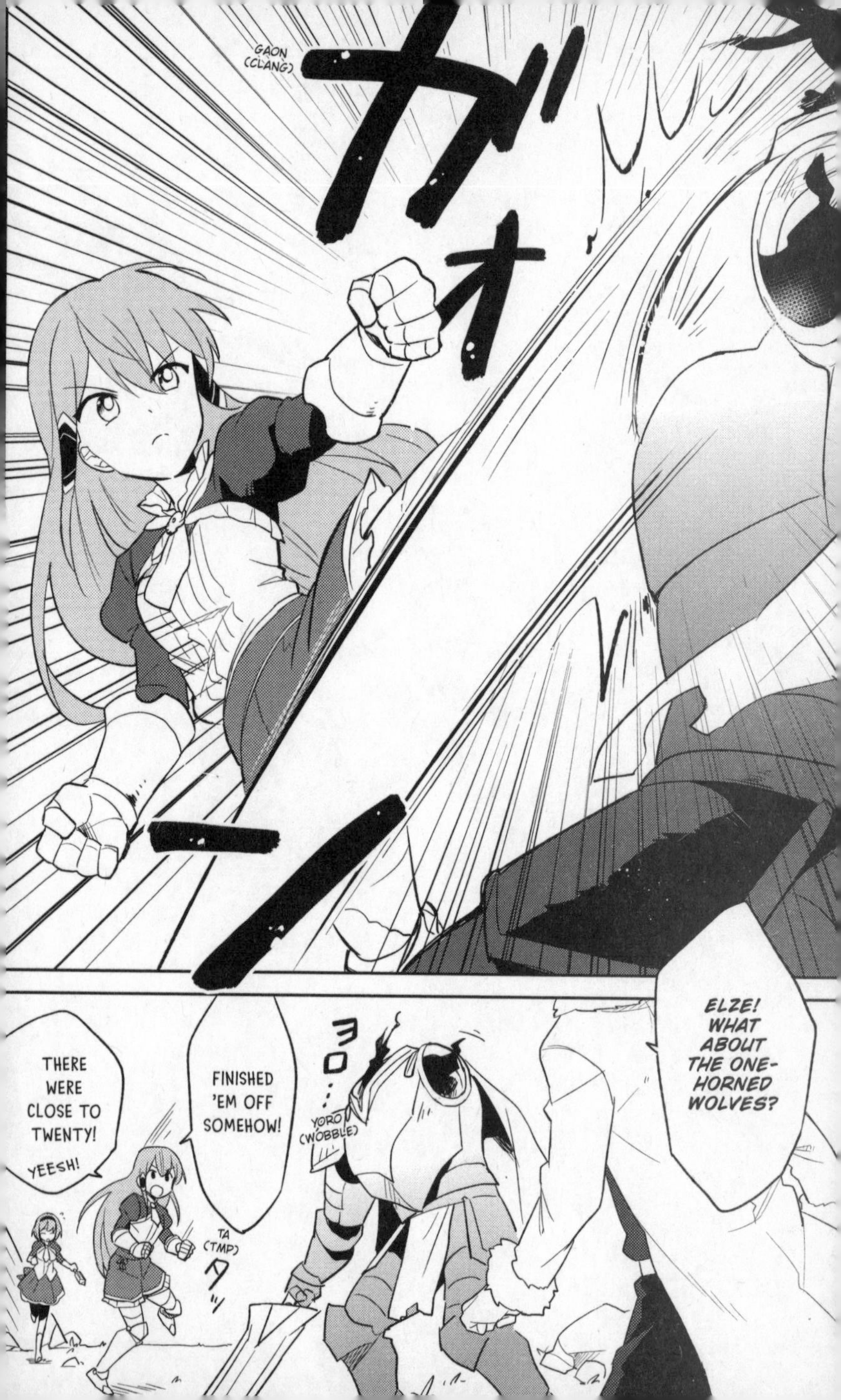
ガオー
GAON (CLANG)
ELZE! WHAT ABOUT THE ONE-HORNED WOLVES?
ヨロ…
YORO (WOBBLE)
FINISHED 'EM OFF SOMEHOW!
THERE WERE CLOSE TO TWENTY! YEESH!
タッ
TA (TMP)

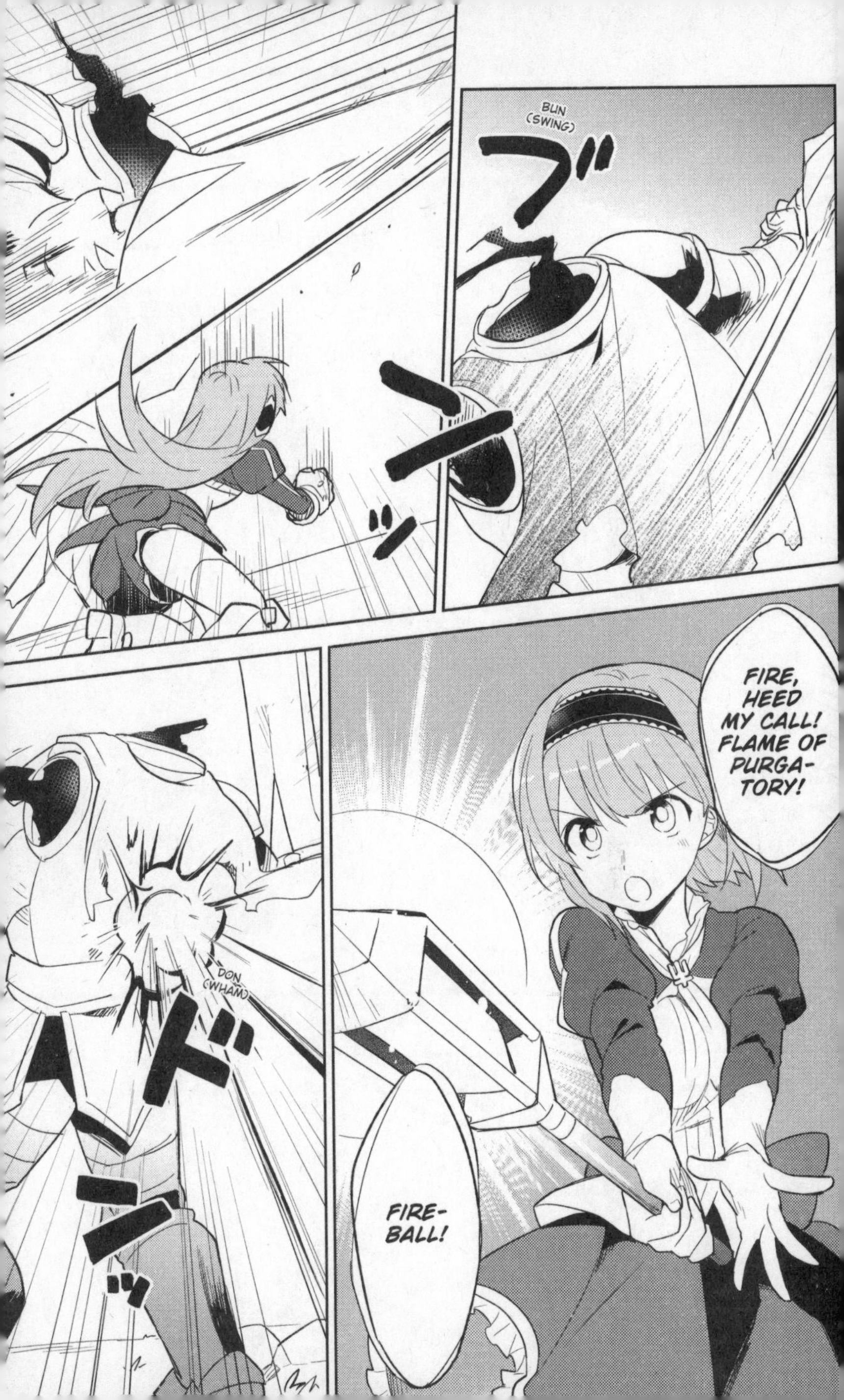
BUN (SWING)
FIRE, HEED MY CALL! FLAME OF PURGA-TORY!
FIRE-BALL!
DON (WHAM)

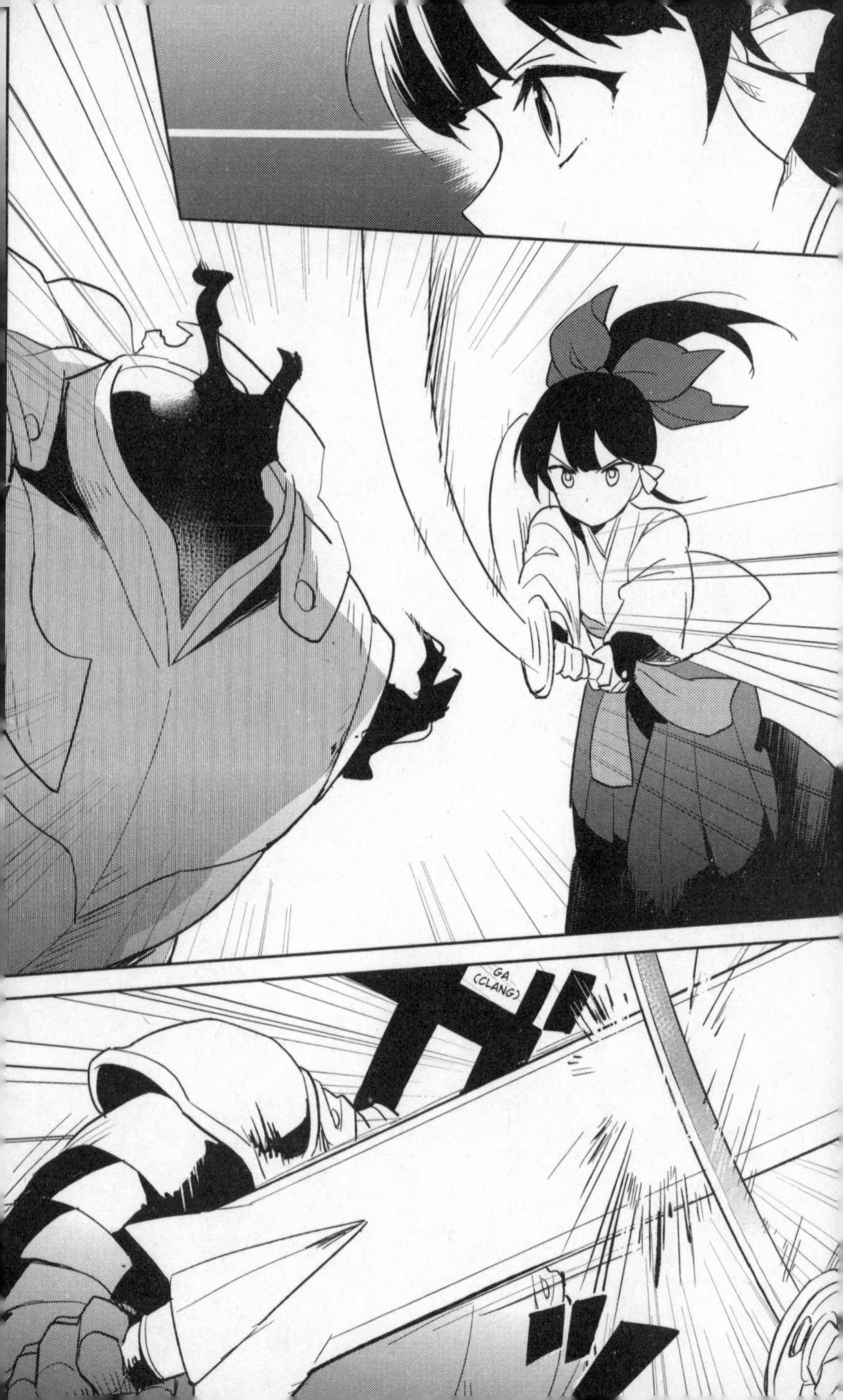
GA (CLANG)

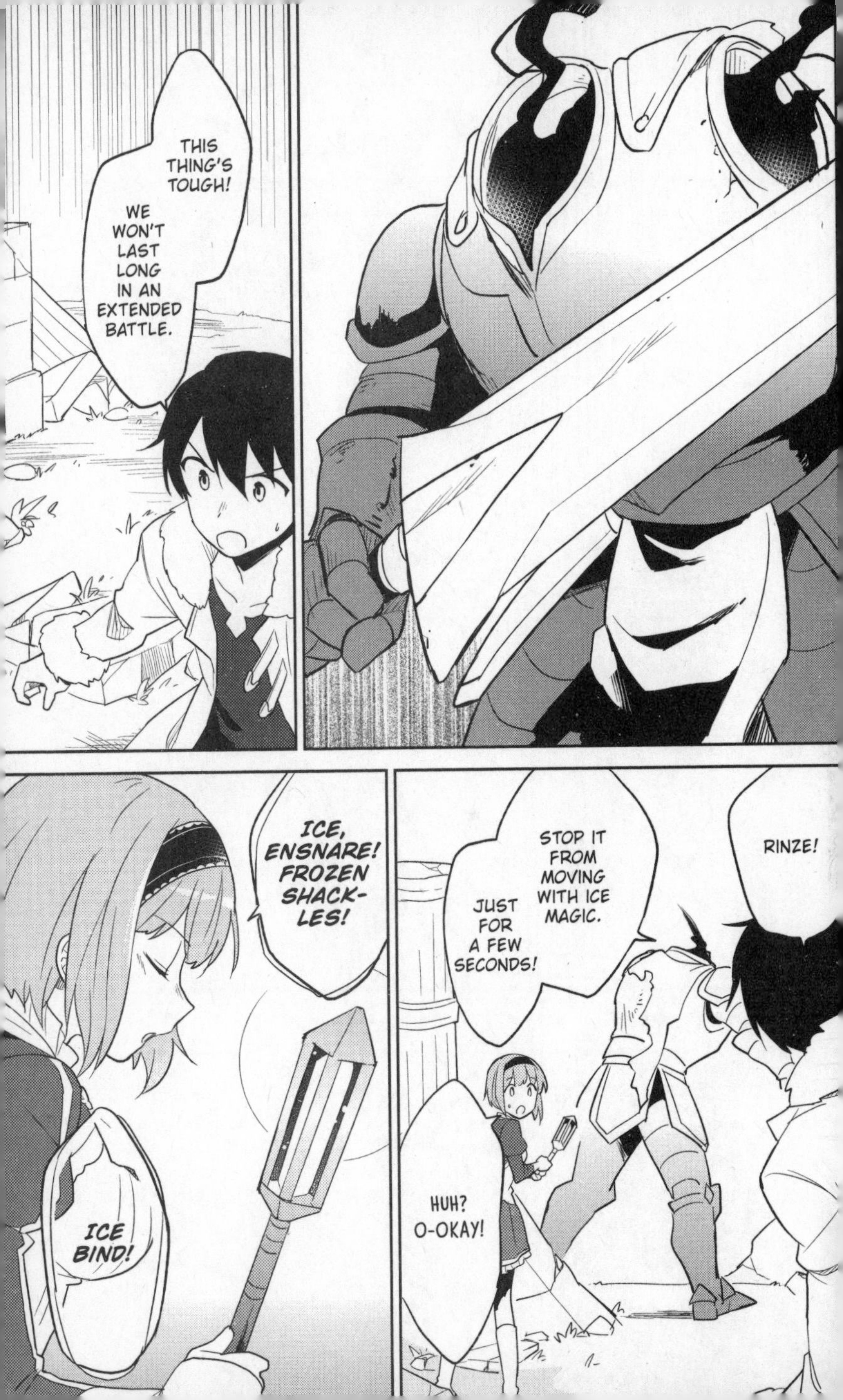
THIS THING'S TOUGH!
WE WON'T LAST LONG IN AN EXTENDED BATTLE.
RINZE!
STOP IT FROM MOVING WITH ICE MAGIC.
JUST FOR A FEW SECONDS!
HUH? O-OKAY!
ICE, ENSNARE! FROZEN SHACK-LES!
ICE BIND!

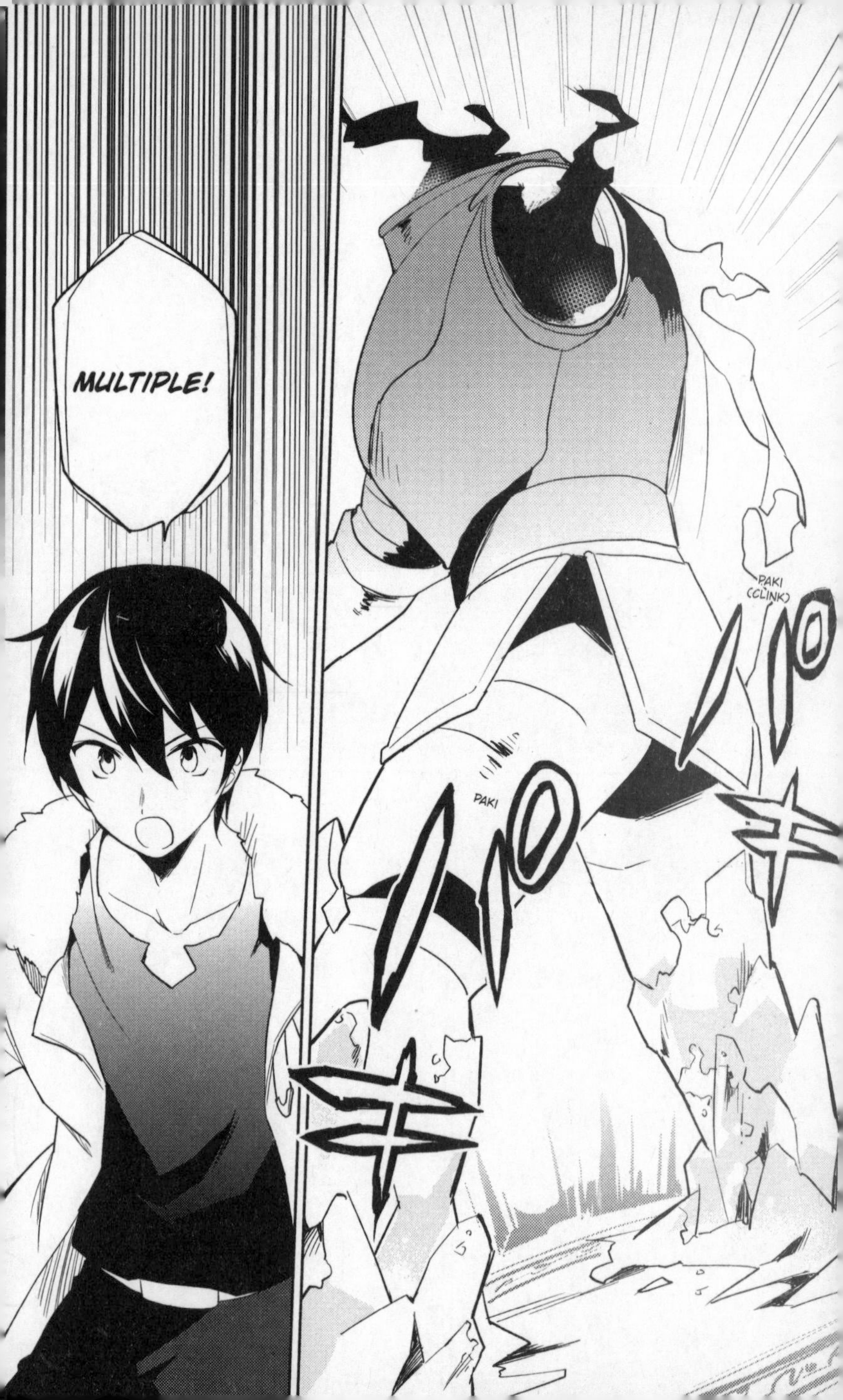
PAKI
(CLINK)
PAKI
MULTIPLE!

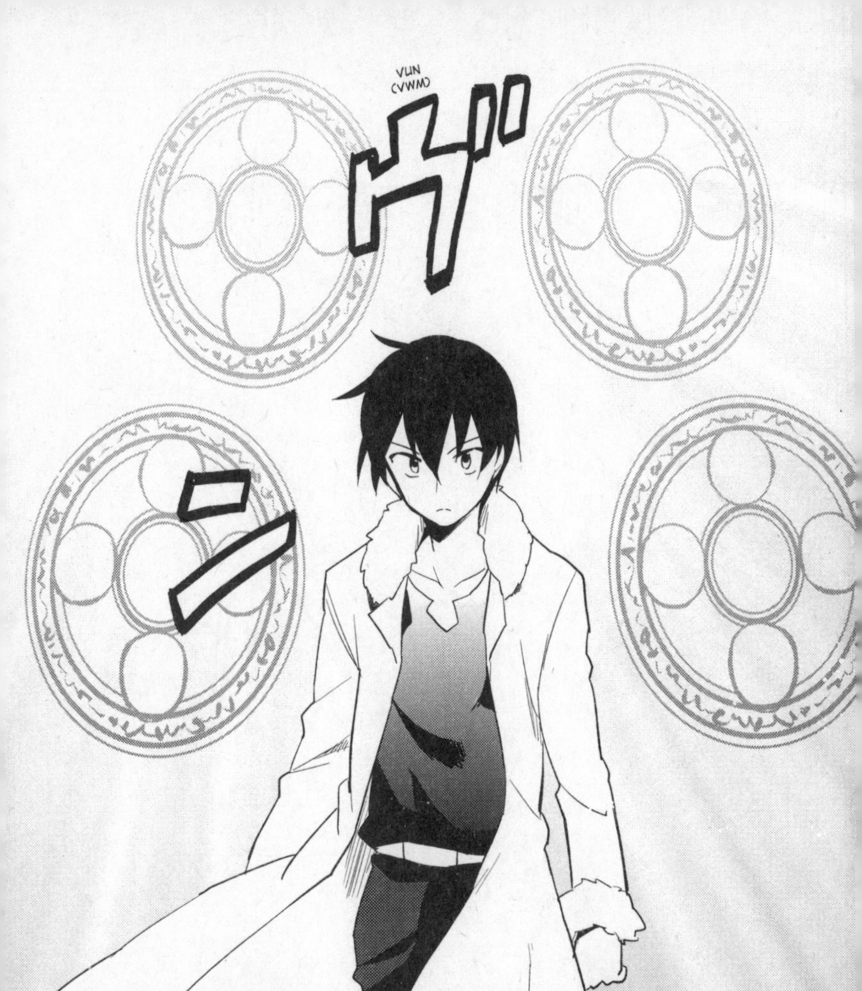
VUN (VWM)

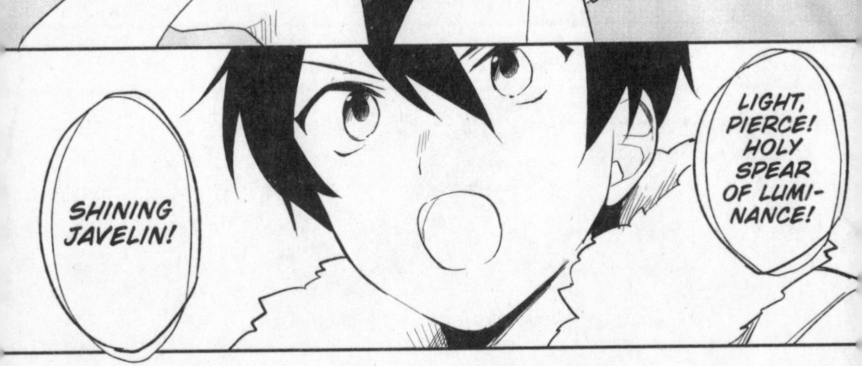
LIGHT, PIERCE! HOLY SPEAR OF LUMI-NANCE!
SHINING JAVELIN!

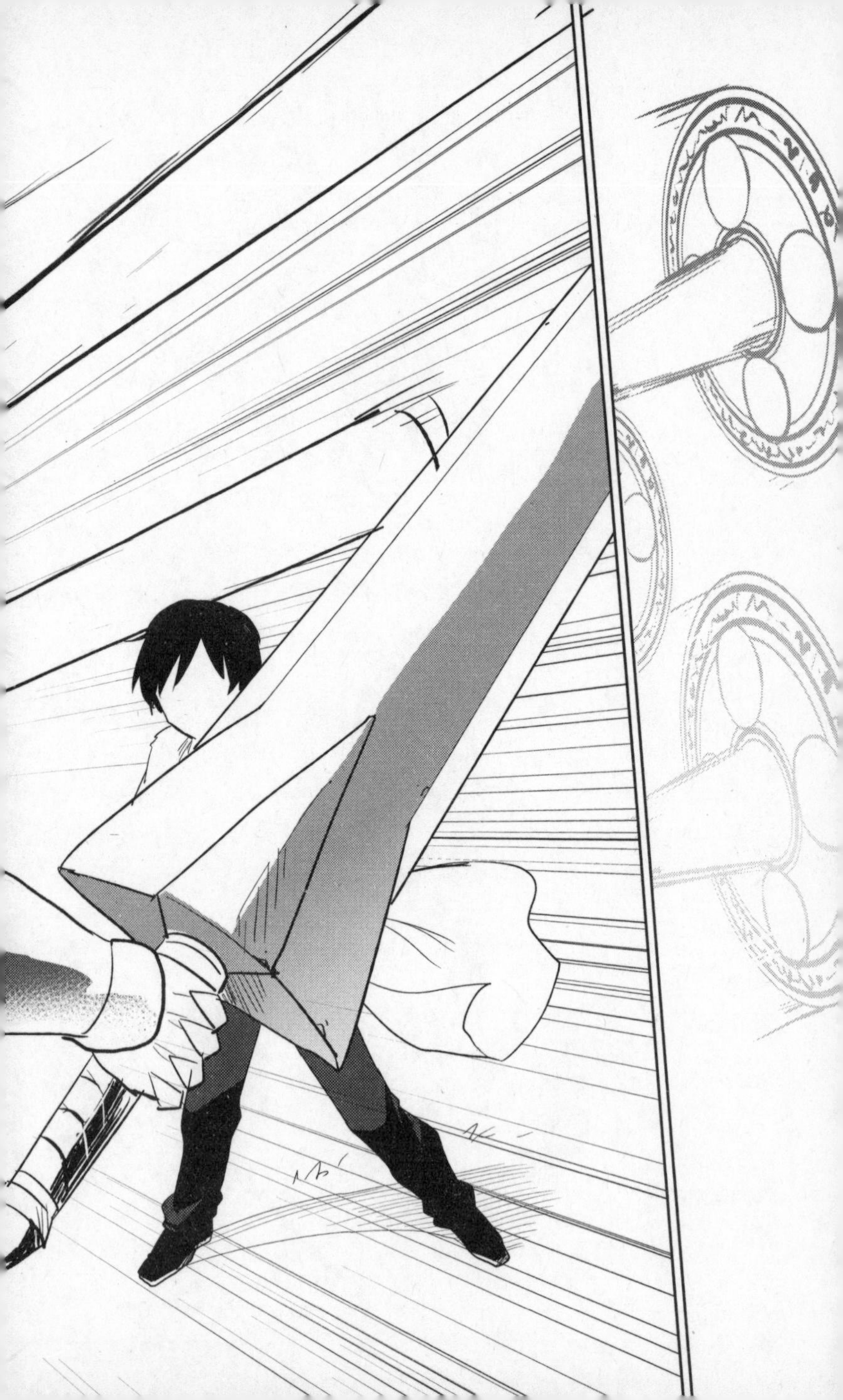

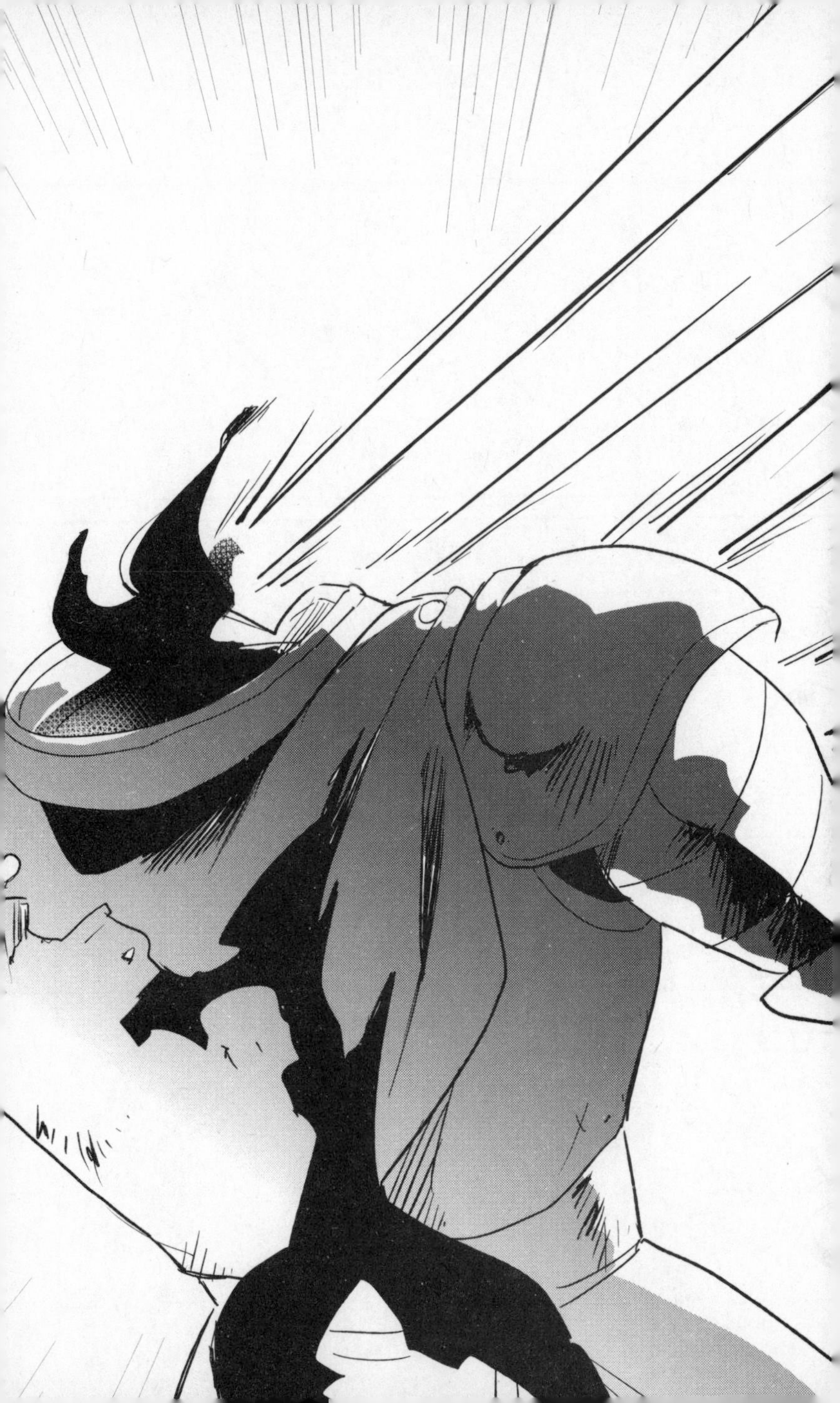

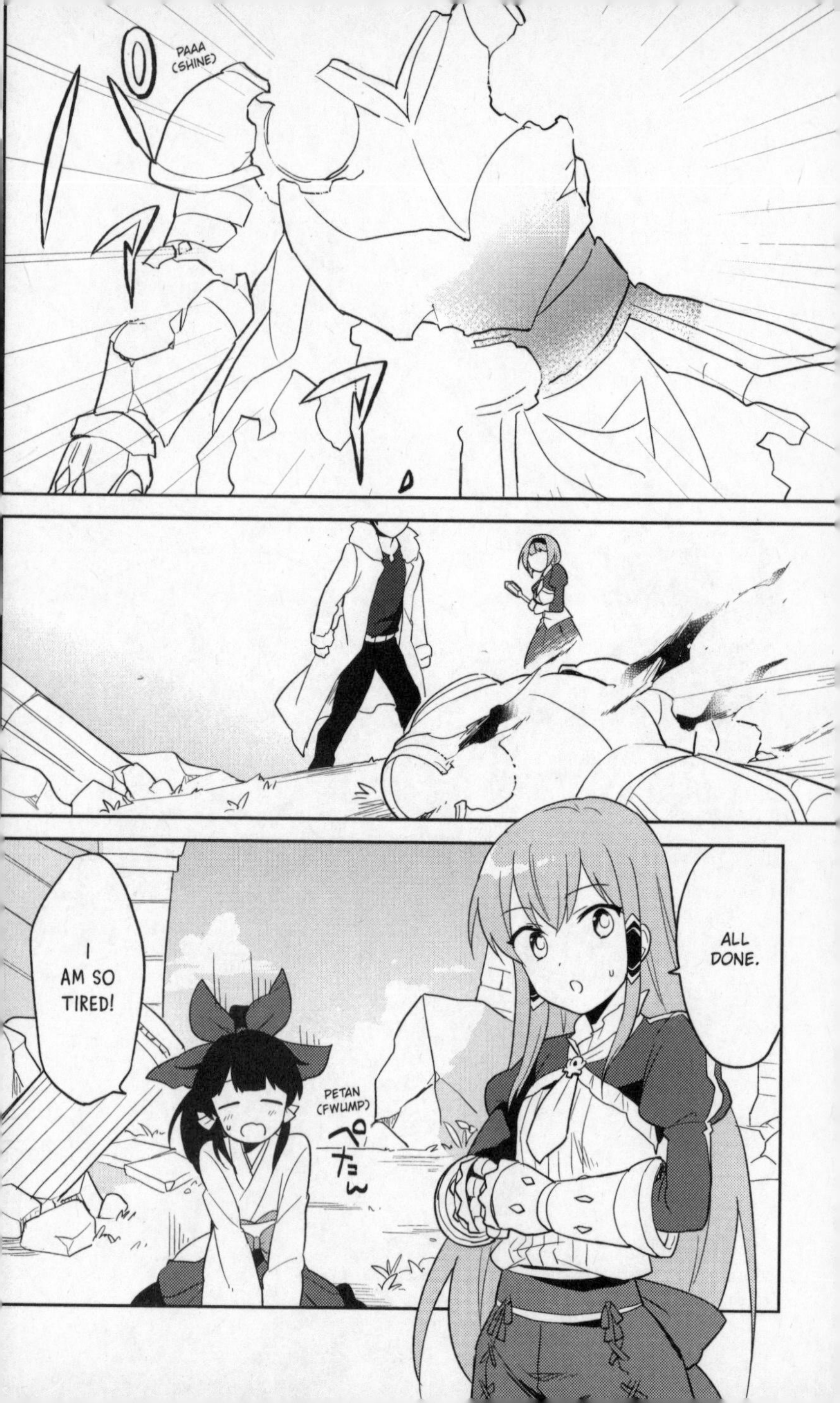
PAAA (SHINE)
ALL DONE.
PETAN (FWUMP)
ぺたん
I AM SO TIRED!

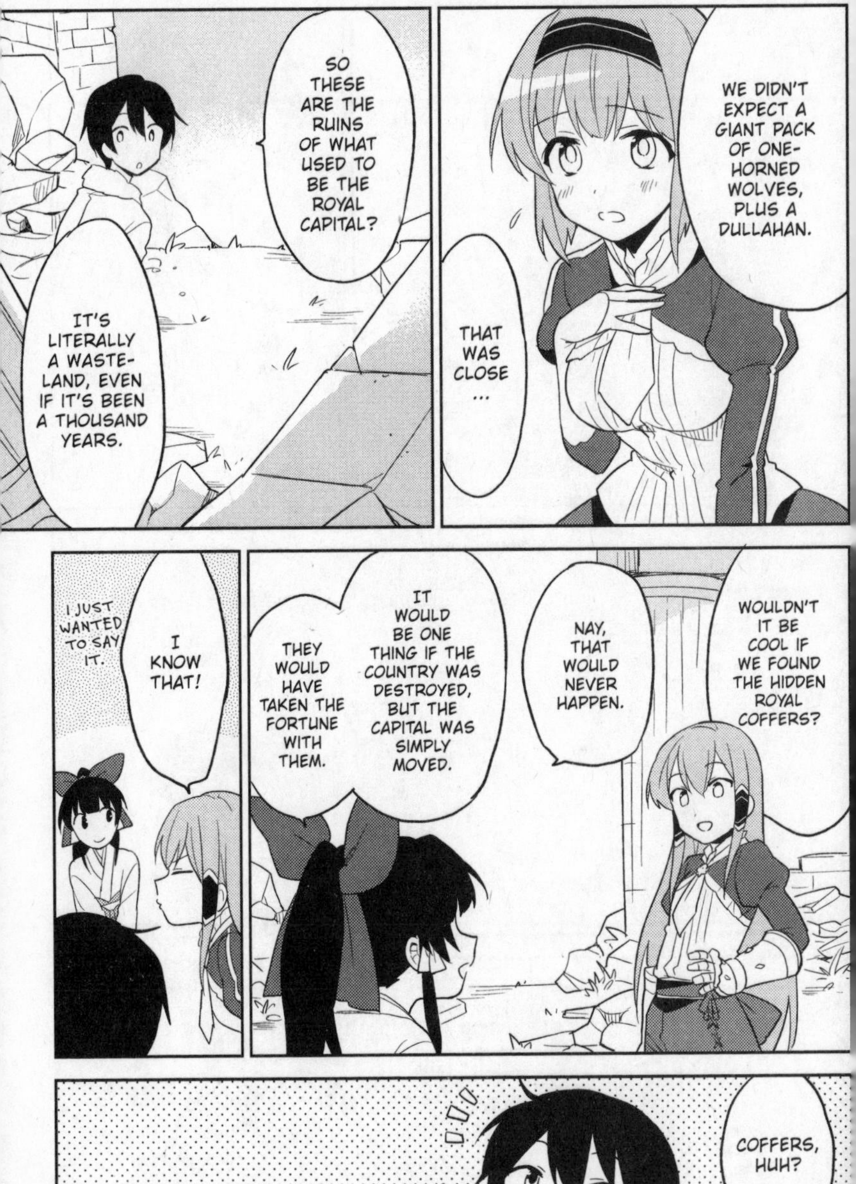
WE DIDN'T EXPECT A GIANT PACK OF ONE-HORNED WOLVES, PLUS A DULLAHAN.
THAT WAS CLOSE...
SO THESE ARE THE RUINS OF WHAT USED TO BE THE ROYAL CAPITAL?
IT'S LITERALLY A WASTELAND, EVEN IF IT'S BEEN A THOUSAND YEARS.
WOULDN'T IT BE COOL IF WE FOUND THE HIDDEN ROYAL COFFERS?
NAY, THAT WOULD NEVER HAPPEN.
IT WOULD BE ONE THING IF THE COUNTRY WAS DESTROYED, BUT THE CAPITAL WAS SIMPLY MOVED.
THEY WOULD HAVE TAKEN THE FORTUNE WITH THEM.
I KNOW THAT!
I JUST WANTED TO SAY IT.
COFFERS, HUH?
OH!

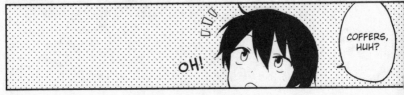

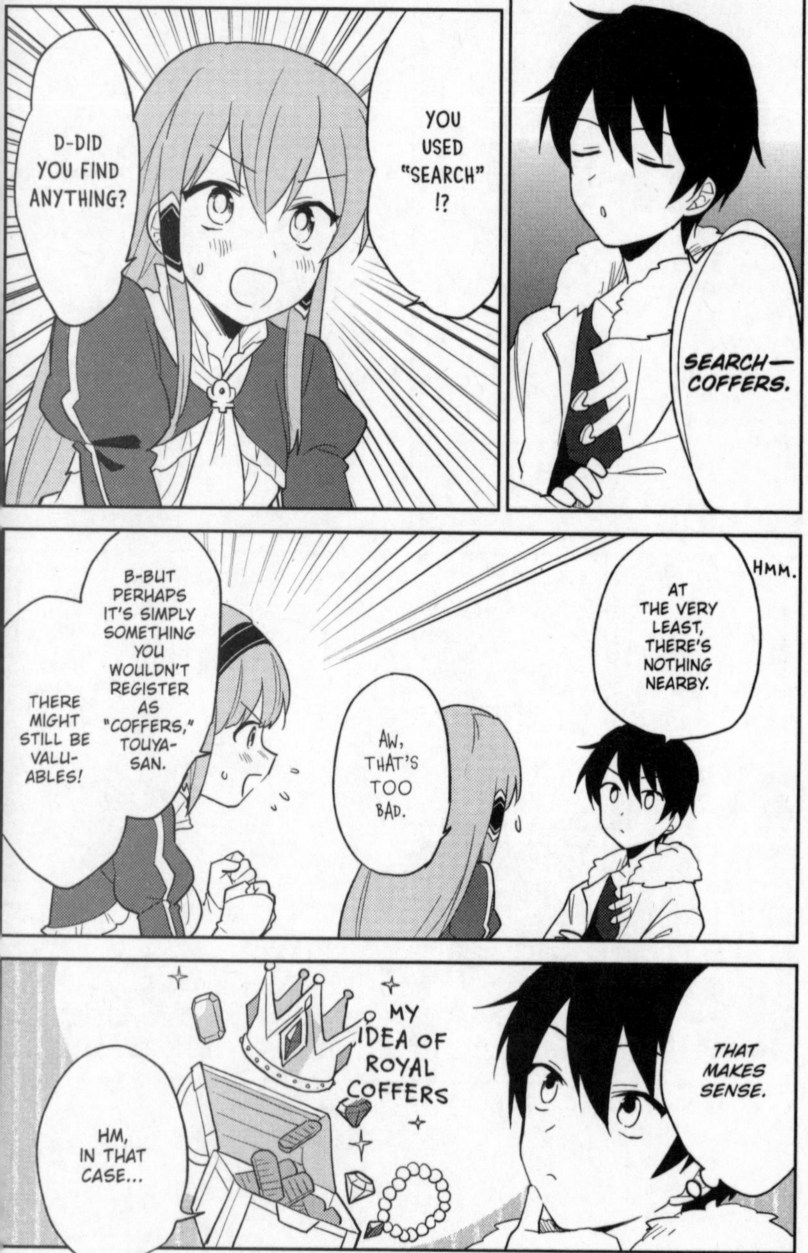
SEARCH—COFFERS.
YOU USED "SEARCH" !?
D-DID YOU FIND ANYTHING?
HMM.
AT THE VERY LEAST, THERE'S NOTHING NEARBY.
AW, THAT'S TOO BAD.
B-BUT PERHAPS IT'S SIMPLY SOMETHING YOU WOULDN'T REGISTER AS "COFFERS," TOUYA-SAN.
THERE MIGHT STILL BE VALU-ABLES!
THAT MAKES SENSE.
MY IDEA OF ROYAL COFFERS
HM, IN THAT CASE...

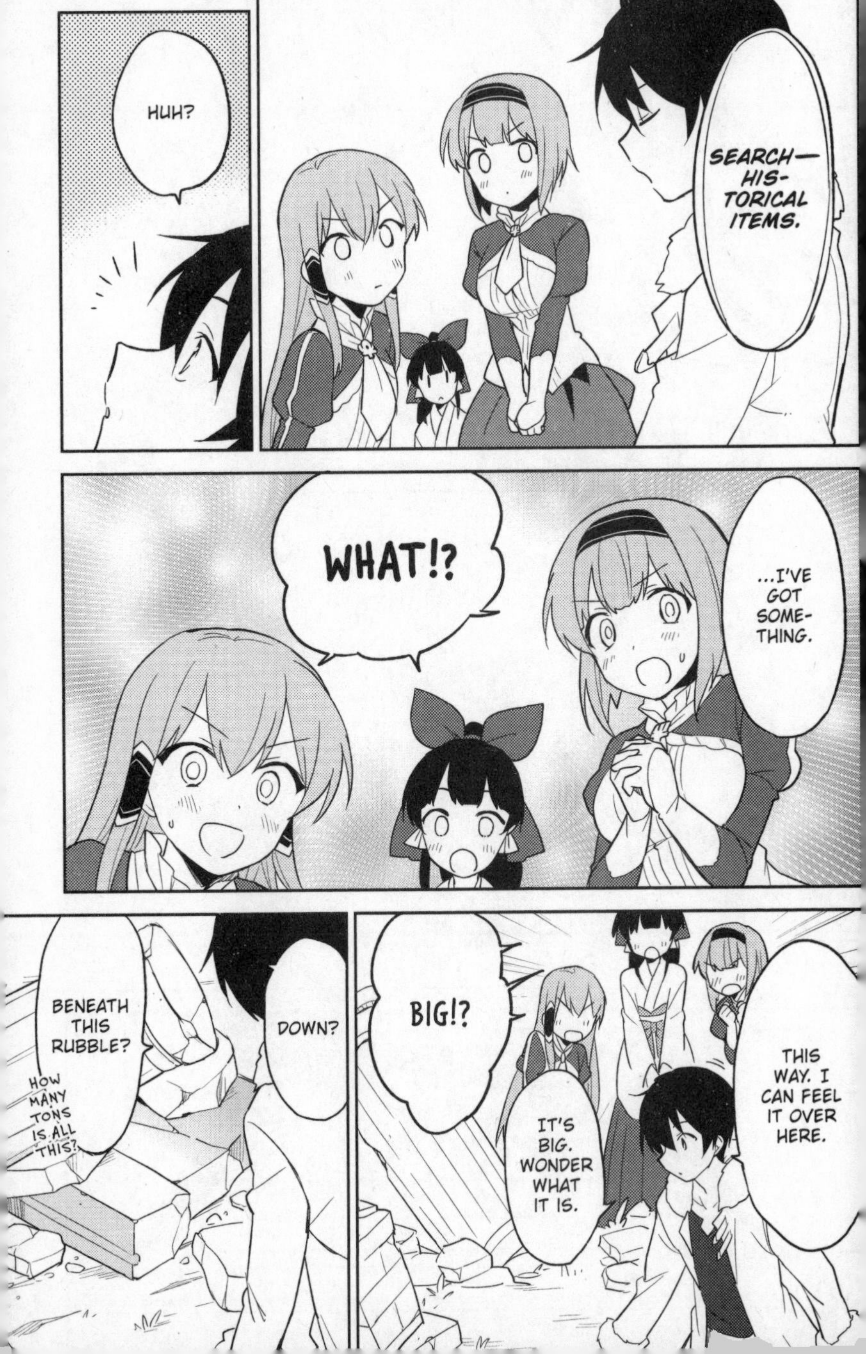

SEARCH— HIS-TORICAL ITEMS.
HUH?
...I'VE GOT SOME-THING.
WHAT!?
THIS WAY. I CAN FEEL IT OVER HERE.
BIG!?
IT'S BIG. WONDER WHAT IT IS.
DOWN?
BENEATH THIS RUBBLE?
HOW MANY TONS IS ALL THIS?

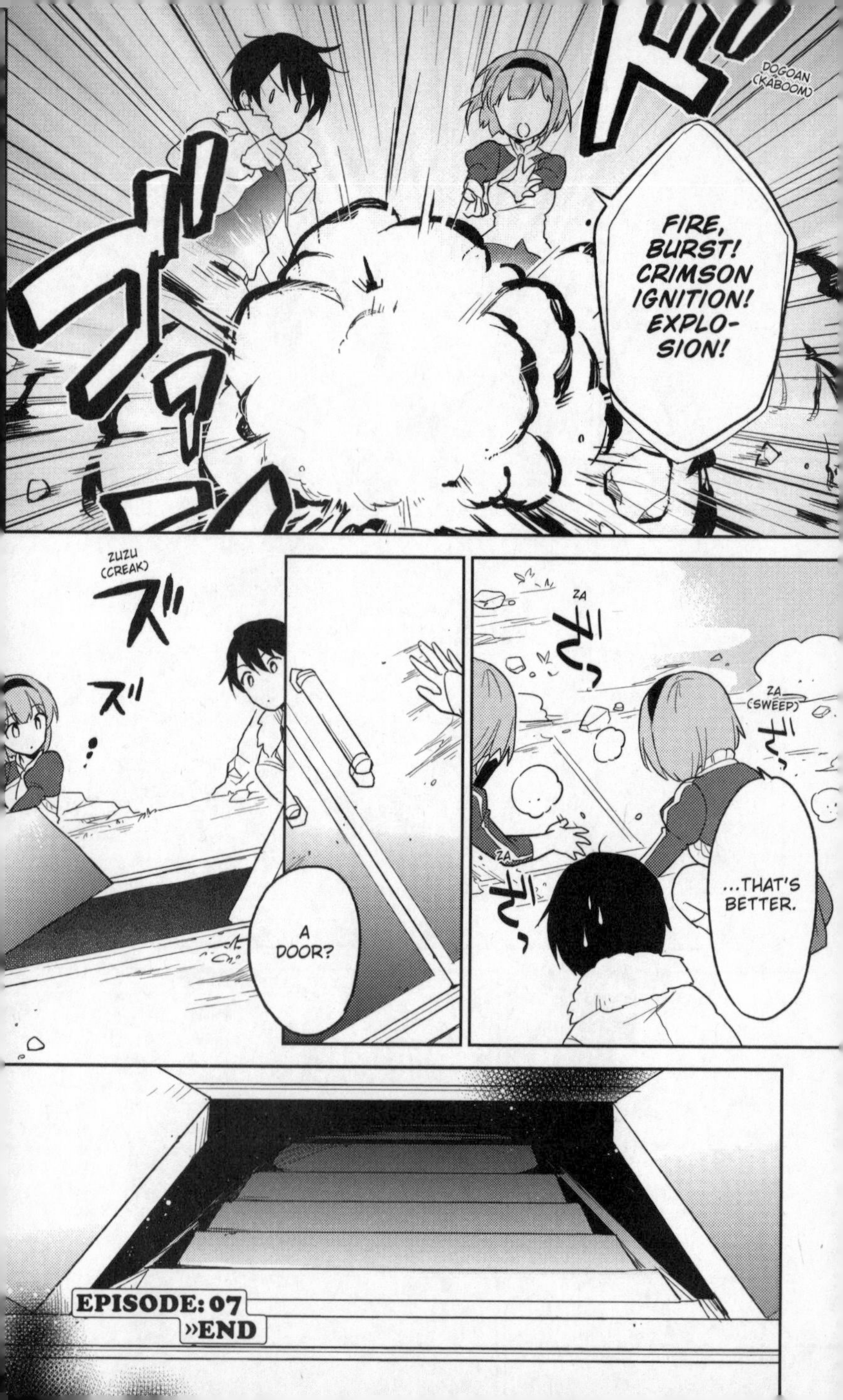
DOGOAN (KABOOM)
FIRE, BURST! CRIMSON IGNITION! EXPLOSION!
ZA
ZA (SWEEP)
ZA
...THAT'S BETTER.
A DOOR?
ZUZU (CREAK)
EPISODE: 07 »END

In Another World with
My Smartphone

In Another World with My Smartphone

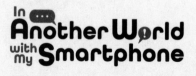

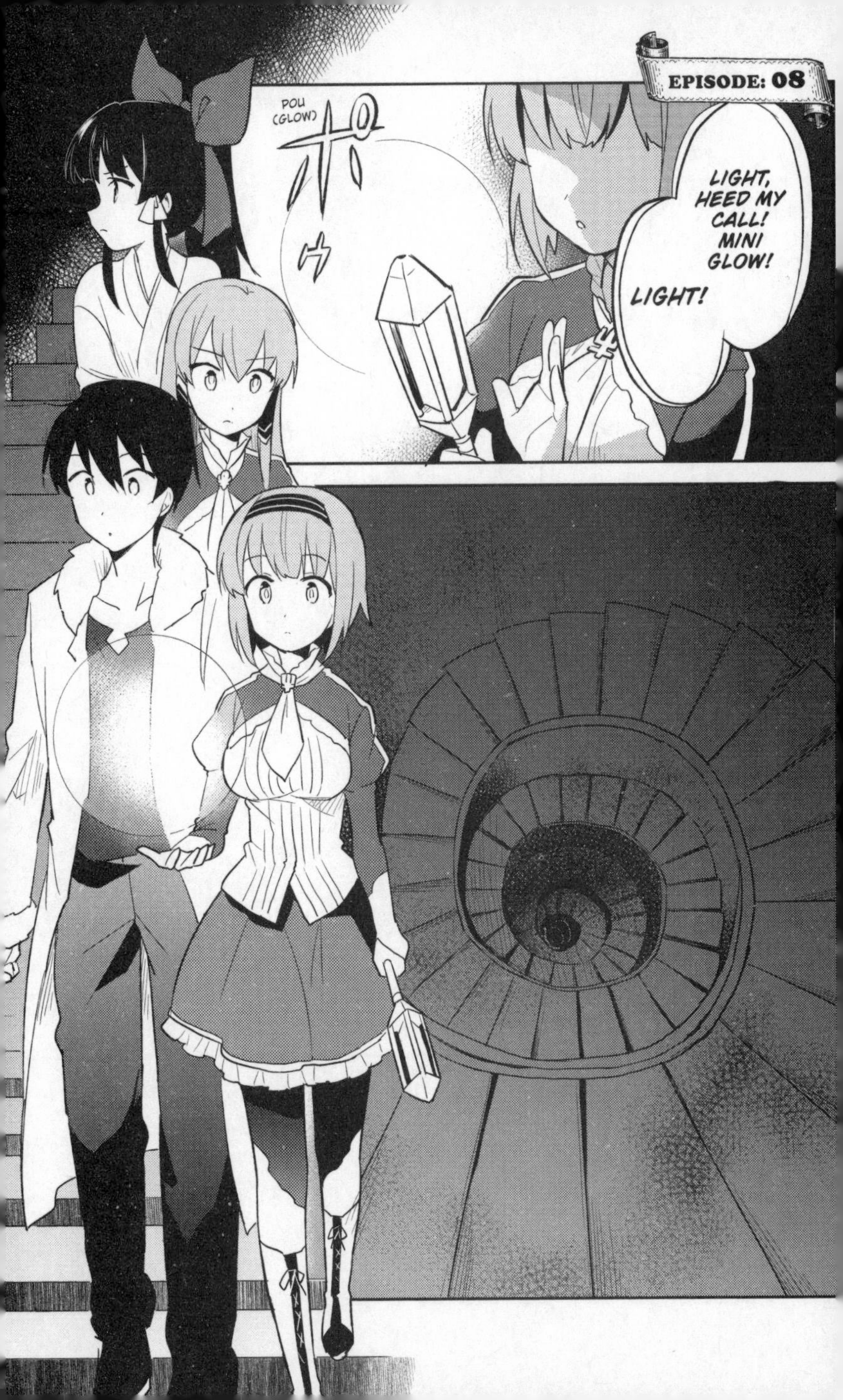
EPISODE: 08
LIGHT, HEED MY CALL! MINI GLOW!
LIGHT!
POU (GLOW)

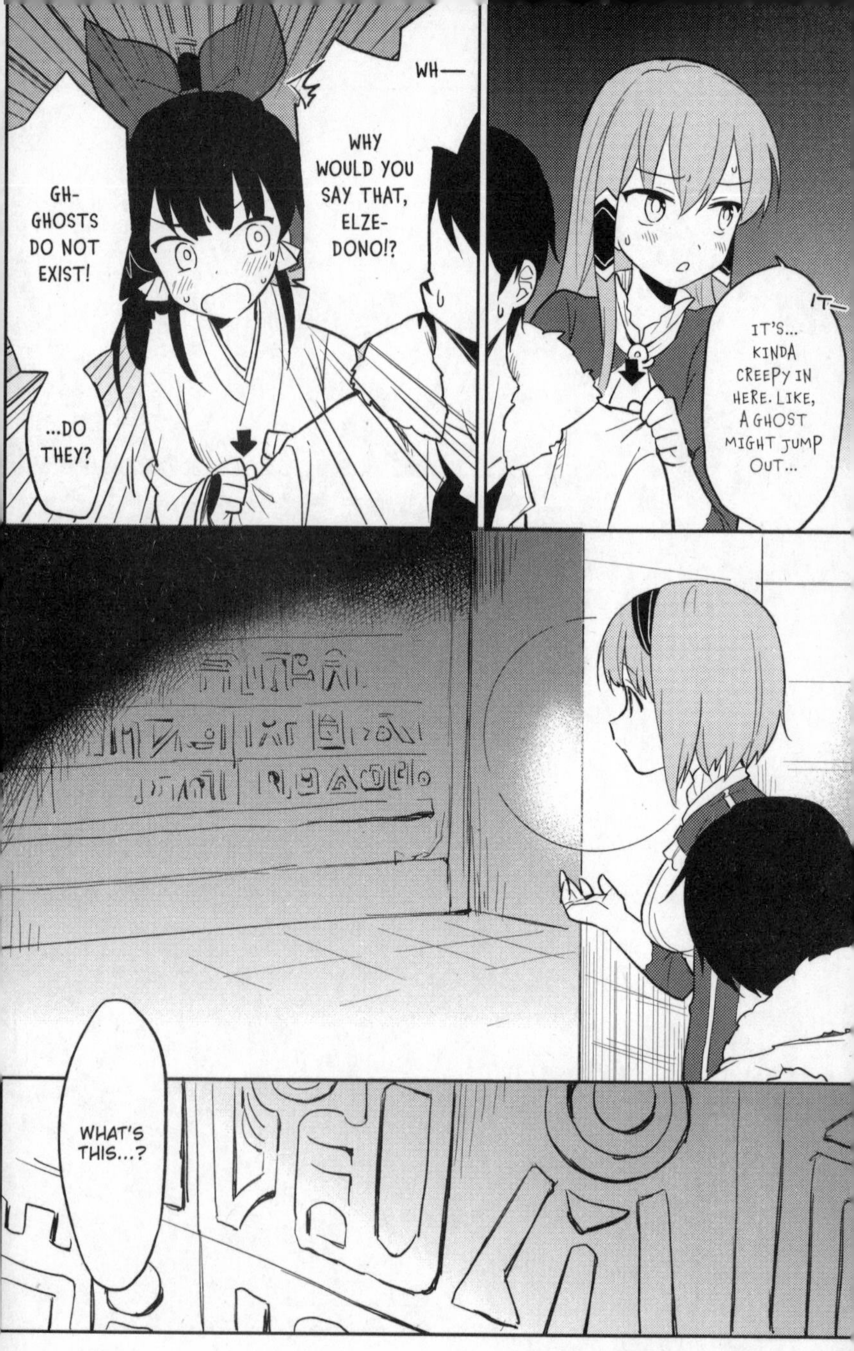
IT—
IT'S... KINDA CREEPY IN HERE. LIKE, A GHOST MIGHT JUMP OUT...
WH—
WHY WOULD YOU SAY THAT, ELZE-DONO!?
GH-GHOSTS DO NOT EXIST!
...DO THEY?
WHAT'S THIS...?

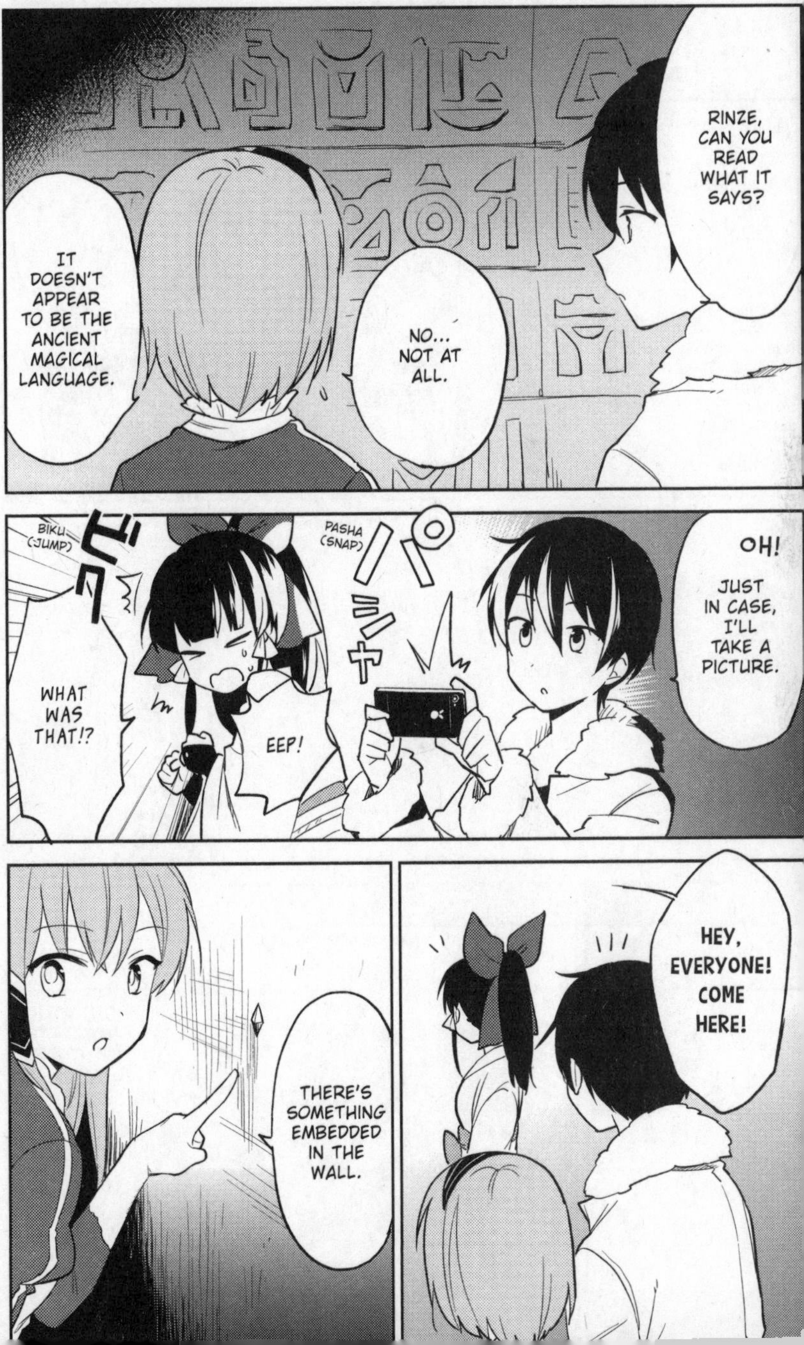
RINZE, CAN YOU READ WHAT IT SAYS?
NO... NOT AT ALL.
IT DOESN'T APPEAR TO BE THE ANCIENT MAGICAL LANGUAGE.
OH!
JUST IN CASE, I'LL TAKE A PICTURE.
PASHA (SNAP)
BIKU (JUMP)
EEP!
WHAT WAS THAT!?
HEY, EVERYONE! COME HERE!
THERE'S SOMETHING EMBEDDED IN THE WALL.

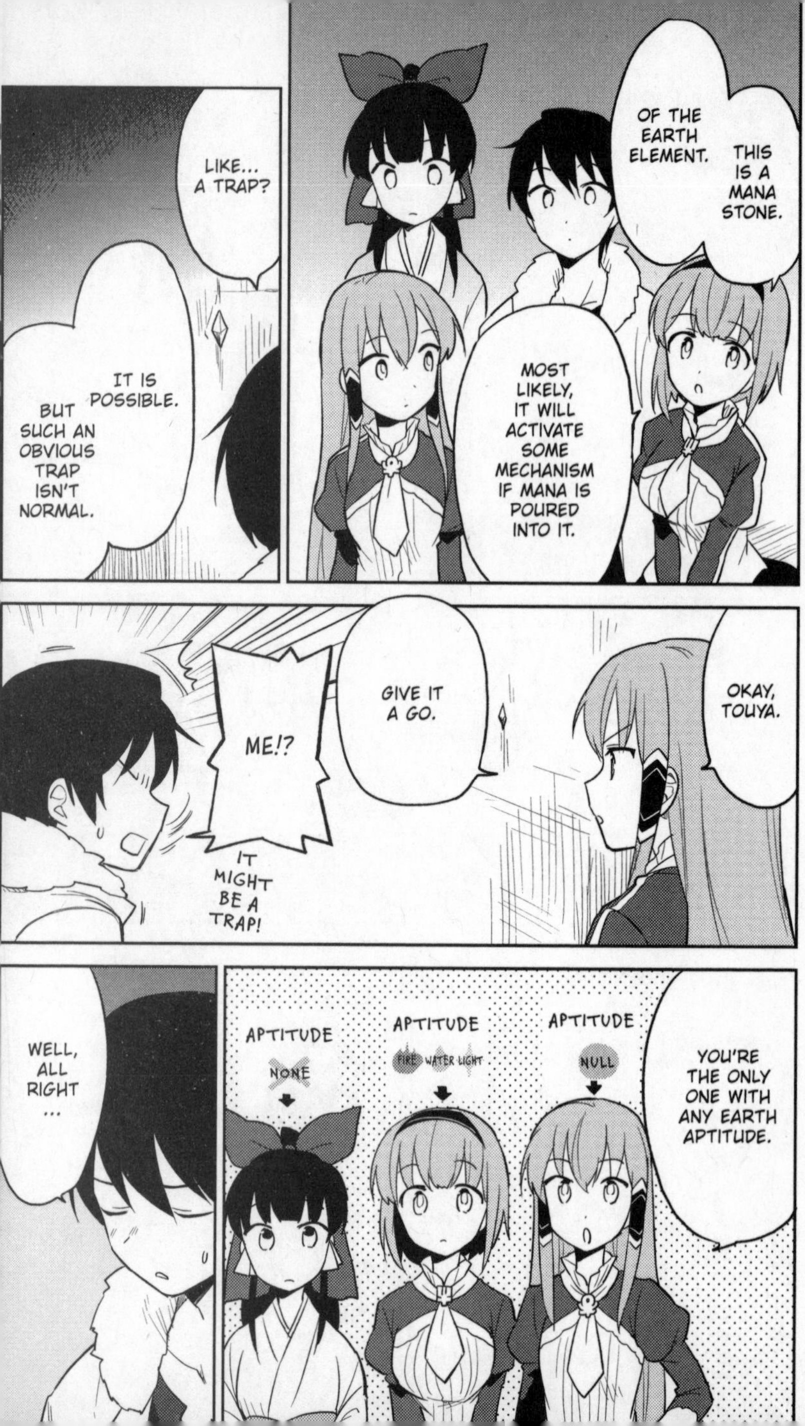
THIS IS A MANA STONE.
OF THE EARTH ELEMENT.
MOST LIKELY, IT WILL ACTIVATE SOME MECHANISM IF MANA IS POURED INTO IT.
LIKE... A TRAP?
IT IS POSSIBLE.
BUT SUCH AN OBVIOUS TRAP ISN'T NORMAL.
OKAY, TOUYA.
GIVE IT A GO.
ME!?
IT MIGHT BE A TRAP!
YOU'RE THE ONLY ONE WITH ANY EARTH APTITUDE.
APTITUDE
NULL
APTITUDE
FIRE WATER LIGHT
APTITUDE
NONE
WELL, ALL RIGHT ...

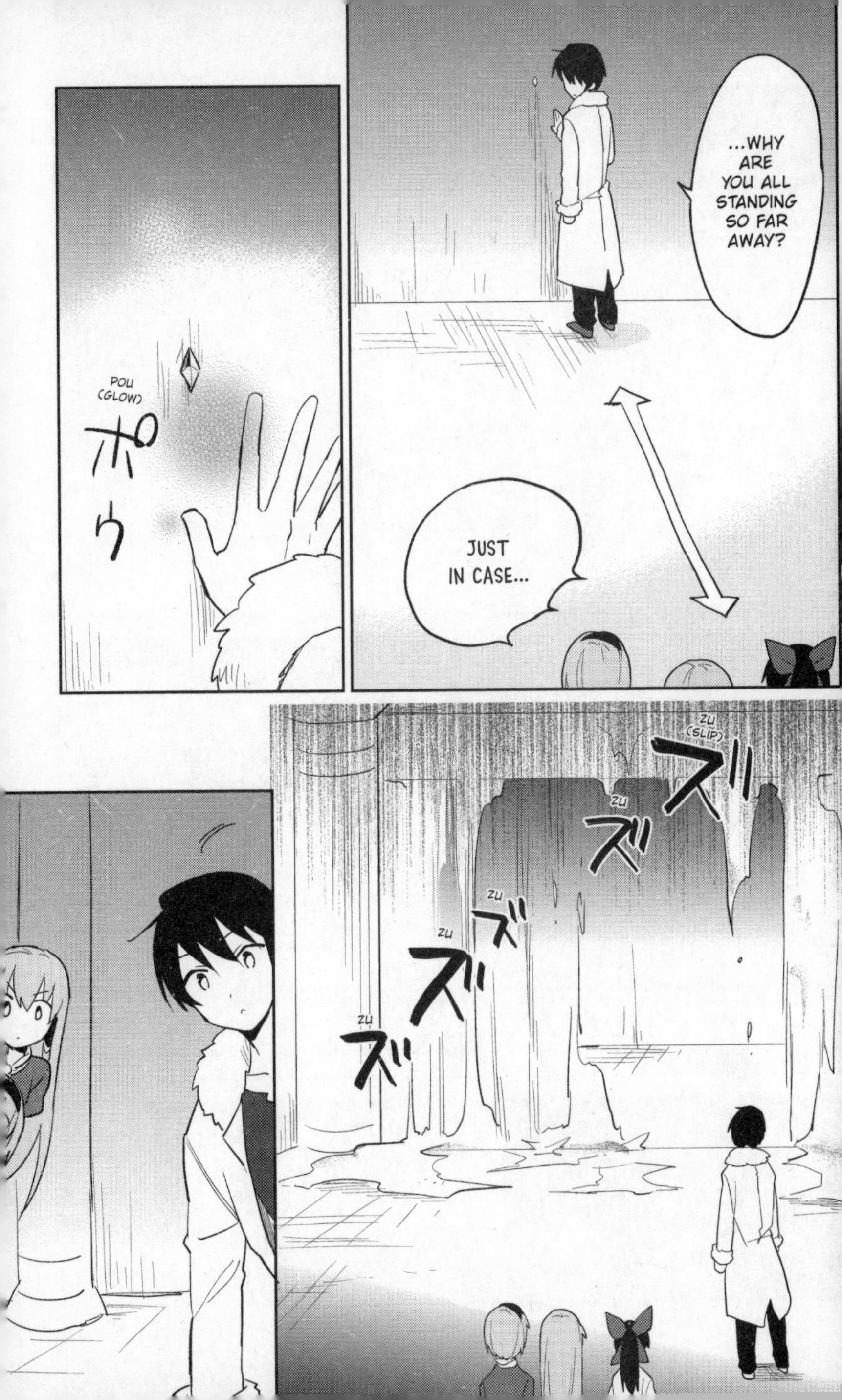
...WHY ARE YOU ALL STANDING SO FAR AWAY?
JUST IN CASE...
POU (GLOW)
ポウ
ZU (SLIP)
ズ
ZU
ズ
ZU
ズ
ZU
ズ
ZU
ズ

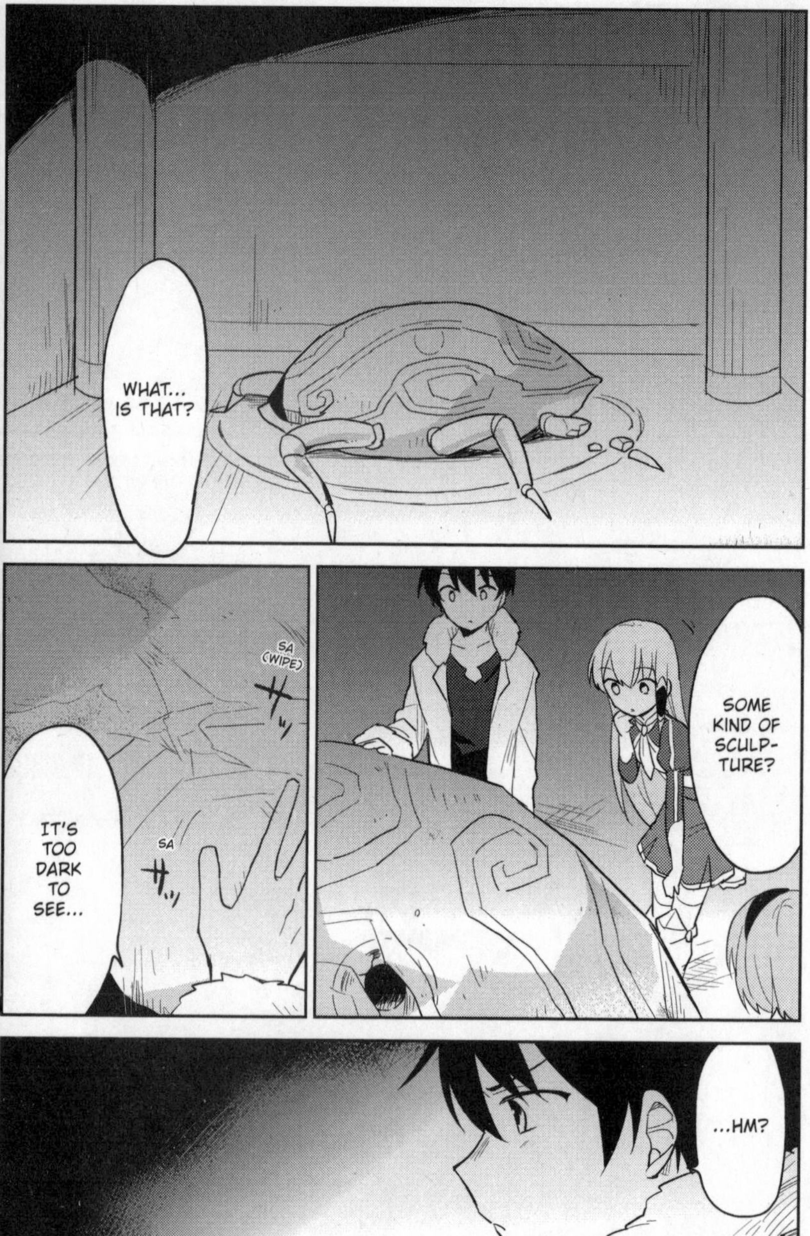
WHAT... IS THAT?
SOME KIND OF SCULP-TURE?
SA (WIPE)
SA
IT'S TOO DARK TO SEE...
...HM?

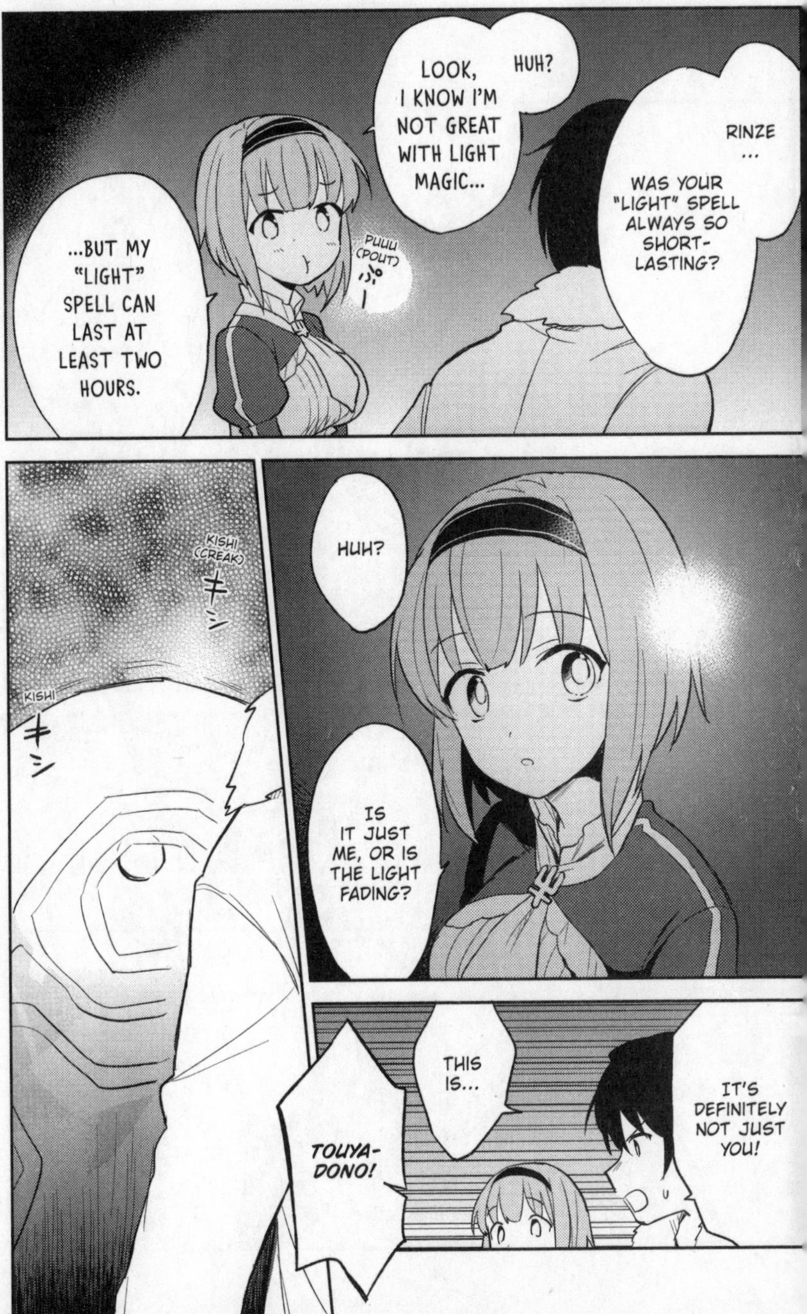
RINZE... WAS YOUR "LIGHT" SPELL ALWAYS SO SHORT-LASTING?
HUH?
LOOK, I KNOW I'M NOT GREAT WITH LIGHT MAGIC...
PUUU (POUT)
...BUT MY "LIGHT" SPELL CAN LAST AT LEAST TWO HOURS.
HUH?
IS IT JUST ME, OR IS THE LIGHT FADING?
IT'S DEFINITELY NOT JUST YOU!
THIS IS...
TOUYA-DONO!
KISHI (CREAK)
KISHI

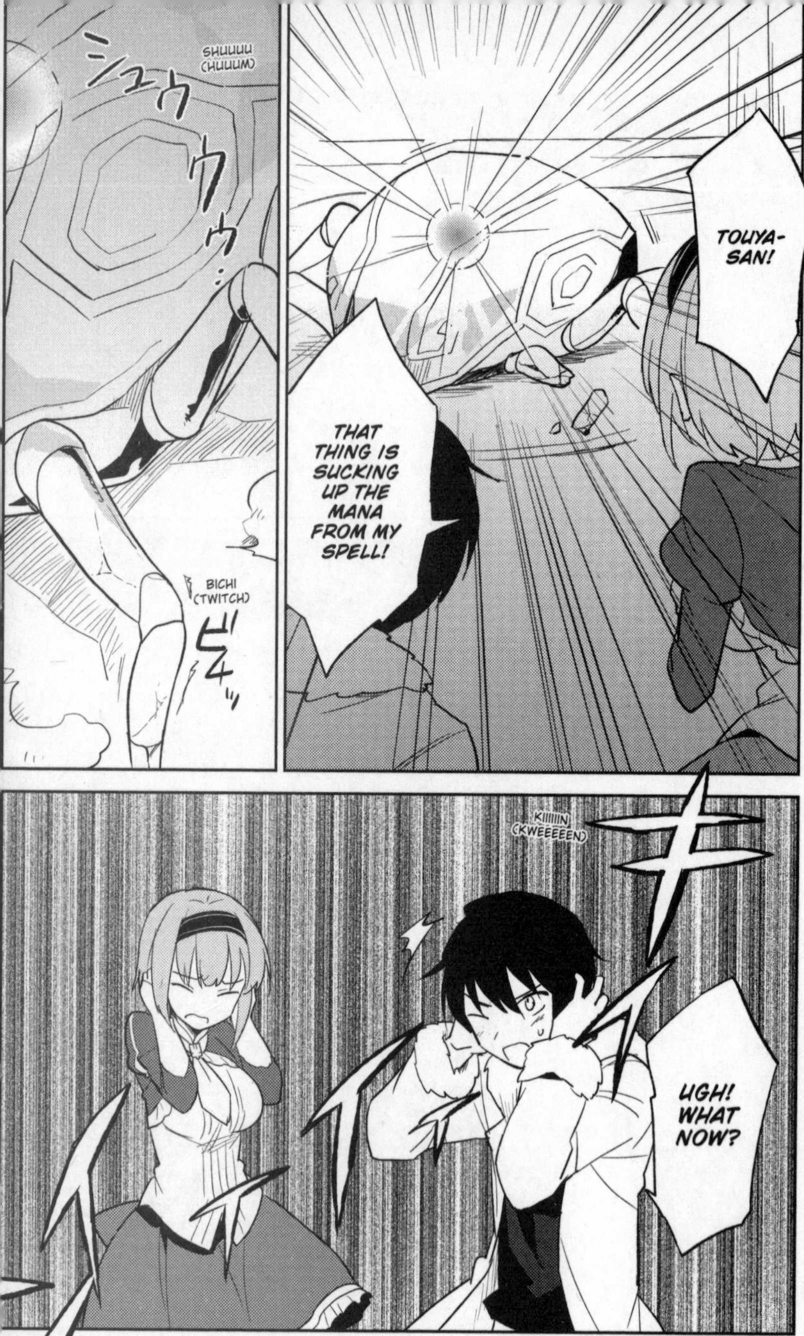
TOUYA-SAN!
THAT THING IS SUCKING UP THE MANA FROM MY SPELL!
SHUUUU (HUUUM)
BICHI (TWITCH)
KIIIIIN (KWEEEEEN)
UGH! WHAT NOW?

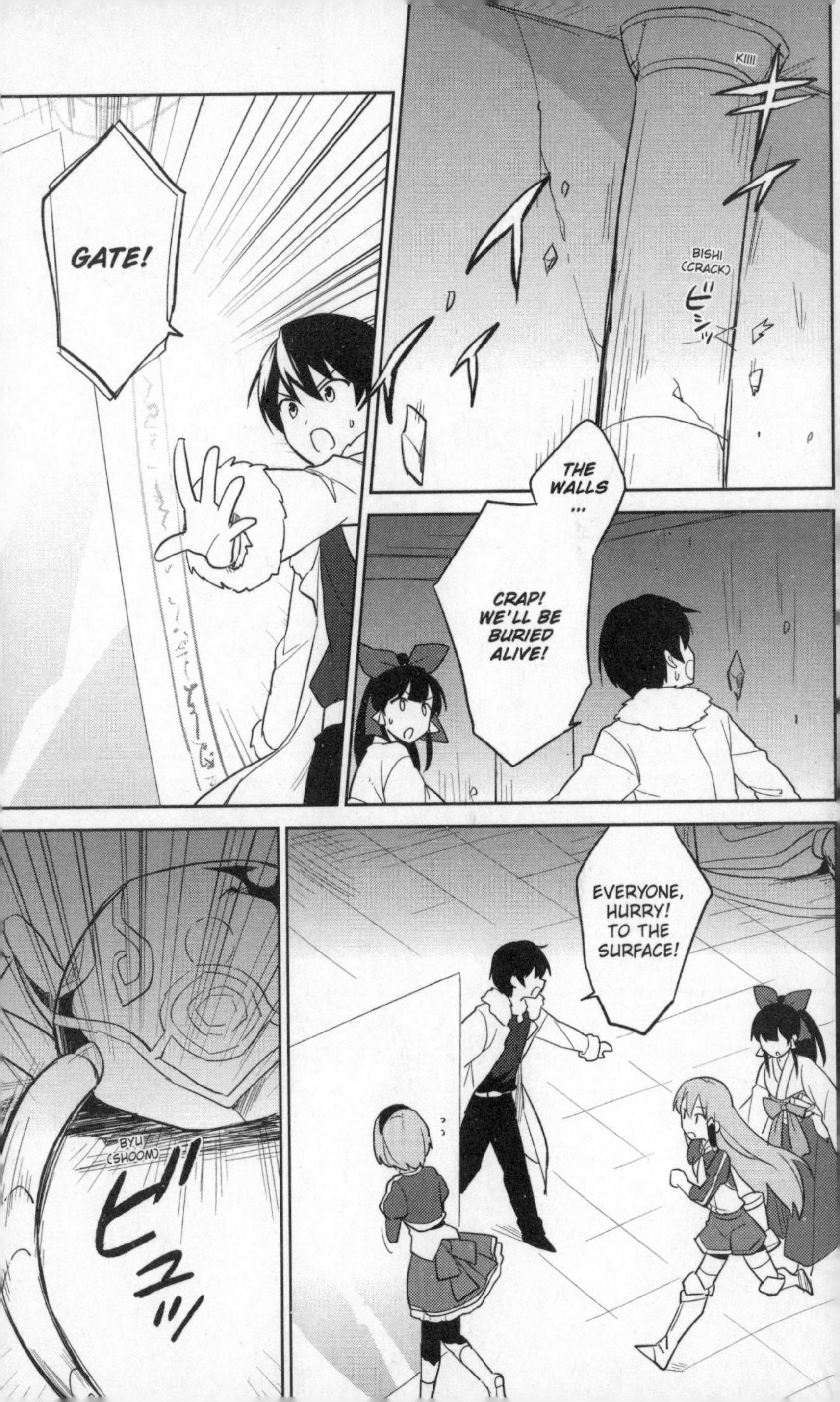
KIIII
BISHI (CRACK)
THE WALLS...
CRAP! WE'LL BE BURIED ALIVE!
GATE!
EVERYONE, HURRY! TO THE SURFACE!
BYU (SHOOM)

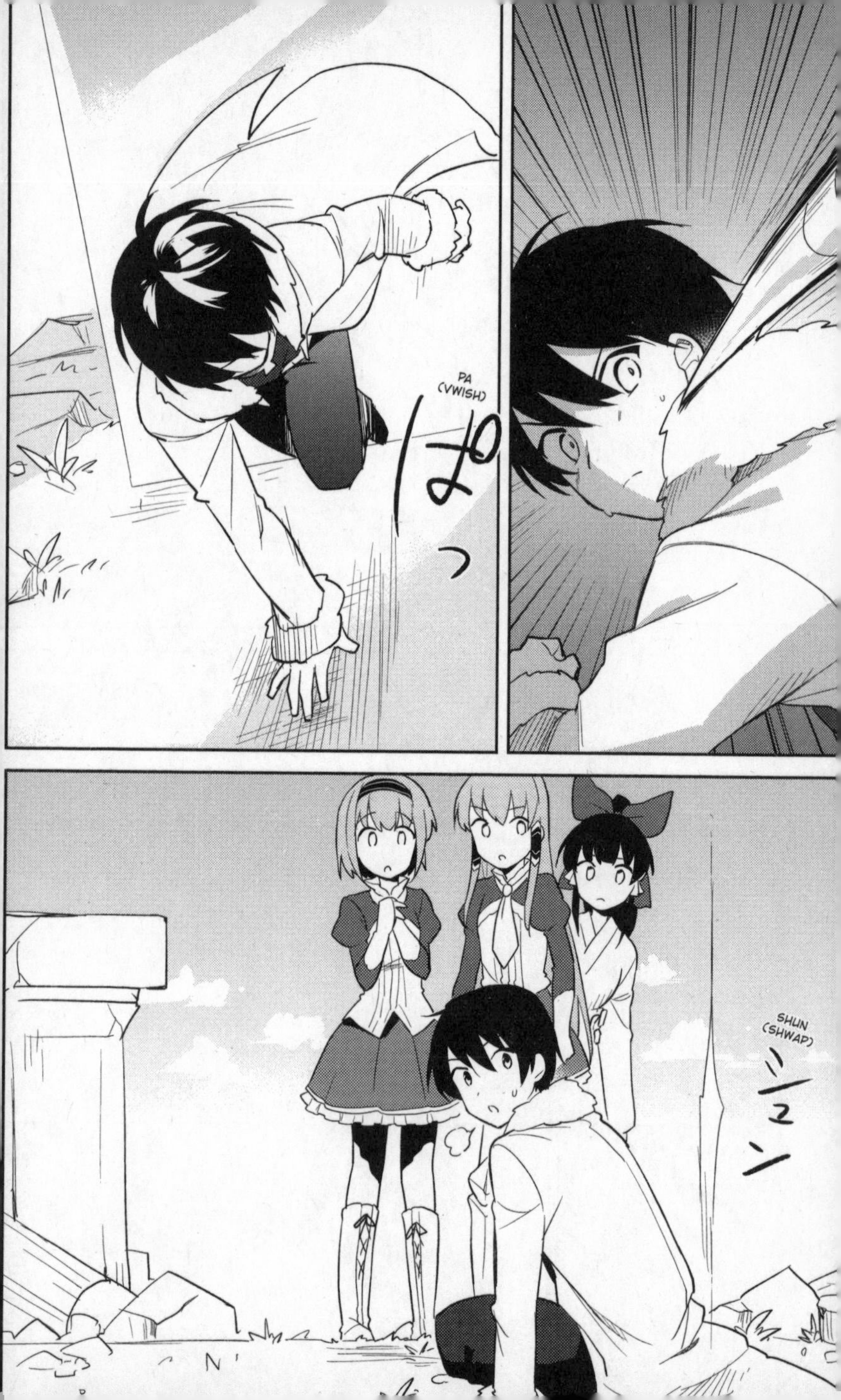
PA (VWISH)
ぱっ
SHUN (SHWAP)
シュン

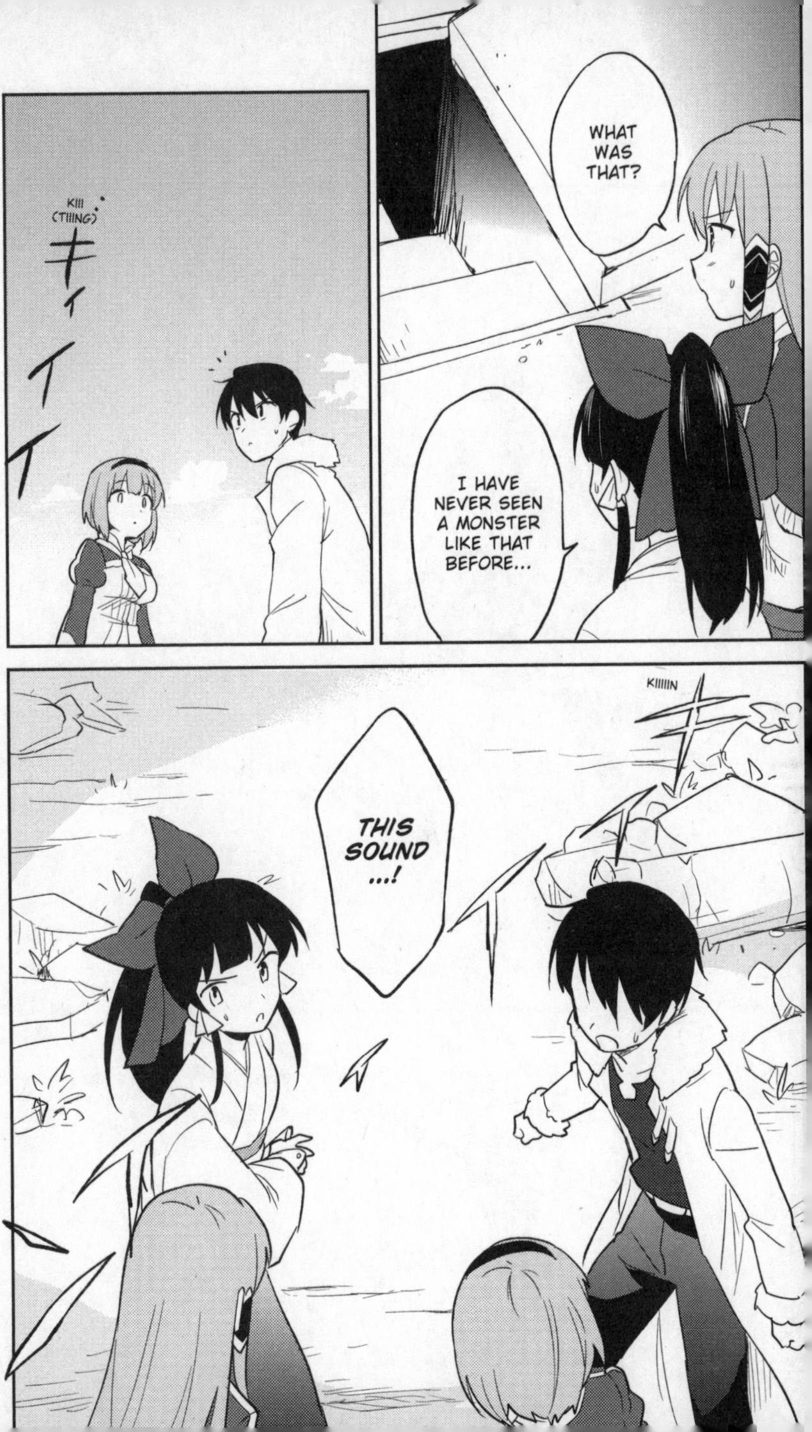
WHAT WAS THAT?
I HAVE NEVER SEEN A MONSTER LIKE THAT BEFORE...
KIII (TIIING)
KIIIIN
THIS SOUND ...!

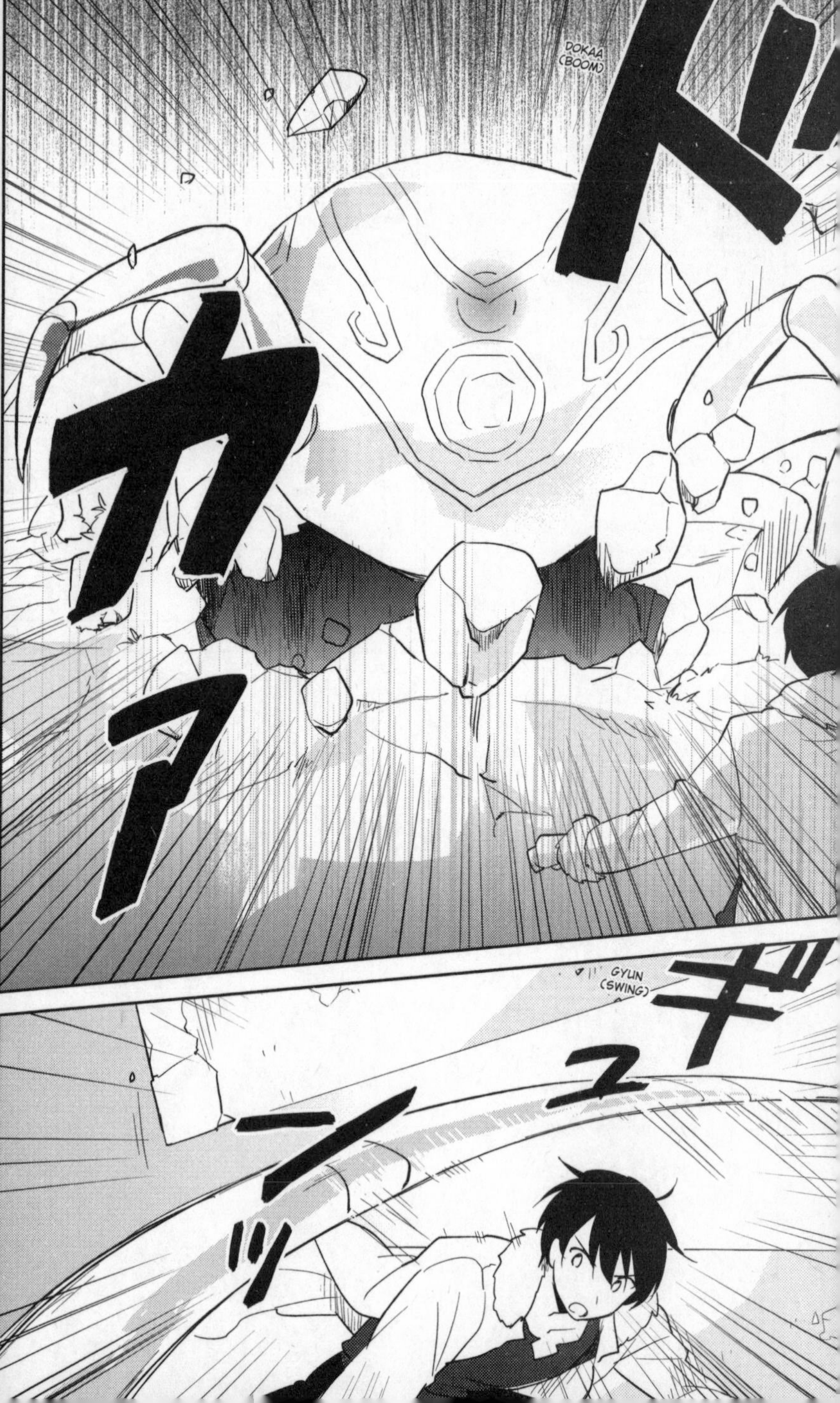
DOKAA (BOOM)
ドカァ
GYUN (SWING)

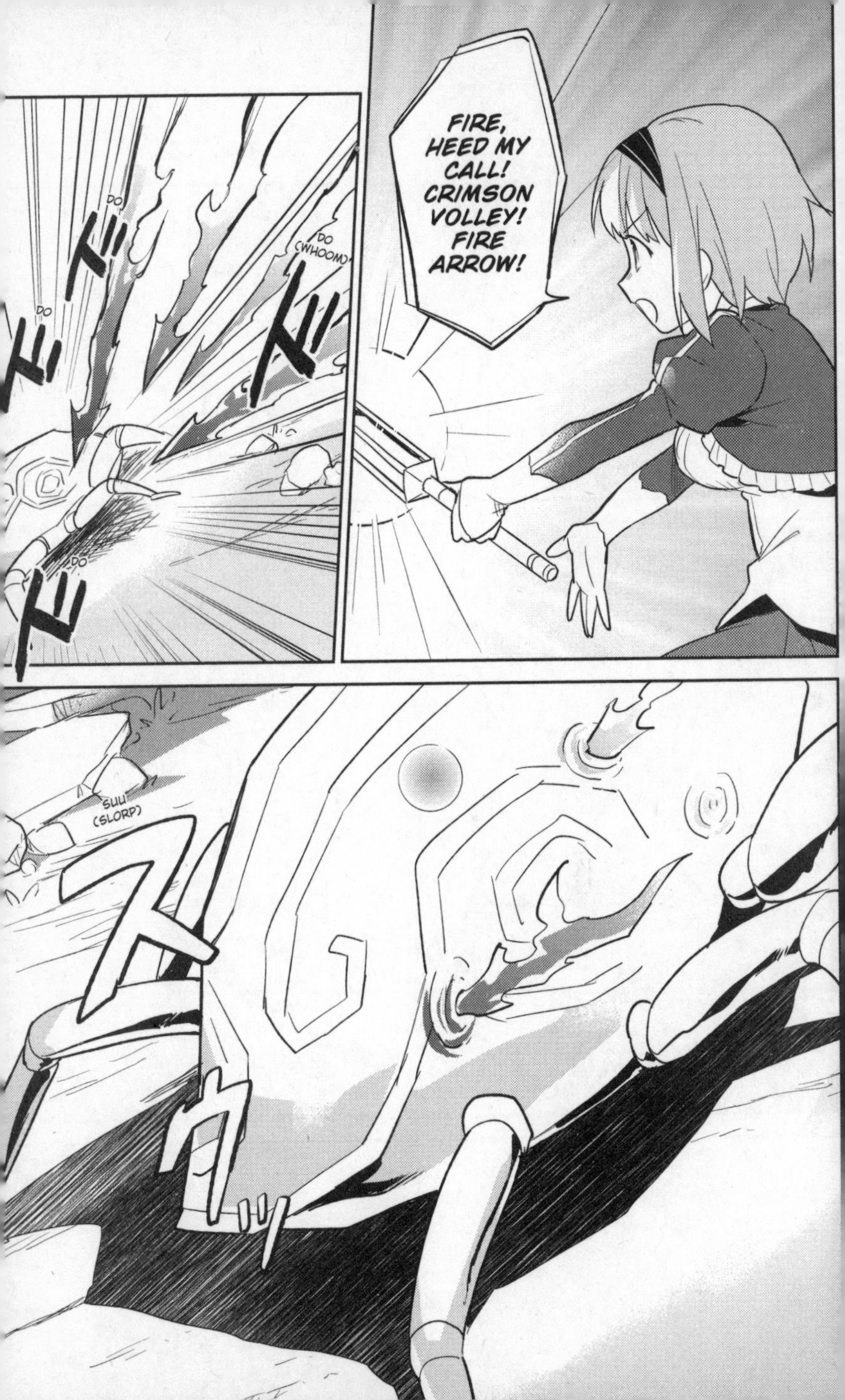
FIRE, HEED MY CALL! CRIMSON VOLLEY! FIRE ARROW!
DO (WHOOM)
DO
DO
DO
SUU (SLORP)

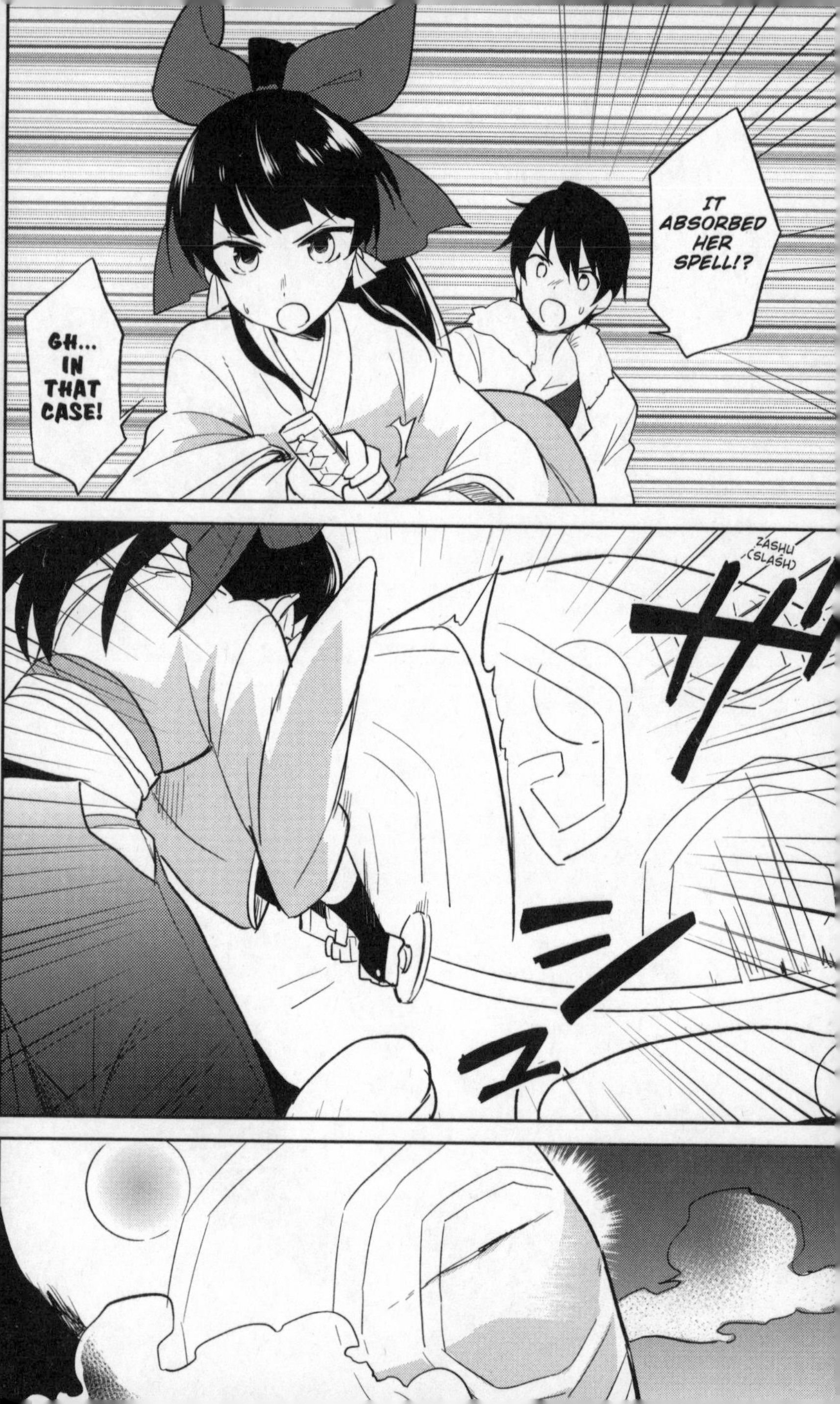
IT ABSORBED HER SPELL!?
GH... IN THAT CASE!
ZASHU (SLASH)

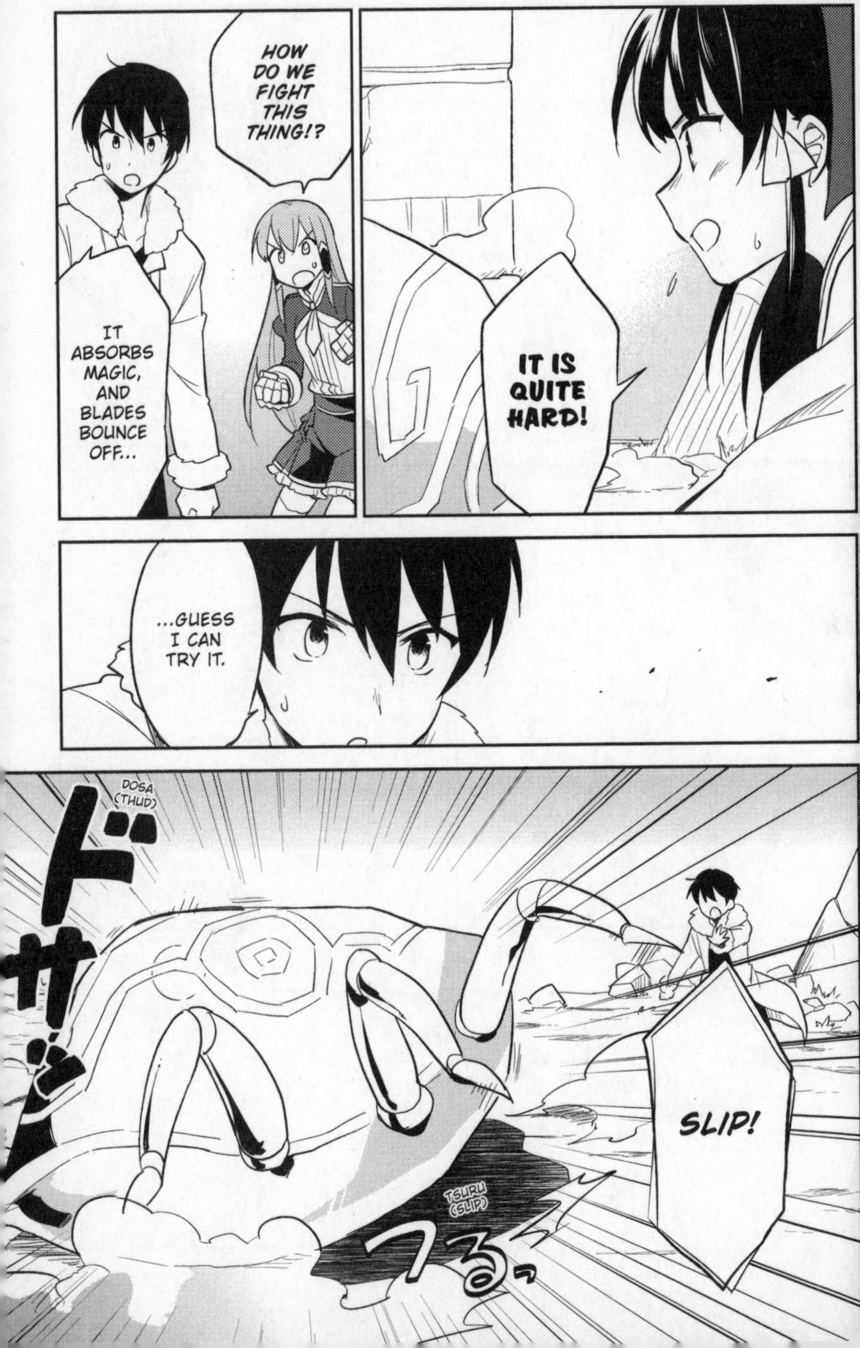
IT IS QUITE HARD!
HOW DO WE FIGHT THIS THING!?
IT ABSORBS MAGIC, AND BLADES BOUNCE OFF...
...GUESS I CAN TRY IT.
DOSA (THUD)
ドサッ
SLIP!
TSURU (SLIP)
つるっ

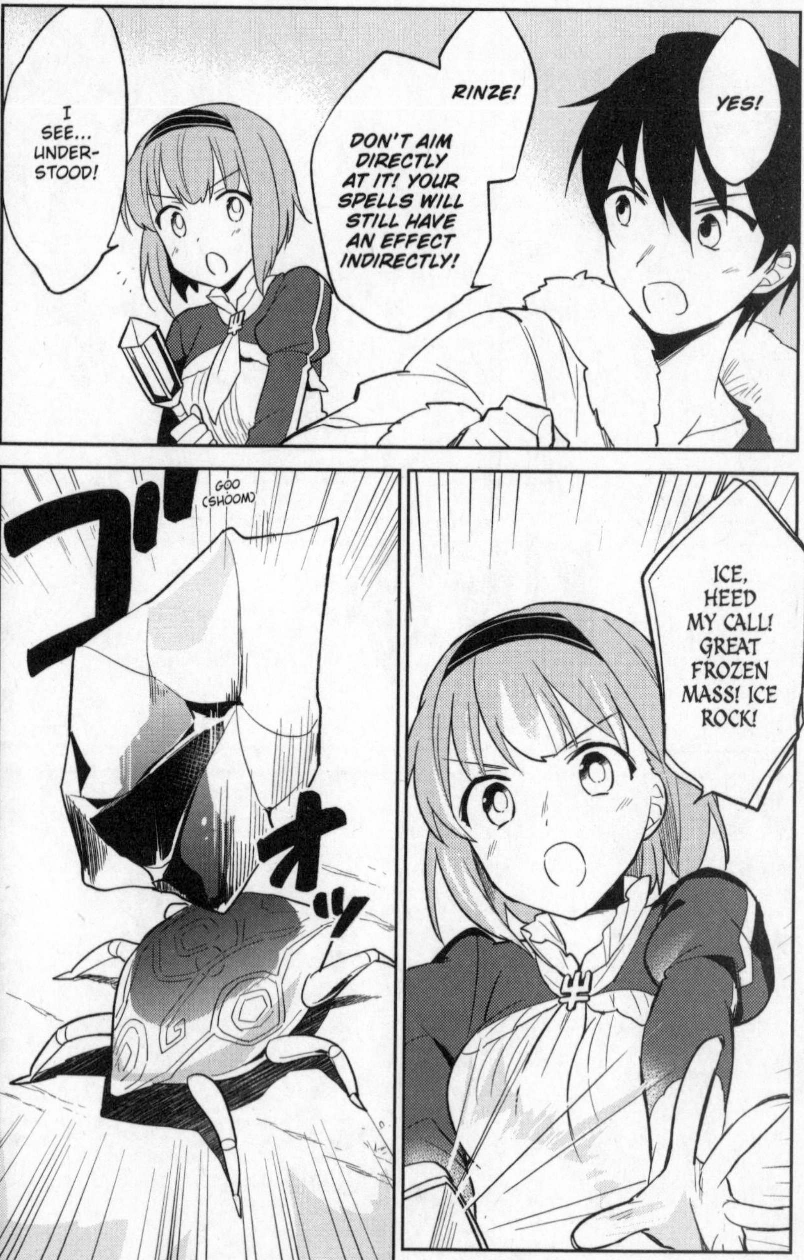
YES!
RINZE!
DON'T AIM DIRECTLY AT IT! YOUR SPELLS WILL STILL HAVE AN EFFECT INDIRECTLY!
I SEE... UNDERSTOOD!
ICE, HEED MY CALL! GREAT FROZEN MASS! ICE ROCK!
GOO (SHOOM)

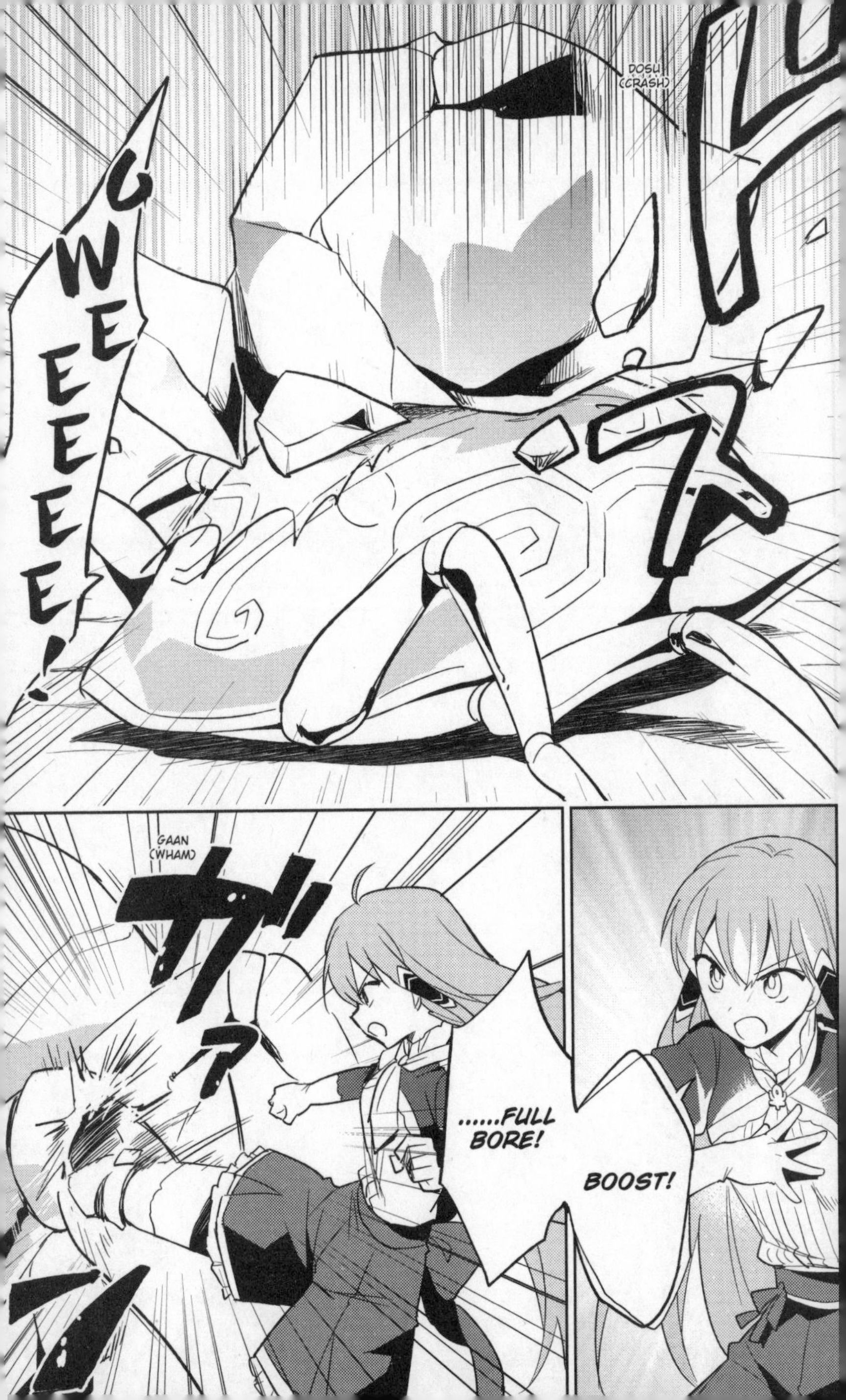
DOSU (CRASH)
GWEEEEEE!!
BOOST!
......FULL BORE!
GAAN (WHAM)

WE
DID IT!

PAKIIN
(CRACK)

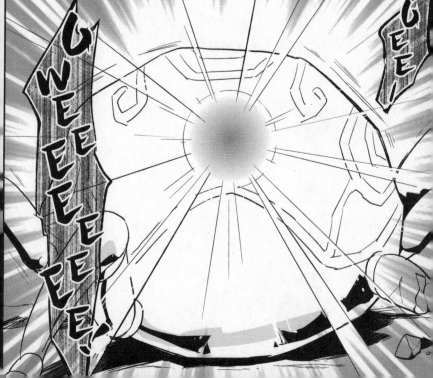

GWEEEEE!

GEE

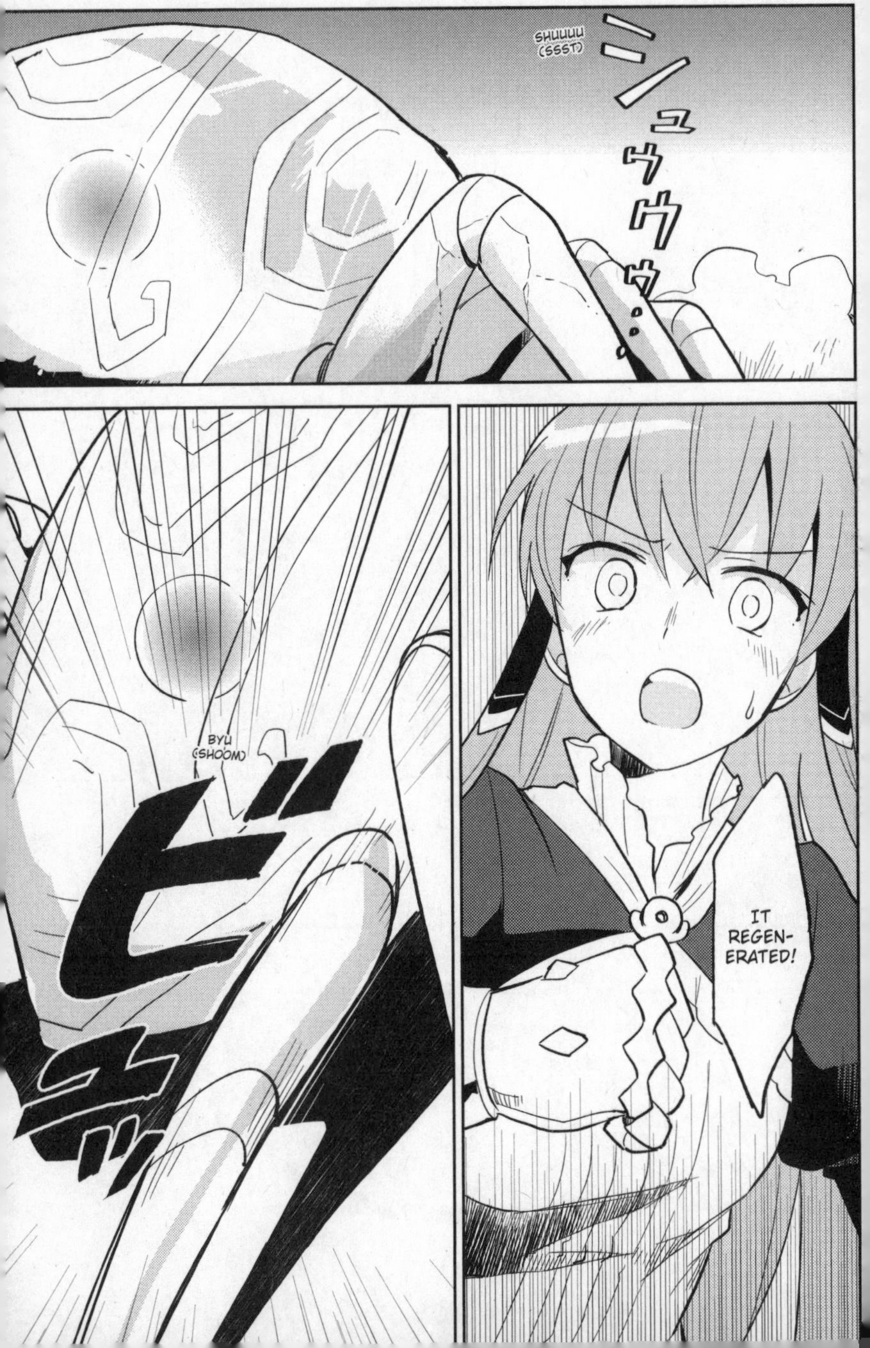
SHUUUU (SSST)
IT REGEN-ERATED!
BYU (SHOOM)

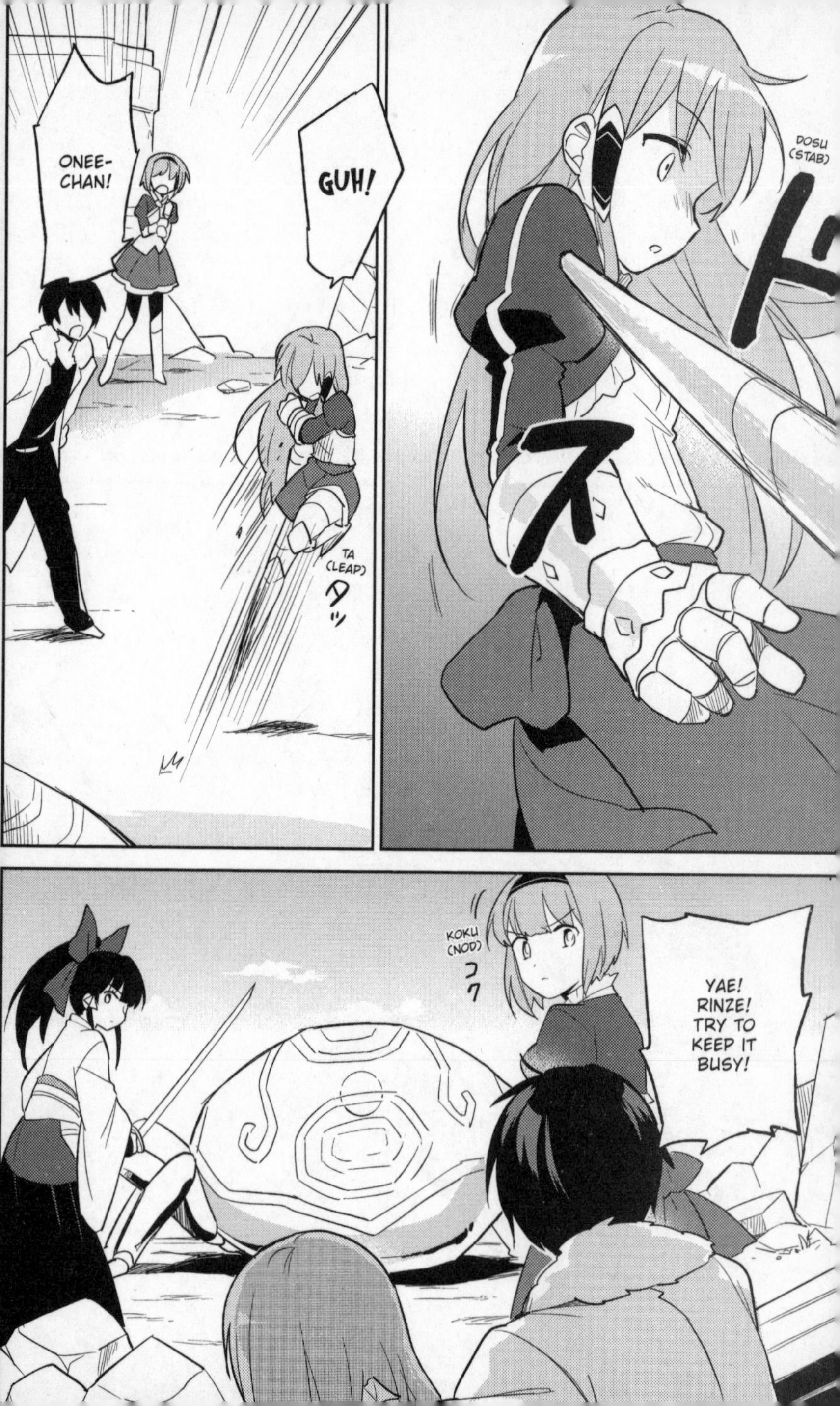
DOSU (STAB)
ドス
GUH!
ONEE-CHAN!
TA (LEAP)
タッ
YAE! RINZE! TRY TO KEEP IT BUSY!
KOKU (NOD)
コク

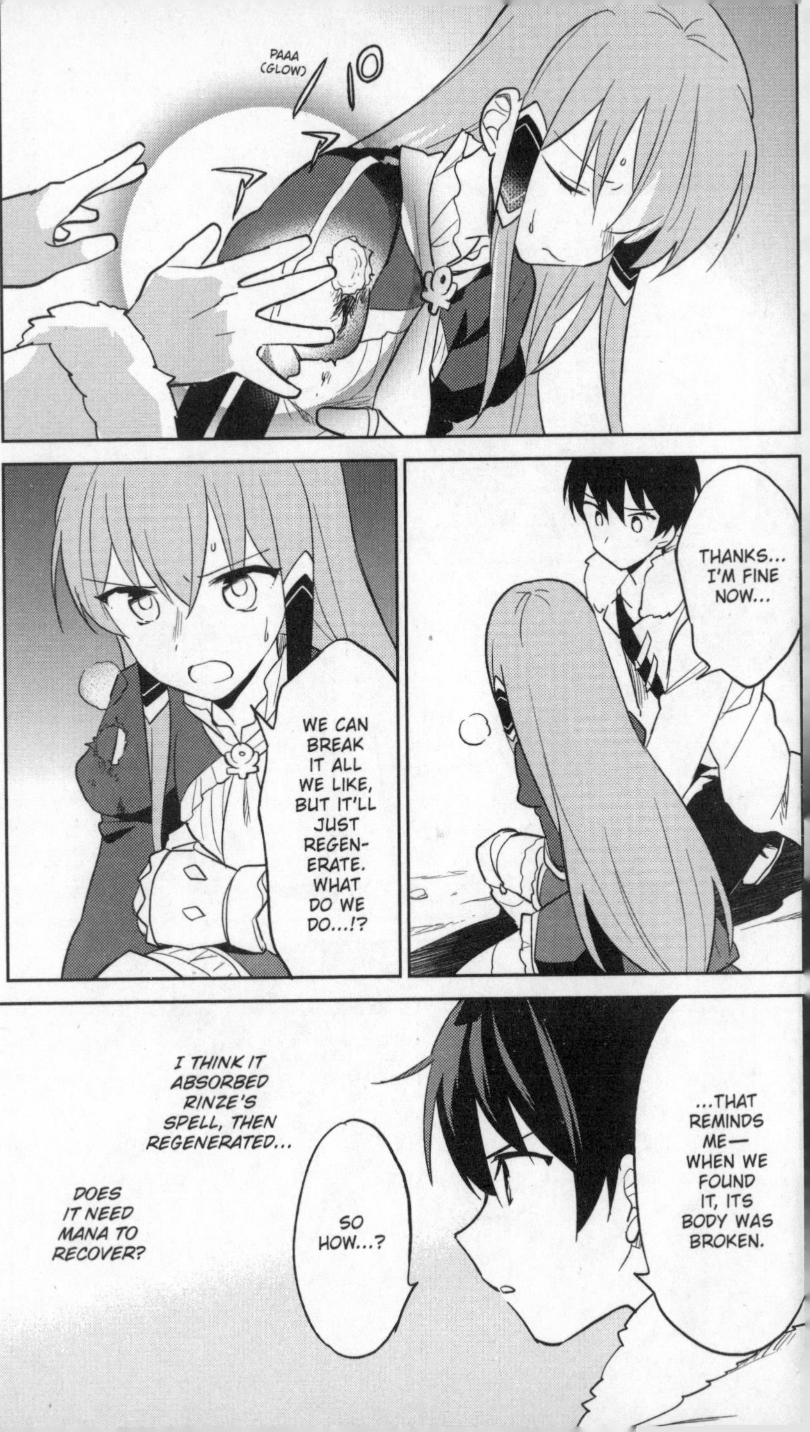
PAAA (GLOW)
THANKS... I'M FINE NOW...
WE CAN BREAK IT ALL WE LIKE, BUT IT'LL JUST REGEN-ERATE. WHAT DO WE DO...!?
...THAT REMINDS ME— WHEN WE FOUND IT, ITS BODY WAS BROKEN.
SO HOW...?
I THINK IT ABSORBED RINZE'S SPELL, THEN REGENERATED...
DOES IT NEED MANA TO RECOVER?

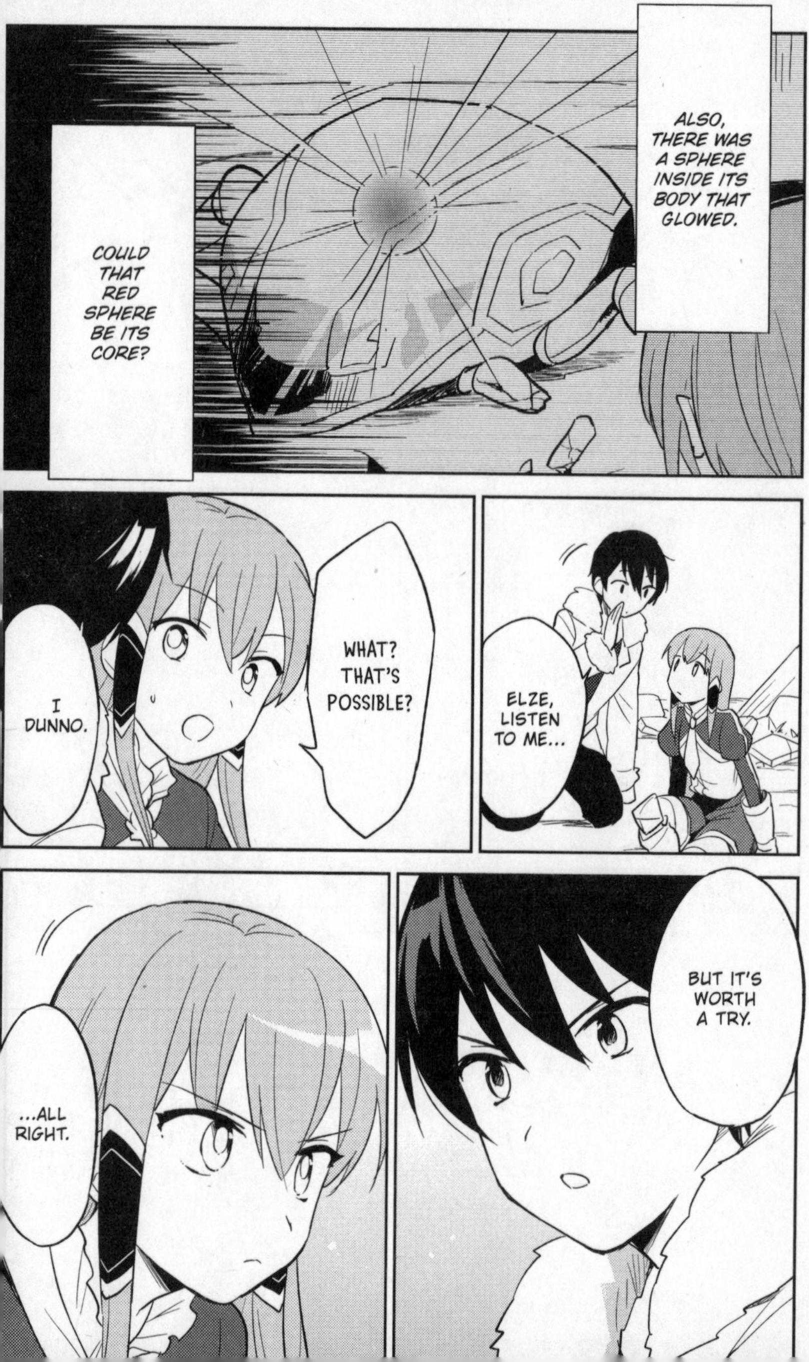
ALSO, THERE WAS A SPHERE INSIDE ITS BODY THAT GLOWED.
COULD THAT RED SPHERE BE ITS CORE?
ELZE, LISTEN TO ME...
WHAT? THAT'S POSSIBLE?
I DUNNO.
BUT IT'S WORTH A TRY.
...ALL RIGHT.

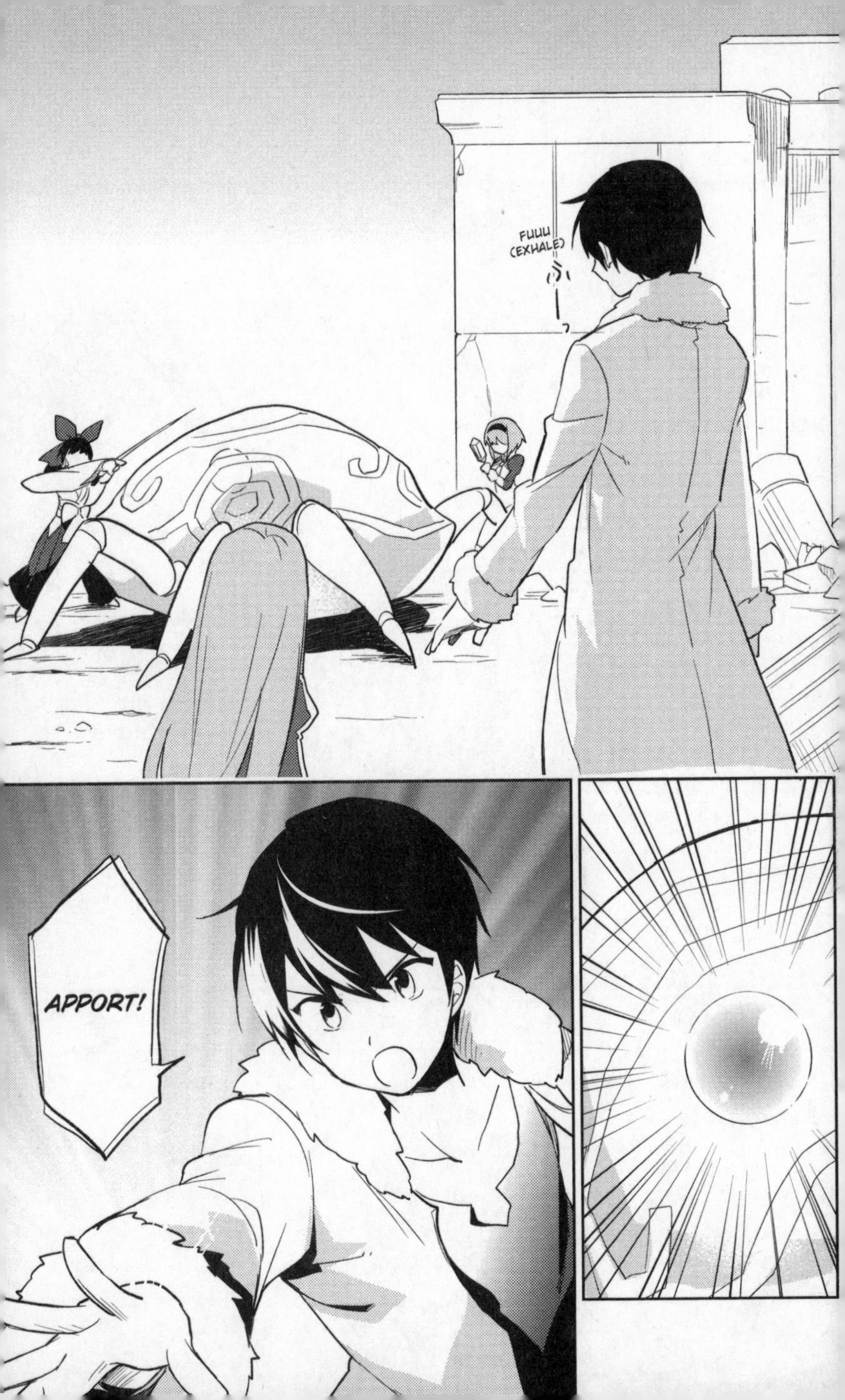
FUUU (EXHALE)
ふーっ
APPORT!

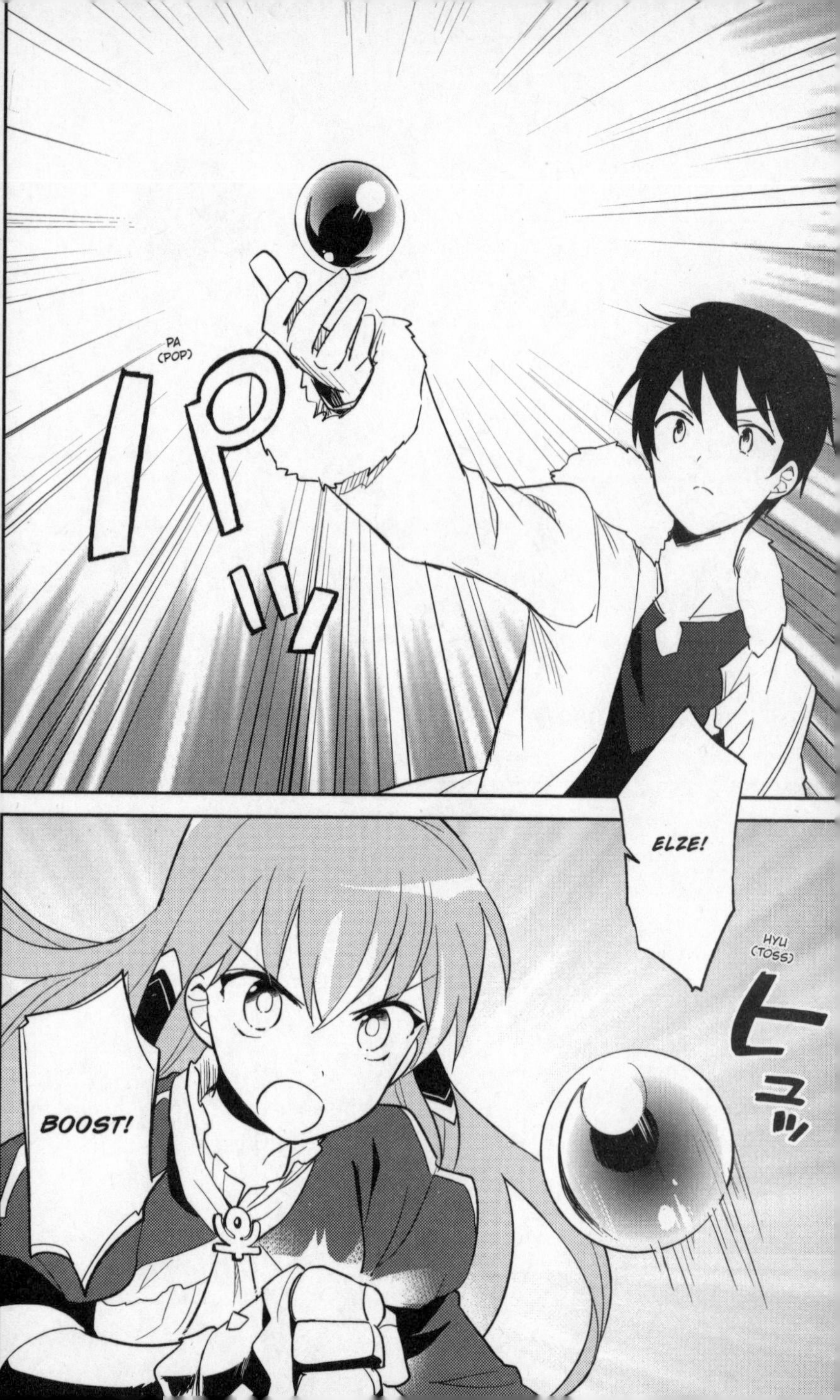
PA
(POP)
パッ
ELZE!
HYU
(TOSS)
ヒュッ
BOOST!

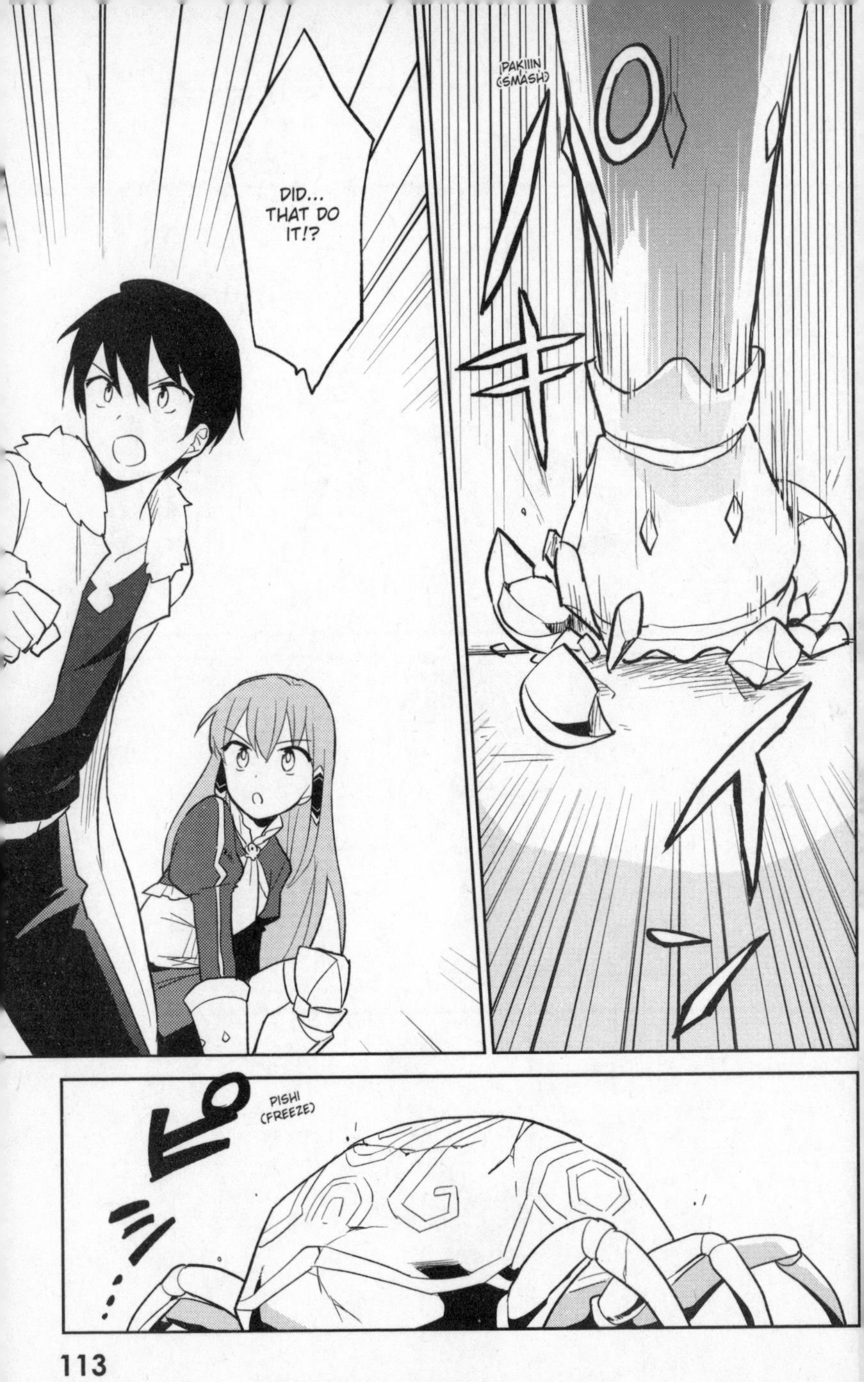
PAKIIIN
(SMASH)
DID... THAT DO IT!?
PISHI
(FREEZE)

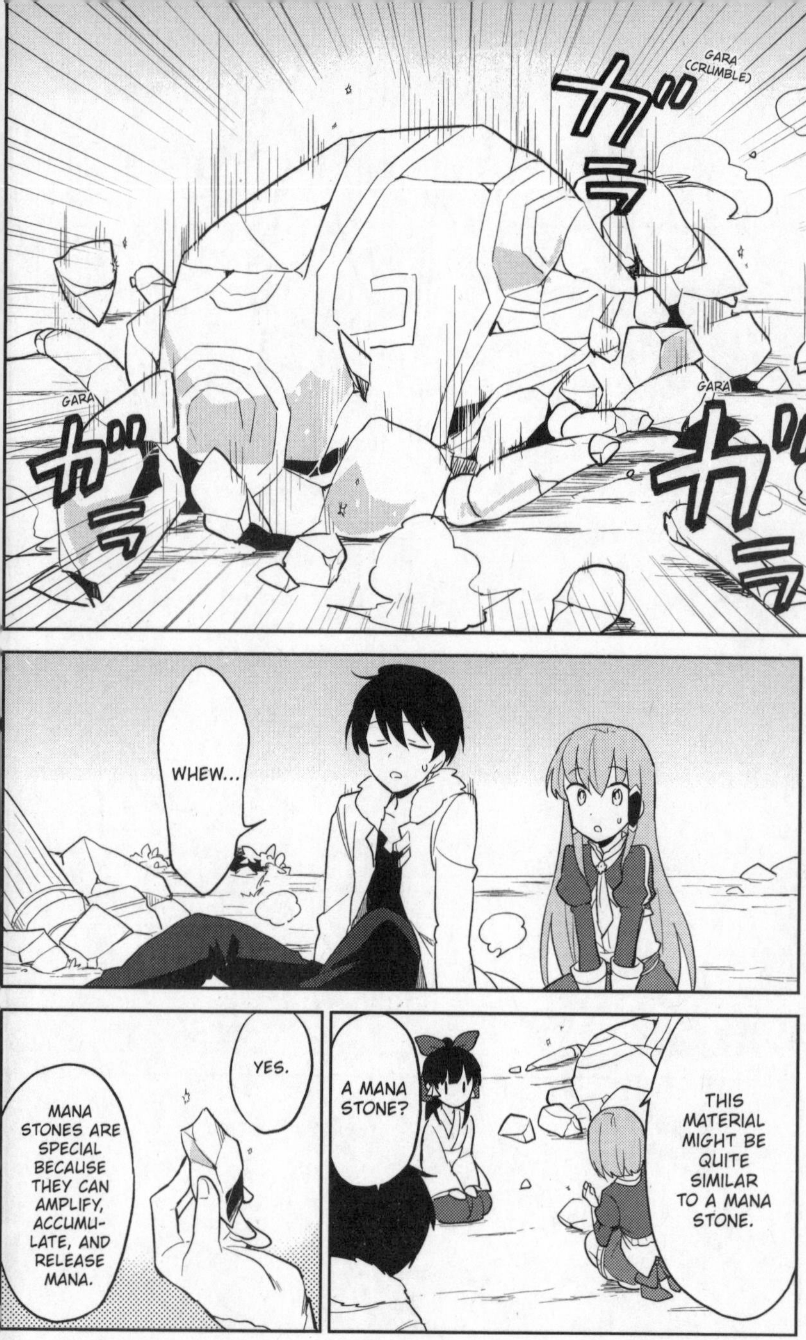
GARA (CRUMBLE)
ガラ
GARA
ガラ
GARA
ガラ
WHEW...
THIS MATERIAL MIGHT BE QUITE SIMILAR TO A MANA STONE.
A MANA STONE?
YES.
MANA STONES ARE SPECIAL BECAUSE THEY CAN AMPLIFY, ACCUMULATE, AND RELEASE MANA.

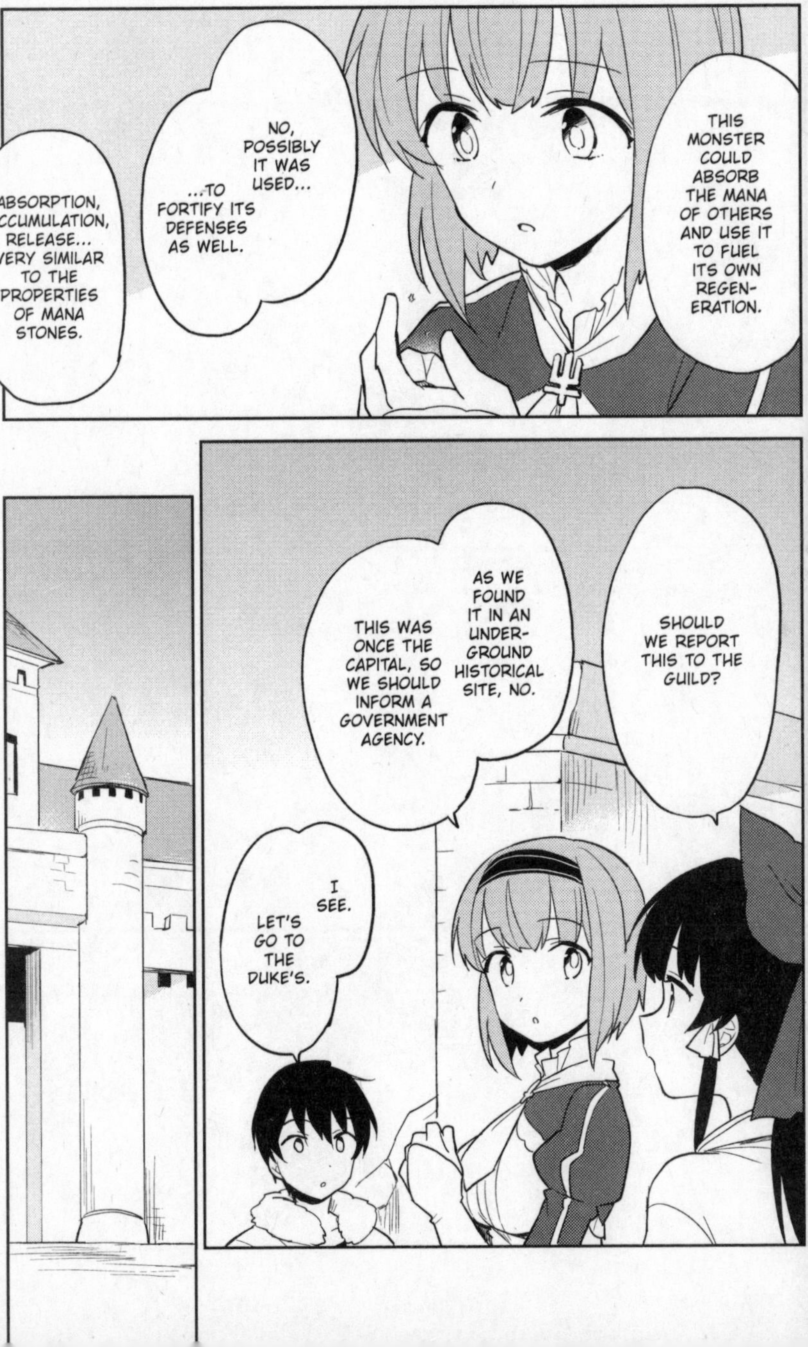
THIS MONSTER COULD ABSORB THE MANA OF OTHERS AND USE IT TO FUEL ITS OWN REGEN-ERATION.
NO, POSSIBLY IT WAS USED...
...TO FORTIFY ITS DEFENSES AS WELL.
ABSORPTION, ACCUMULATION, RELEASE... VERY SIMILAR TO THE PROPERTIES OF MANA STONES.
SHOULD WE REPORT THIS TO THE GUILD?
AS WE FOUND IT IN AN UNDER-GROUND HISTORICAL SITE, NO.
THIS WAS ONCE THE CAPITAL, SO WE SHOULD INFORM A GOVERNMENT AGENCY.
I SEE.
LET'S GO TO THE DUKE'S.

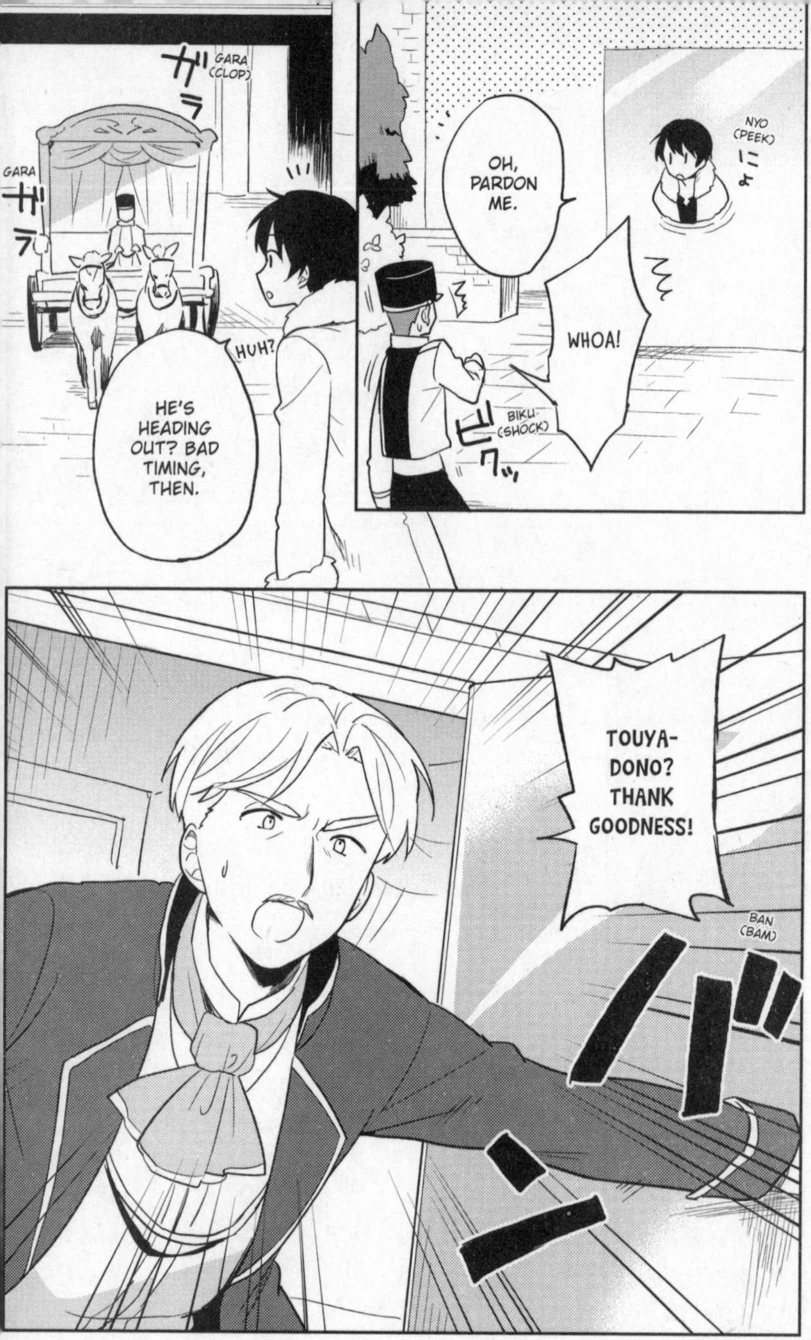
NYO (PEEK)
にょ
OH, PARDON ME.
WHOA!
BIKU (SHOCK)
ビクッ
GARA (CLOP)
ガラ
GARA
ガラ
HUH?
HE'S HEADING OUT? BAD TIMING, THEN.
TOUYA-DONO? THANK GOODNESS!
BAN (BAM)
バーン

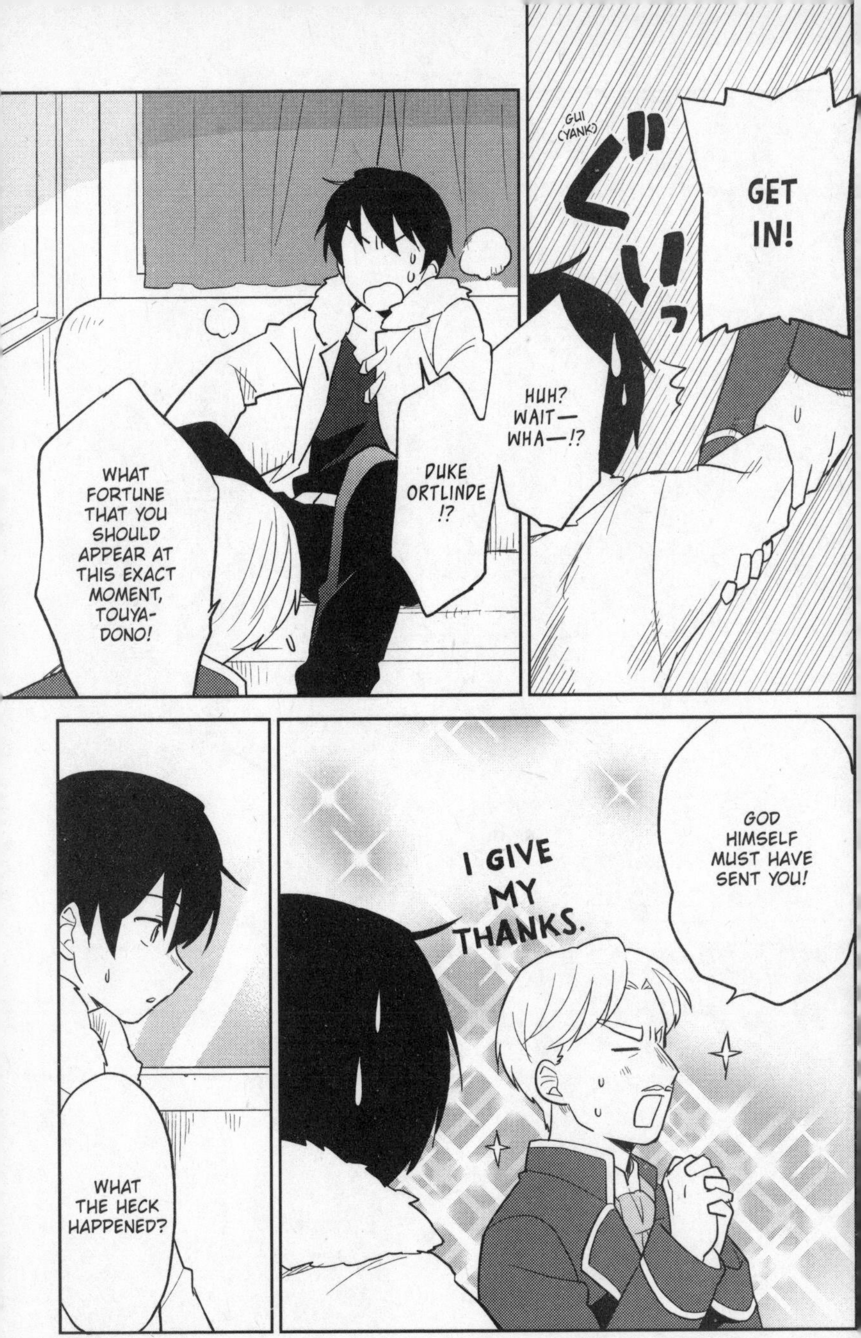
GUI (YANK)
GET IN!
HUH? WAIT— WHA—!?
DUKE ORTLINDE !?
WHAT FORTUNE THAT YOU SHOULD APPEAR AT THIS EXACT MOMENT, TOUYA-DONO!
GOD HIMSELF MUST HAVE SENT YOU!
I GIVE MY THANKS.
WHAT THE HECK HAPPENED?

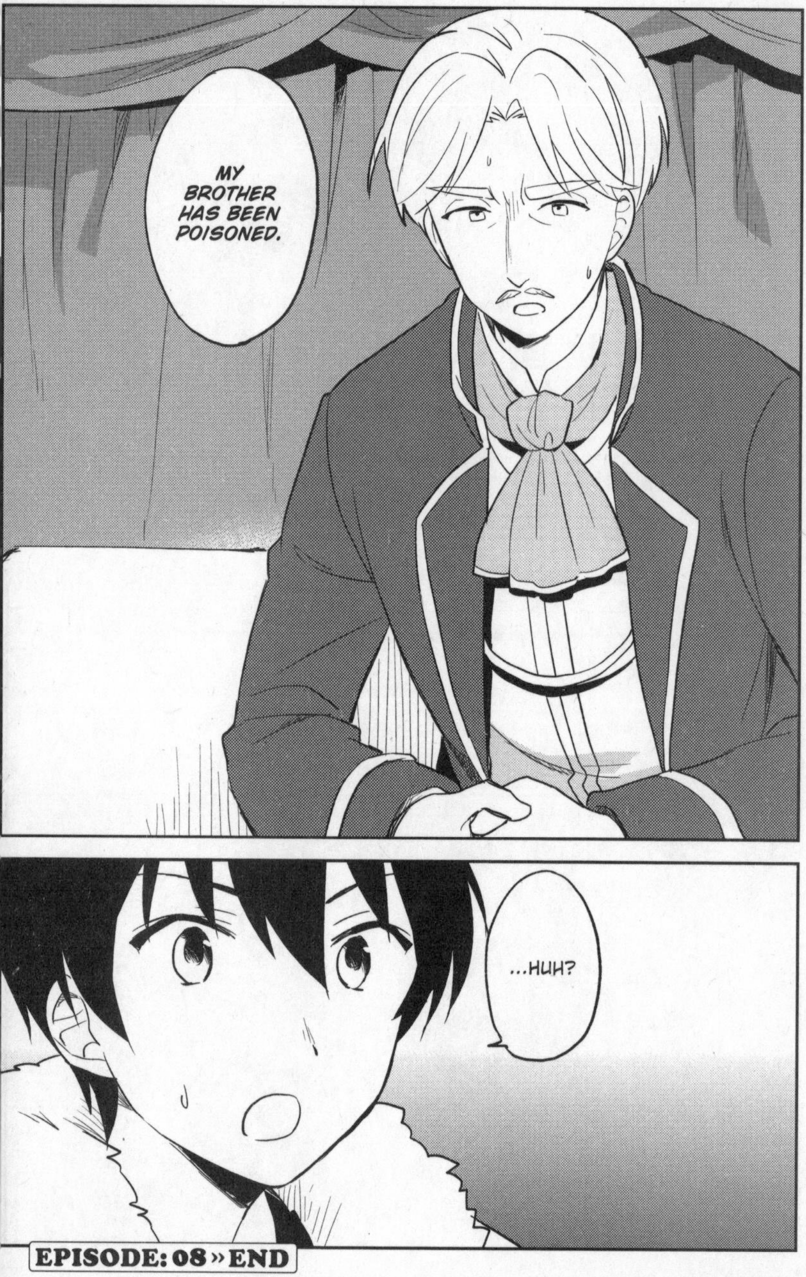
MY BROTHER HAS BEEN POISONED.
...HUH?

EPISODE: 08 » END

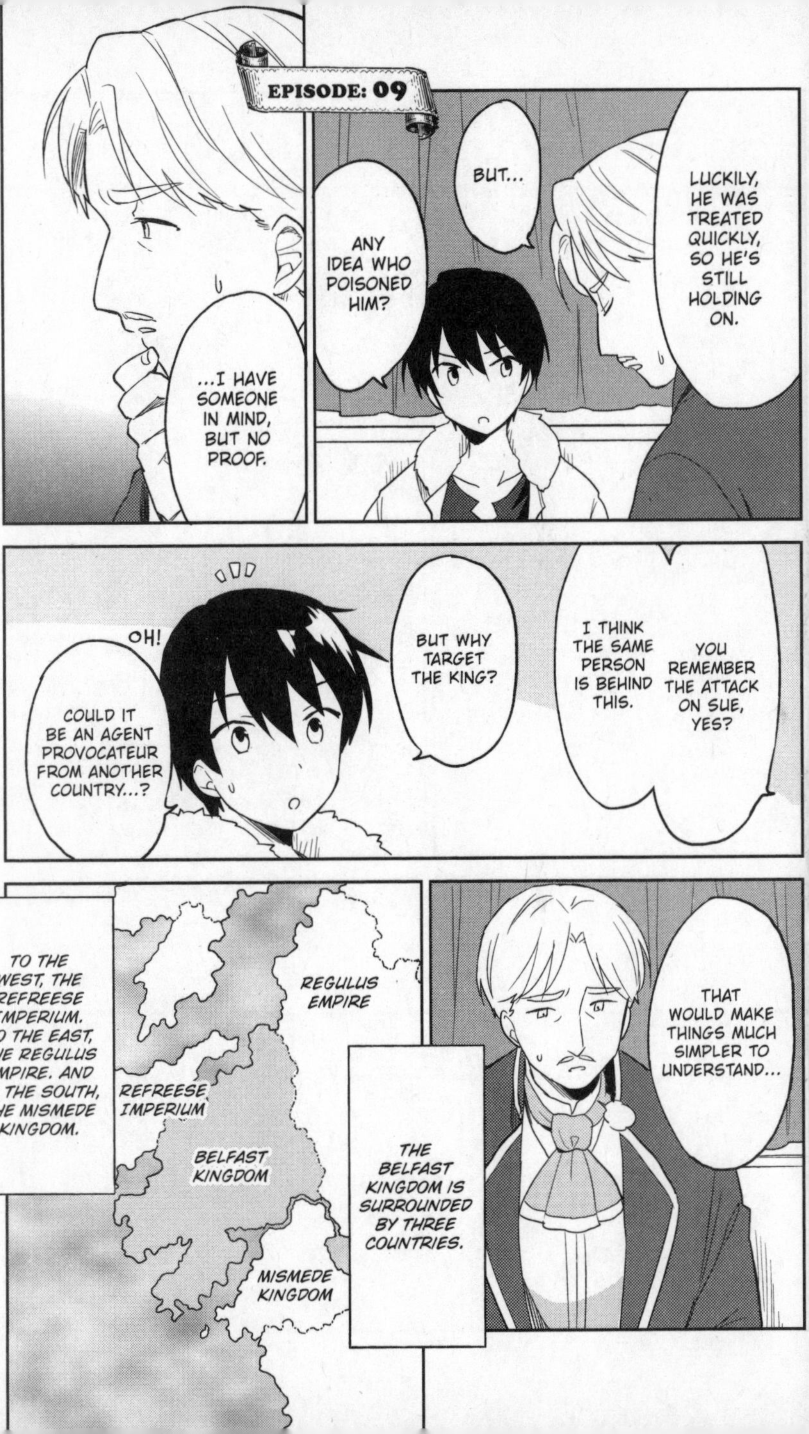
EPISODE: 09
LUCKILY, HE WAS TREATED QUICKLY, SO HE'S STILL HOLDING ON.
BUT...
ANY IDEA WHO POISONED HIM?
...I HAVE SOMEONE IN MIND, BUT NO PROOF.
YOU REMEMBER THE ATTACK ON SUE, YES?
I THINK THE SAME PERSON IS BEHIND THIS.
BUT WHY TARGET THE KING?
OH!
COULD IT BE AN AGENT PROVOCATEUR FROM ANOTHER COUNTRY...?
THAT WOULD MAKE THINGS MUCH SIMPLER TO UNDERSTAND...
THE BELFAST KINGDOM IS SURROUNDED BY THREE COUNTRIES.
REGULUS EMPIRE
REFREESE IMPERIUM
BELFAST KINGDOM
MISMEDE KINGDOM
TO THE WEST, THE REFREESE IMPERIUM. TO THE EAST, THE REGULUS EMPIRE. AND TO THE SOUTH, THE MISMEDE KINGDOM.

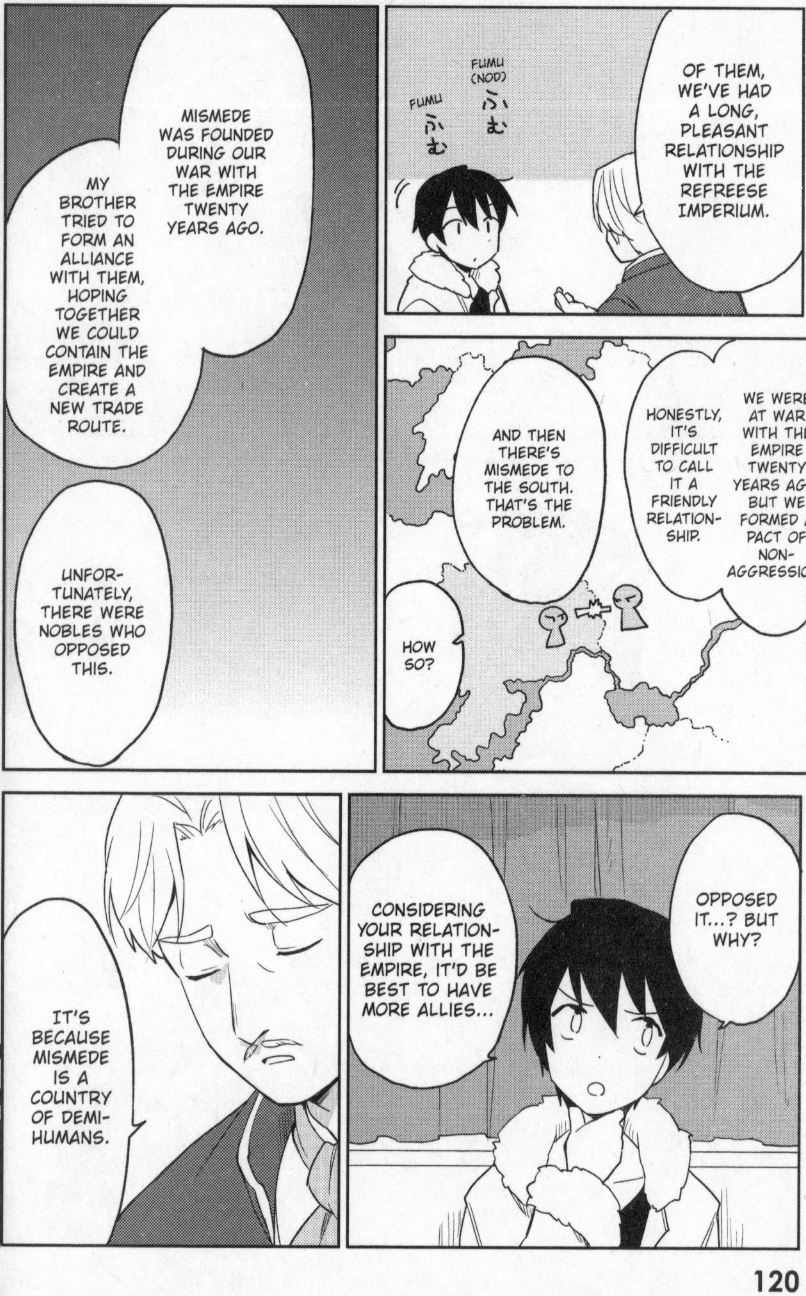
OF THEM, WE'VE HAD A LONG, PLEASANT RELATIONSHIP WITH THE REFREESE IMPERIUM.
FUMU (NOD) ふむ
FUMU ふむ
WE WERE AT WAR WITH THE EMPIRE TWENTY YEARS AGO, BUT WE FORMED A PACT OF NON-AGGRESSION.
HONESTLY, IT'S DIFFICULT TO CALL IT A FRIENDLY RELATIONSHIP.
AND THEN THERE'S MISMEDE TO THE SOUTH. THAT'S THE PROBLEM.
HOW SO?
MISMEDE WAS FOUNDED DURING OUR WAR WITH THE EMPIRE TWENTY YEARS AGO.
MY BROTHER TRIED TO FORM AN ALLIANCE WITH THEM, HOPING TOGETHER WE COULD CONTAIN THE EMPIRE AND CREATE A NEW TRADE ROUTE.
UNFORTUNATELY, THERE WERE NOBLES WHO OPPOSED THIS.
OPPOSED IT...? BUT WHY?
CONSIDERING YOUR RELATIONSHIP WITH THE EMPIRE, IT'D BE BEST TO HAVE MORE ALLIES...
IT'S BECAUSE MISMEDE IS A COUNTRY OF DEMI-HUMANS.

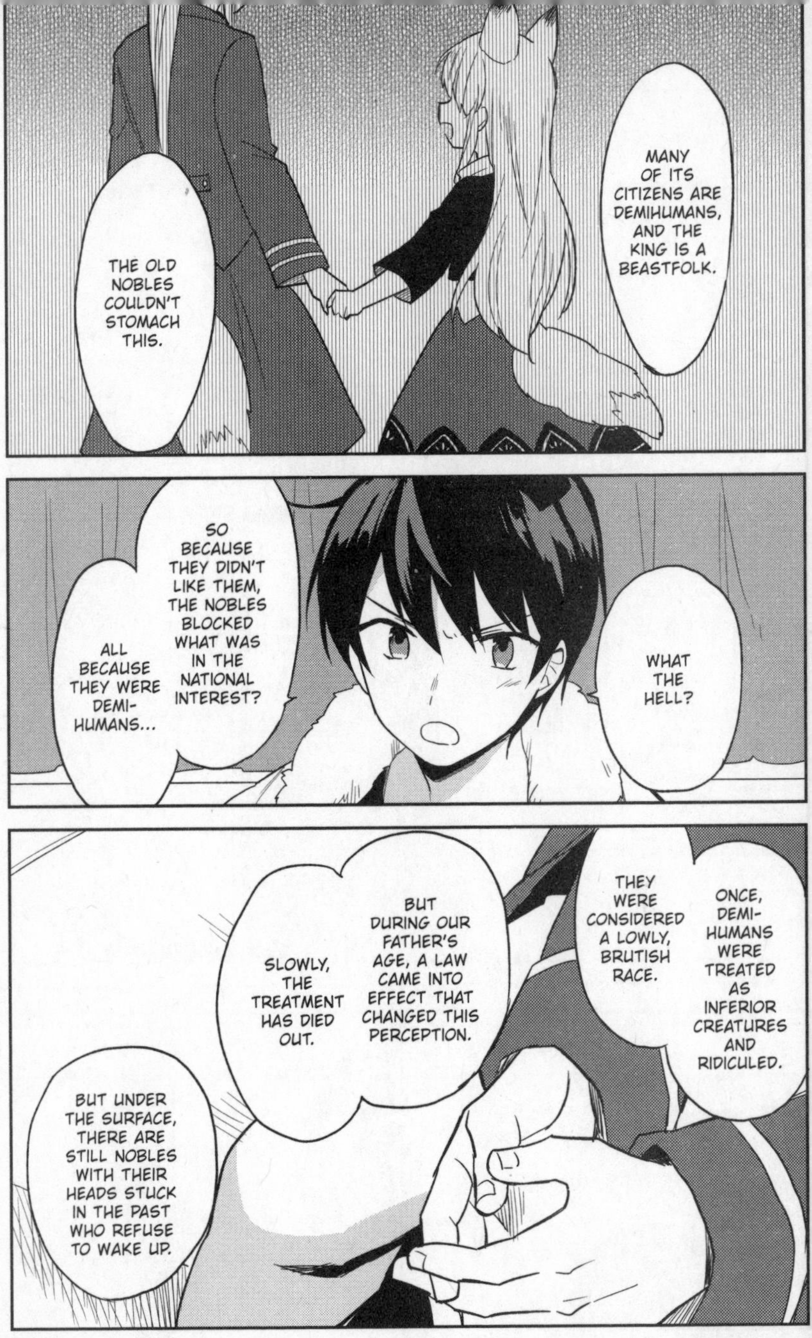
MANY OF ITS CITIZENS ARE DEMIHUMANS, AND THE KING IS A BEASTFOLK.
THE OLD NOBLES COULDN'T STOMACH THIS.
WHAT THE HELL?
SO BECAUSE THEY DIDN'T LIKE THEM, THE NOBLES BLOCKED WHAT WAS IN THE NATIONAL INTEREST?
ALL BECAUSE THEY WERE DEMI-HUMANS...
ONCE, DEMI-HUMANS WERE TREATED AS INFERIOR CREATURES AND RIDICULED.
THEY WERE CONSIDERED A LOWLY, BRUTISH RACE.
BUT DURING OUR FATHER'S AGE, A LAW CAME INTO EFFECT THAT CHANGED THIS PERCEPTION.
SLOWLY, THE TREATMENT HAS DIED OUT.
BUT UNDER THE SURFACE, THERE ARE STILL NOBLES WITH THEIR HEADS STUCK IN THE PAST WHO REFUSE TO WAKE UP.

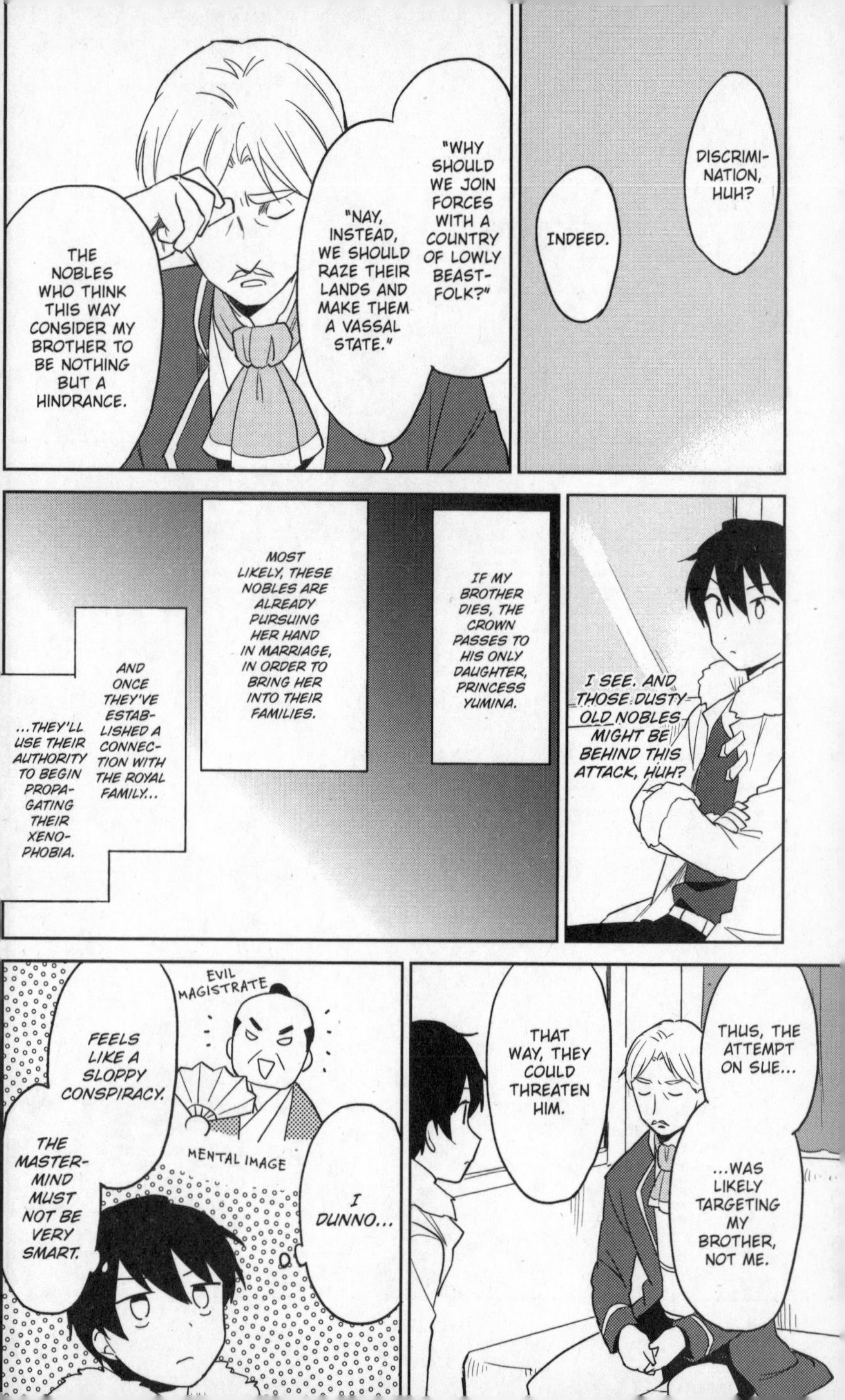
DISCRIMINATION, HUH?
INDEED.
"WHY SHOULD WE JOIN FORCES WITH A COUNTRY OF LOWLY BEAST-FOLK?"
"NAY, INSTEAD, WE SHOULD RAZE THEIR LANDS AND MAKE THEM A VASSAL STATE."
THE NOBLES WHO THINK THIS WAY CONSIDER MY BROTHER TO BE NOTHING BUT A HINDRANCE.
I SEE. AND THOSE DUSTY OLD NOBLES MIGHT BE BEHIND THIS ATTACK, HUH?
IF MY BROTHER DIES, THE CROWN PASSES TO HIS ONLY DAUGHTER, PRINCESS YUMINA.
MOST LIKELY, THESE NOBLES ARE ALREADY PURSUING HER HAND IN MARRIAGE, IN ORDER TO BRING HER INTO THEIR FAMILIES.
AND ONCE THEY'VE ESTABLISHED A CONNECTION WITH THE ROYAL FAMILY...
...THEY'LL USE THEIR AUTHORITY TO BEGIN PROPAGATING THEIR XENOPHOBIA.
THUS, THE ATTEMPT ON SUE...
...WAS LIKELY TARGETING MY BROTHER, NOT ME.
THAT WAY, THEY COULD THREATEN HIM.
I DUNNO...
EVIL MAGISTRATE
FEELS LIKE A SLOPPY CONSPIRACY.
MENTAL IMAGE
THE MASTERMIND MUST NOT BE VERY SMART.

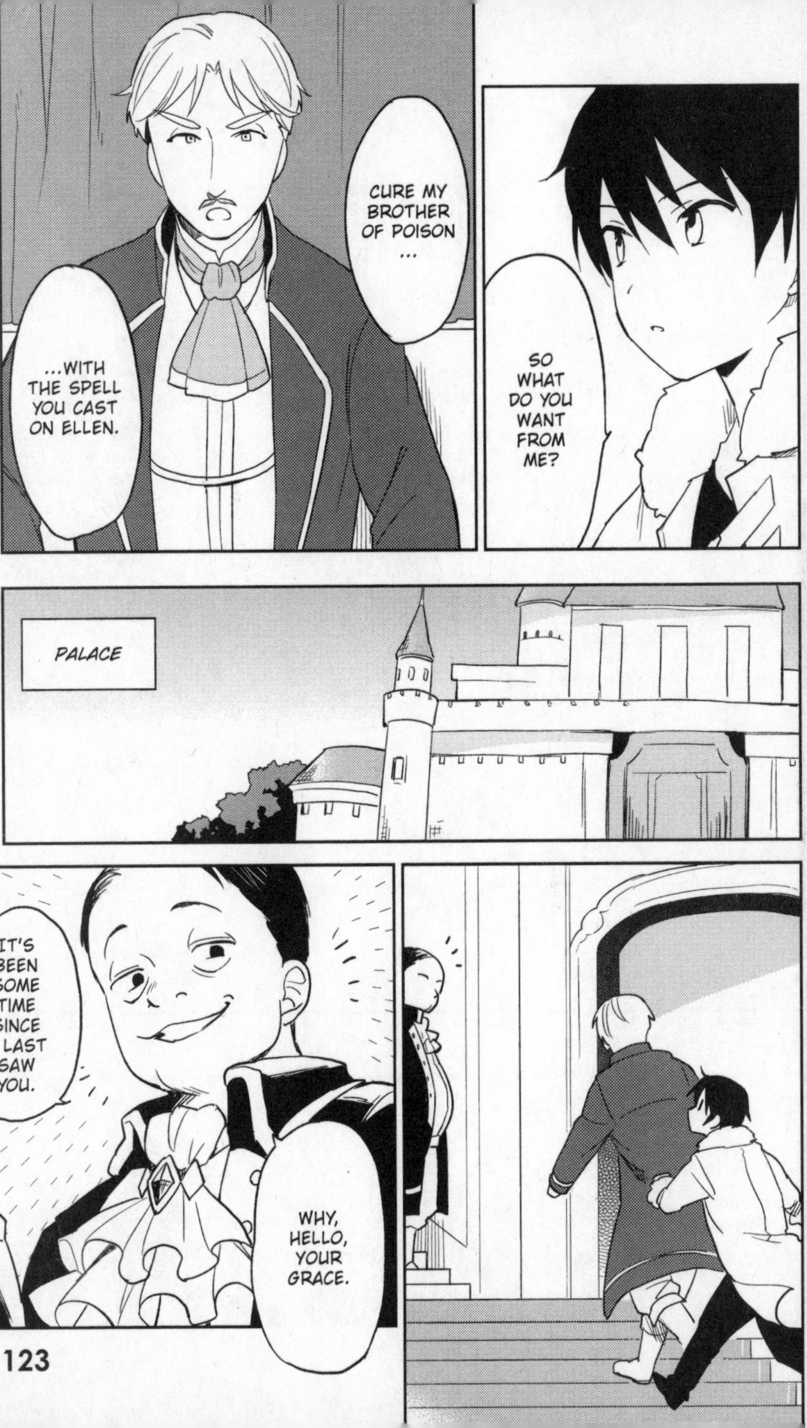
SO WHAT DO YOU WANT FROM ME?
CURE MY BROTHER OF POISON ...
...WITH THE SPELL YOU CAST ON ELLEN.
PALACE
WHY, HELLO, YOUR GRACE.
IT'S BEEN SOME TIME SINCE I LAST SAW YOU.

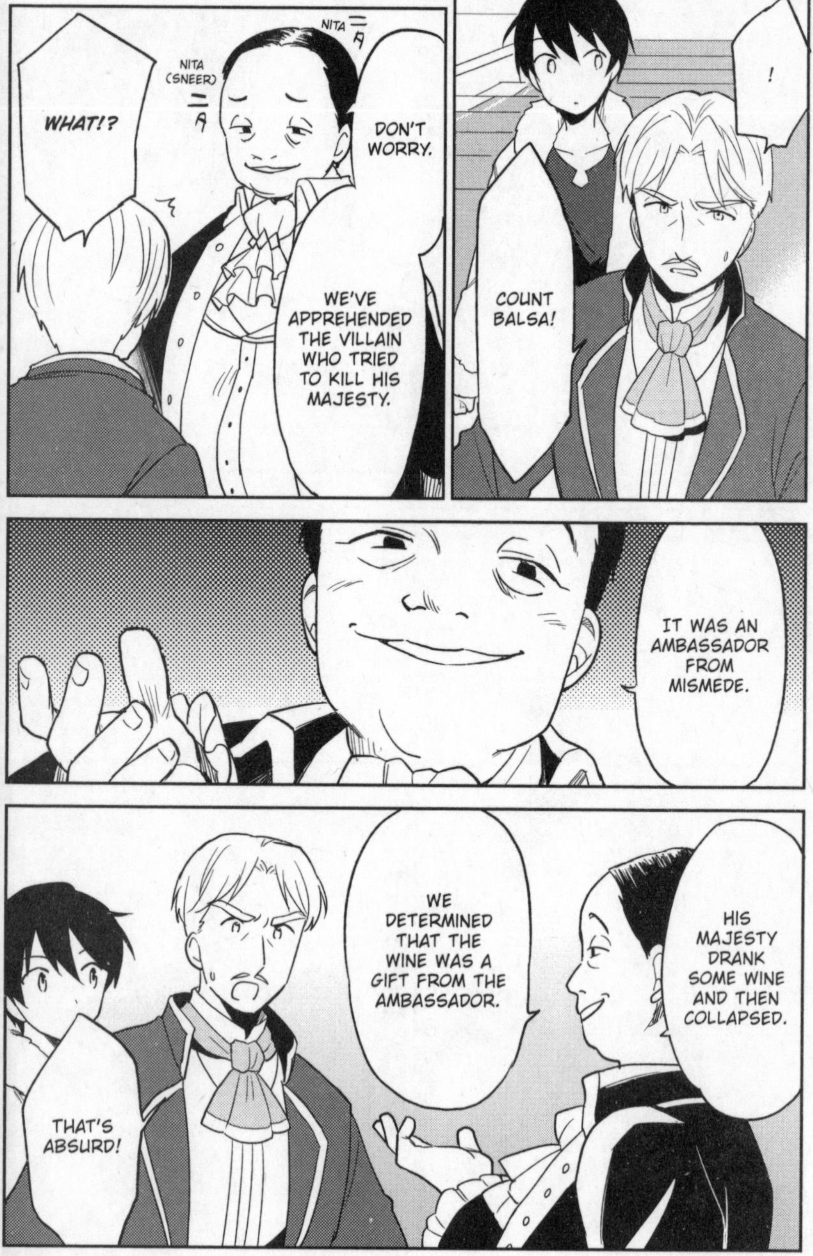
!
COUNT BALSA!
NITA
DON'T WORRY.
WE'VE APPREHENDED THE VILLAIN WHO TRIED TO KILL HIS MAJESTY.
NITA (SNEER)
WHAT!?
IT WAS AN AMBASSADOR FROM MISMEDE.
HIS MAJESTY DRANK SOME WINE AND THEN COLLAPSED.
WE DETERMINED THAT THE WINE WAS A GIFT FROM THE AMBASSADOR.
THAT'S ABSURD!

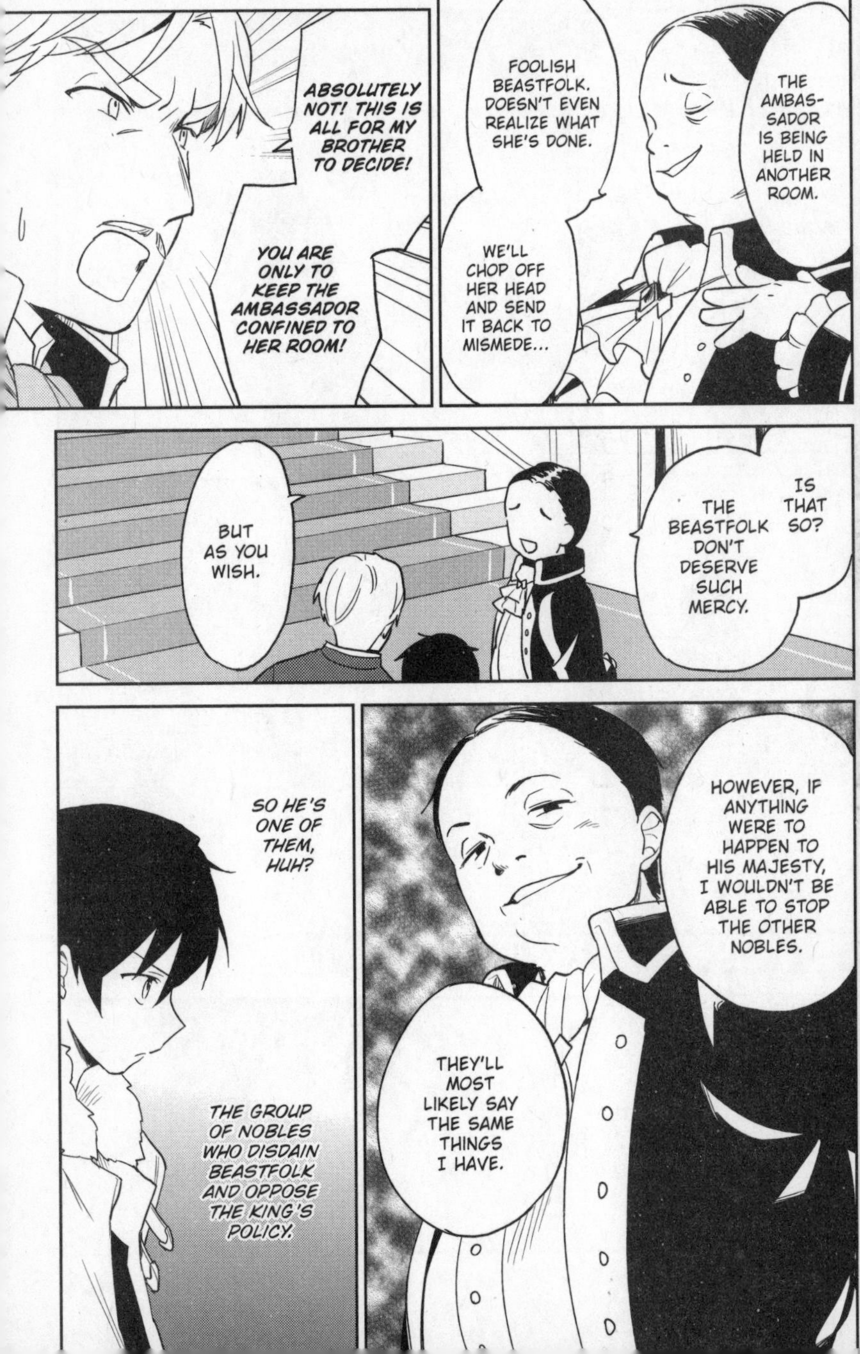
THE AMBASSADOR IS BEING HELD IN ANOTHER ROOM.
FOOLISH BEASTFOLK. DOESN'T EVEN REALIZE WHAT SHE'S DONE.
WE'LL CHOP OFF HER HEAD AND SEND IT BACK TO MISMEDE...
ABSOLUTELY NOT! THIS IS ALL FOR MY BROTHER TO DECIDE!
YOU ARE ONLY TO KEEP THE AMBASSADOR CONFINED TO HER ROOM!
IS THAT SO?
THE BEASTFOLK DON'T DESERVE SUCH MERCY.
BUT AS YOU WISH.
HOWEVER, IF ANYTHING WERE TO HAPPEN TO HIS MAJESTY, I WOULDN'T BE ABLE TO STOP THE OTHER NOBLES.
THEY'LL MOST LIKELY SAY THE SAME THINGS I HAVE.
SO HE'S ONE OF THEM, HUH?
THE GROUP OF NOBLES WHO DISDAIN BEASTFOLK AND OPPOSE THE KING'S POLICY.

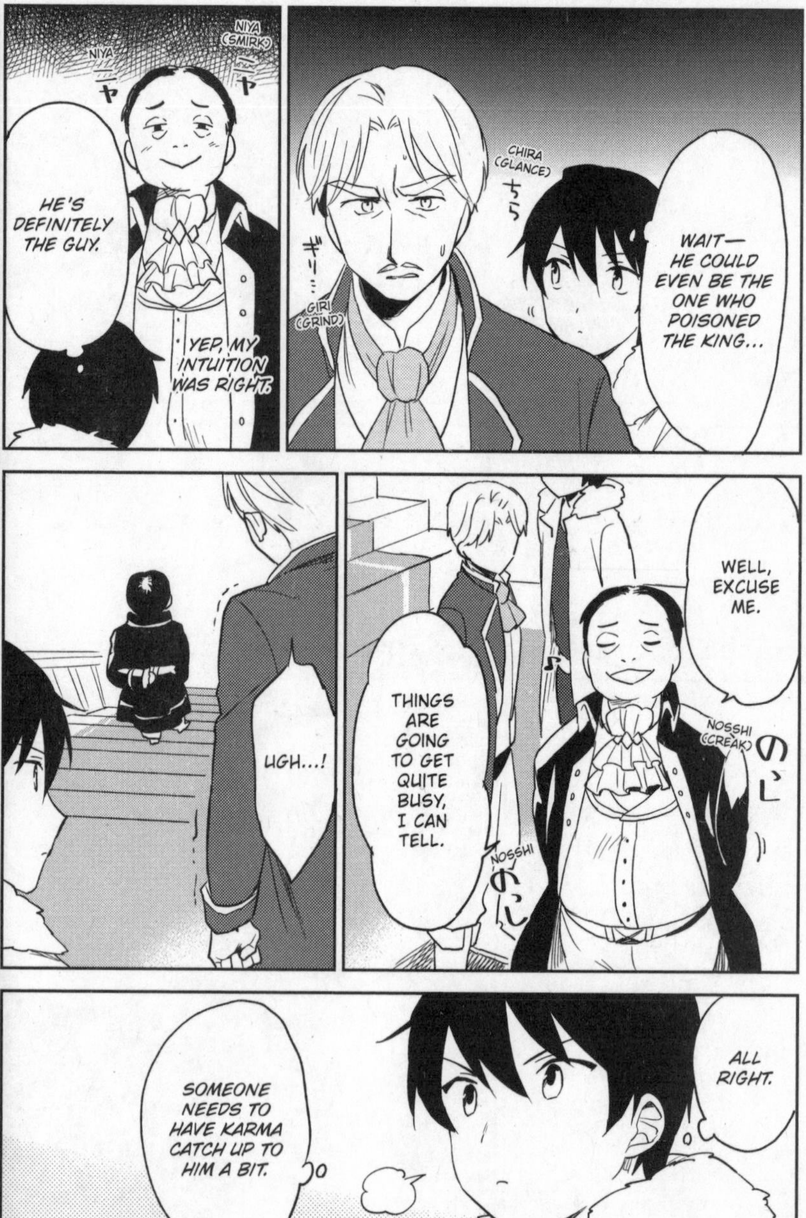
CHIRA (GLANCE)
WAIT— HE COULD EVEN BE THE ONE WHO POISONED THE KING...
GIRI (GRIND)
NIYA (SMIRK)
NIYA
HE'S DEFINITELY THE GUY.
YEP, MY INTUITION WAS RIGHT.
WELL, EXCUSE ME.
NOSSHI (CREAK)
THINGS ARE GOING TO GET QUITE BUSY, I CAN TELL.
NOSSHI
UGH...!
ALL RIGHT.
SOMEONE NEEDS TO HAVE KARMA CATCH UP TO HIM A BIT.

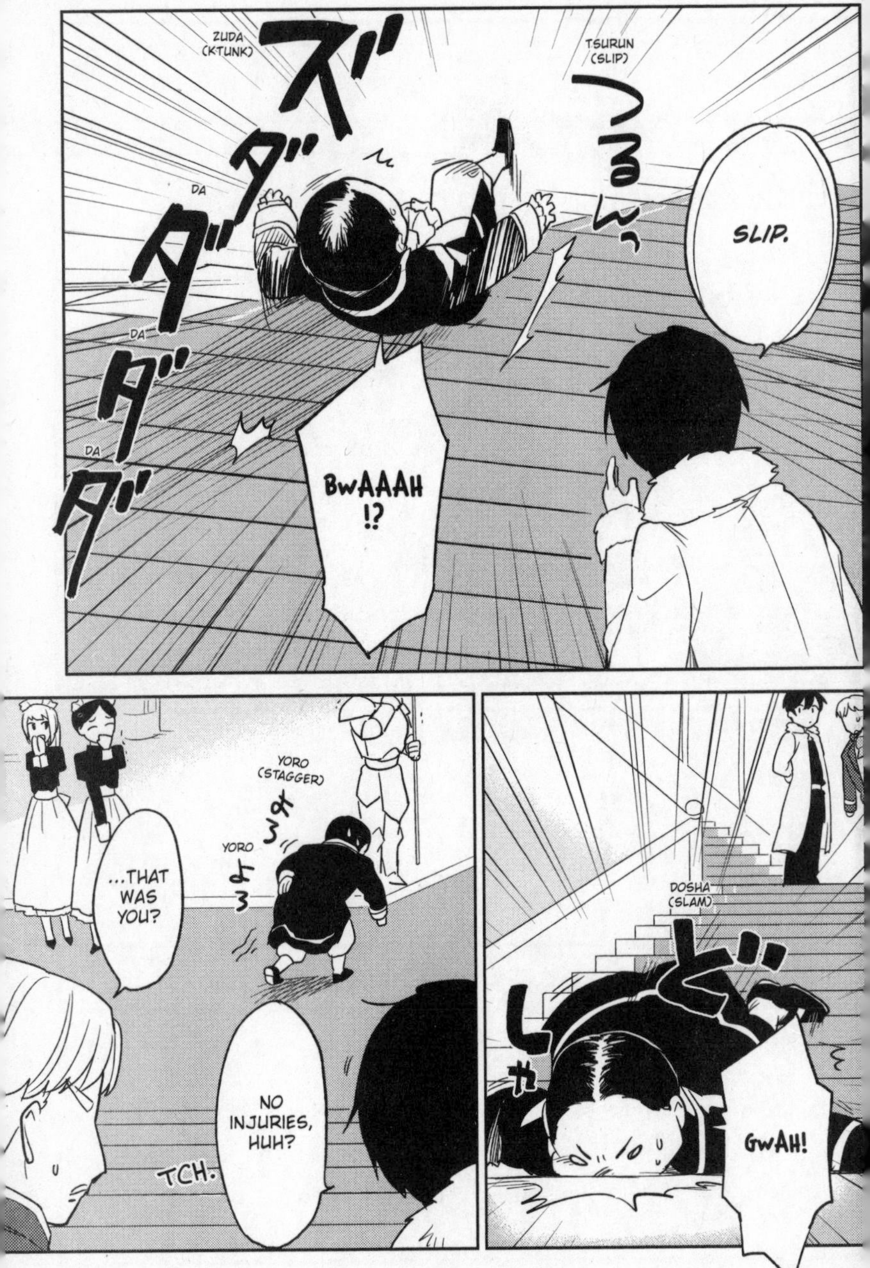
TSURUN (SLIP)
SLIP.
ZUDA (KTUNK)
DA
DA
DA
BWAAAH !?
DOSHA (SLAM)
GWAH!
YORO (STAGGER)
YORO
...THAT WAS YOU?
NO INJURIES, HUH?
TCH.

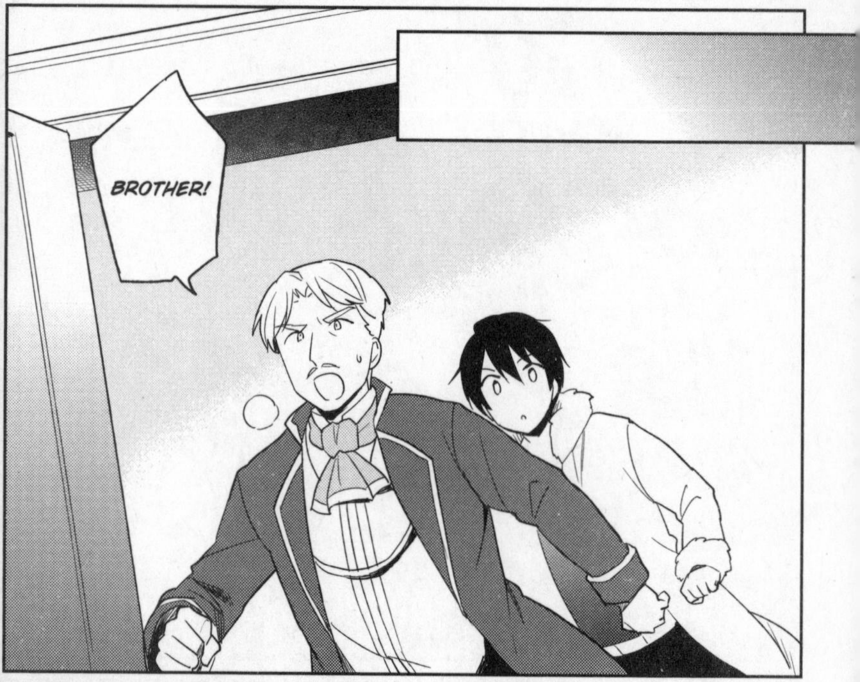
BROTHER!
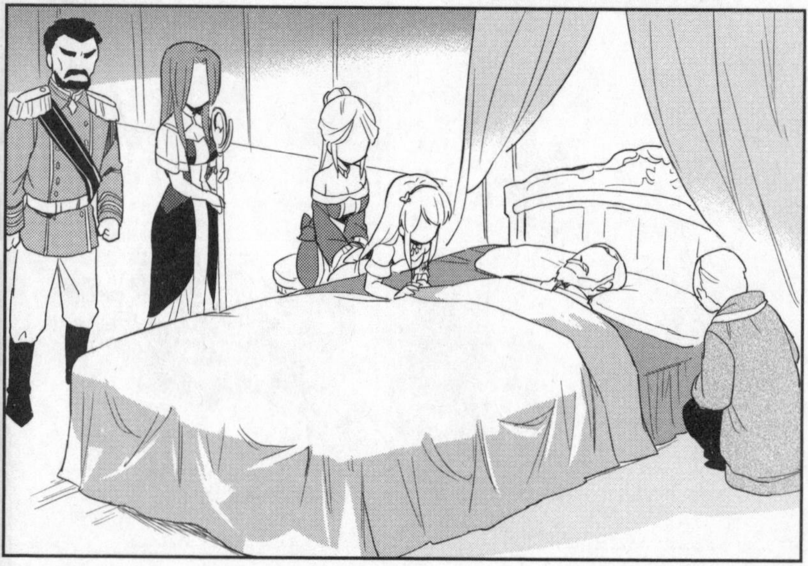

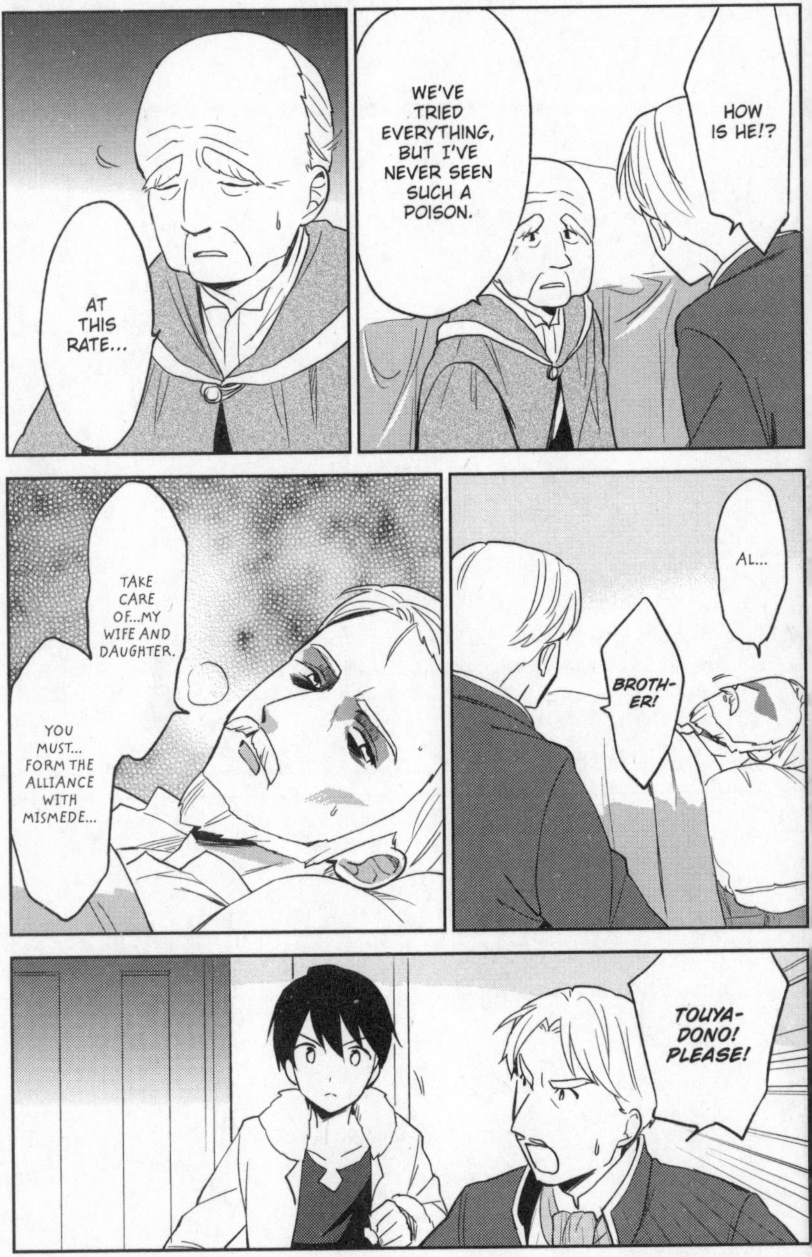
HOW IS HE!?
WE'VE TRIED EVERYTHING, BUT I'VE NEVER SEEN SUCH A POISON.
AT THIS RATE...
AL...
BROTHER!
TAKE CARE OF...MY WIFE AND DAUGHTER.
YOU MUST... FORM THE ALLIANCE WITH MISMEDE...
TOUYA-DONO! PLEASE!

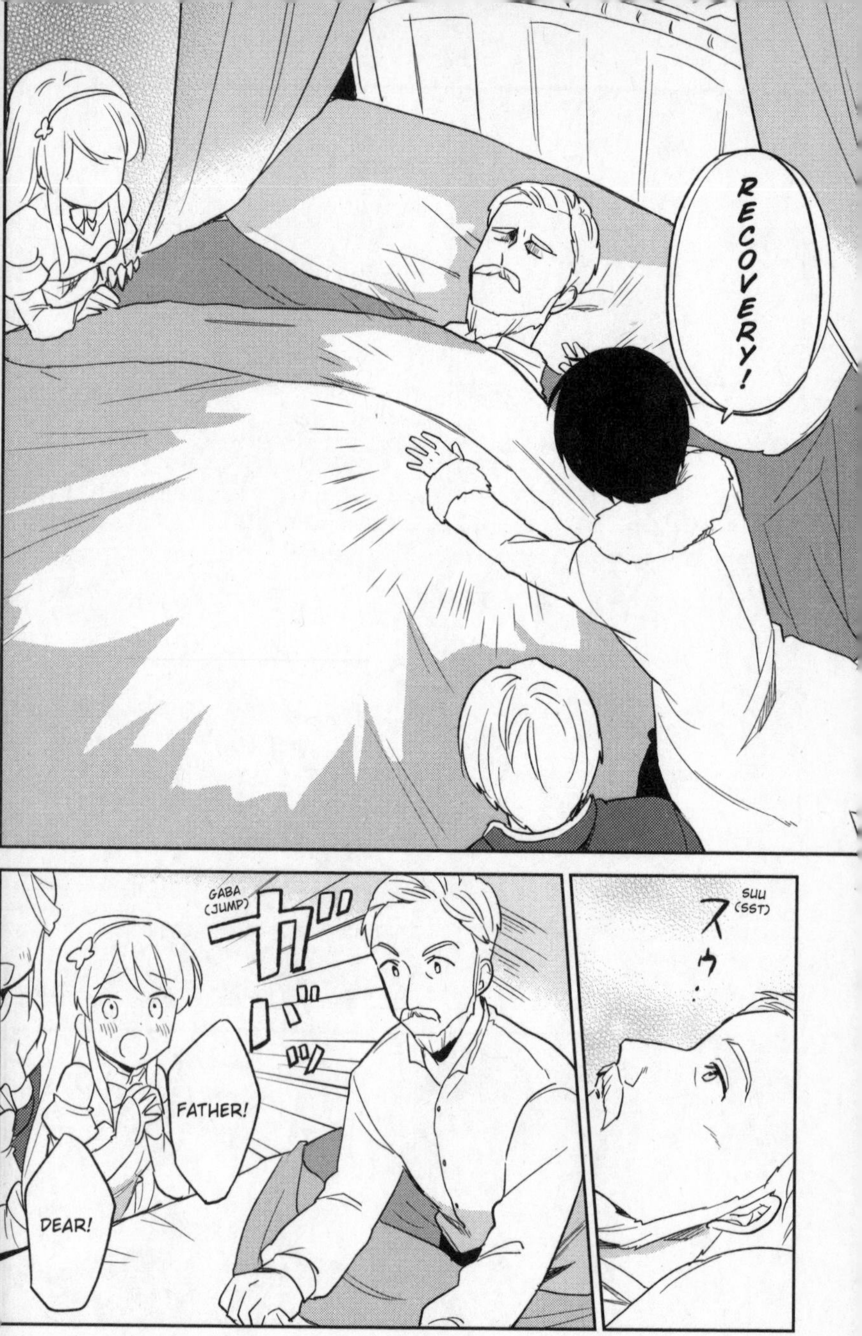
RECOVERY!
SUU (SST)
スゥ…
GABA (JUMP)
ガバッ
FATHER!
DEAR!

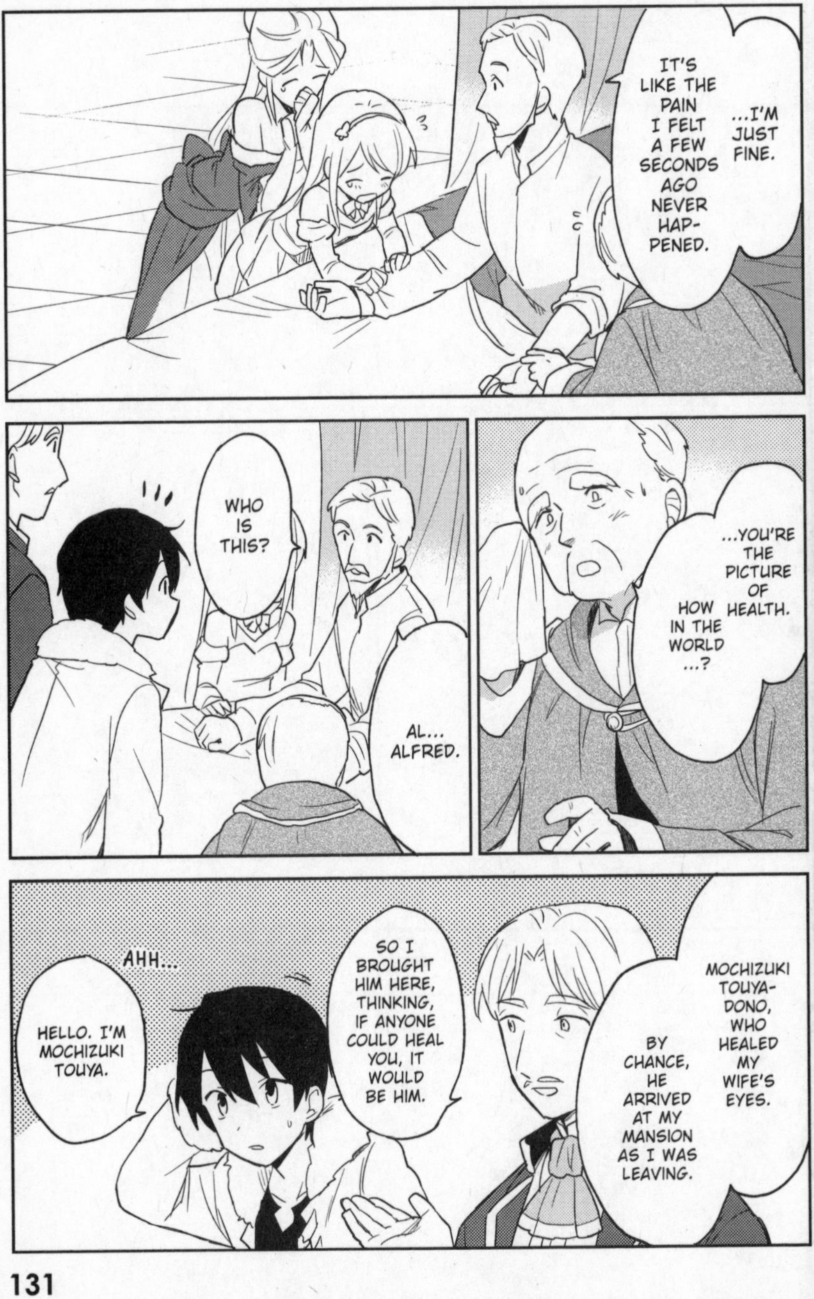
...I'M JUST FINE.
IT'S LIKE THE PAIN I FELT A FEW SECONDS AGO NEVER HAP-PENED.
...YOU'RE THE PICTURE OF HEALTH.
HOW IN THE WORLD ...?
AL... ALFRED.
WHO IS THIS?
MOCHIZUKI TOUYA-DONO, WHO HEALED MY WIFE'S EYES.
BY CHANCE, HE ARRIVED AT MY MANSION AS I WAS LEAVING.
SO I BROUGHT HIM HERE, THINKING, IF ANYONE COULD HEAL YOU, IT WOULD BE HIM.
AHH...
HELLO. I'M MOCHIZUKI TOUYA.

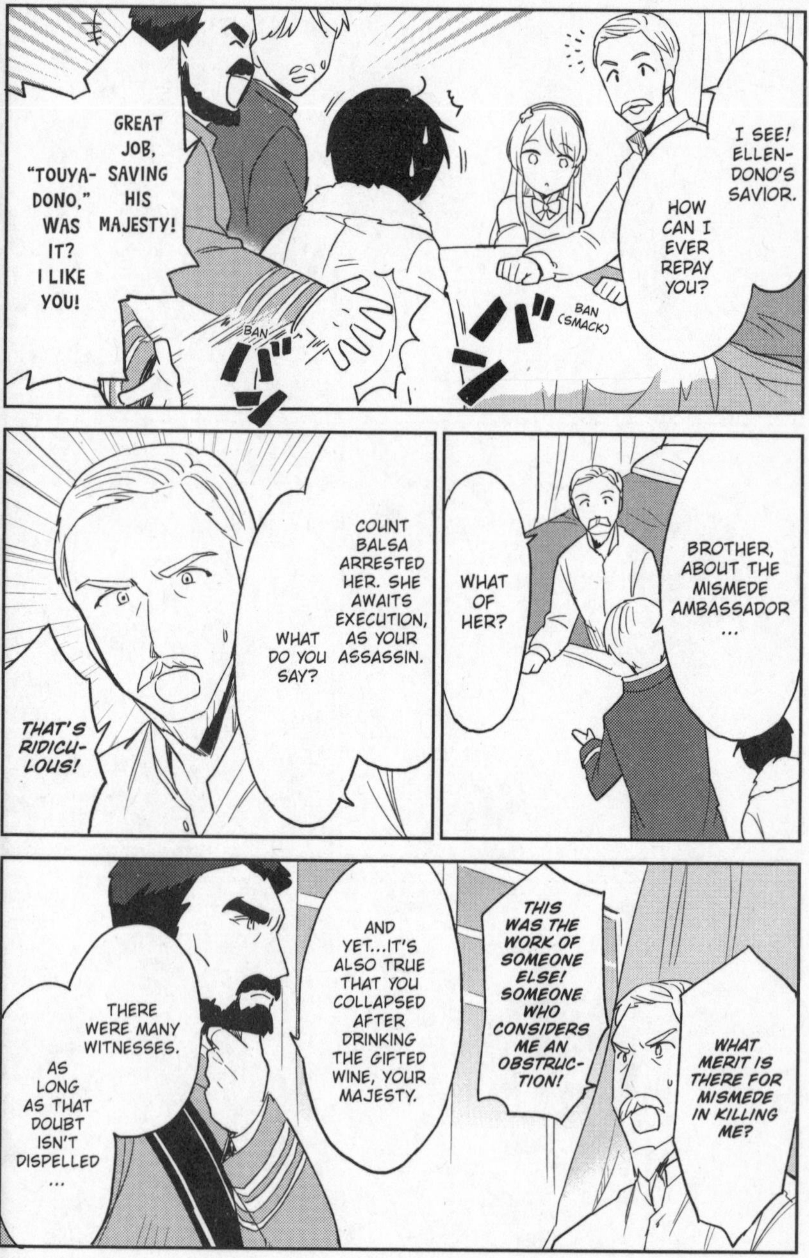
I SEE! ELLEN-DONO'S SAVIOR.
HOW CAN I EVER REPAY YOU?
BAN (SMACK)
GREAT JOB, SAVING HIS MAJESTY!
"TOUYA-DONO," WAS IT? I LIKE YOU!
BAN
BROTHER, ABOUT THE MISMEDE AMBASSADOR ...
WHAT OF HER?
COUNT BALSA ARRESTED HER. SHE AWAITS EXECUTION, AS YOUR ASSASSIN.
WHAT DO YOU SAY?
THAT'S RIDICULOUS!
WHAT MERIT IS THERE FOR MISMEDE IN KILLING ME?
THIS WAS THE WORK OF SOMEONE ELSE! SOMEONE WHO CONSIDERS ME AN OBSTRUCTION!
AND YET...IT'S ALSO TRUE THAT YOU COLLAPSED AFTER DRINKING THE GIFTED WINE, YOUR MAJESTY.
THERE WERE MANY WITNESSES.
AS LONG AS THAT DOUBT ISN'T DISPELLED ...

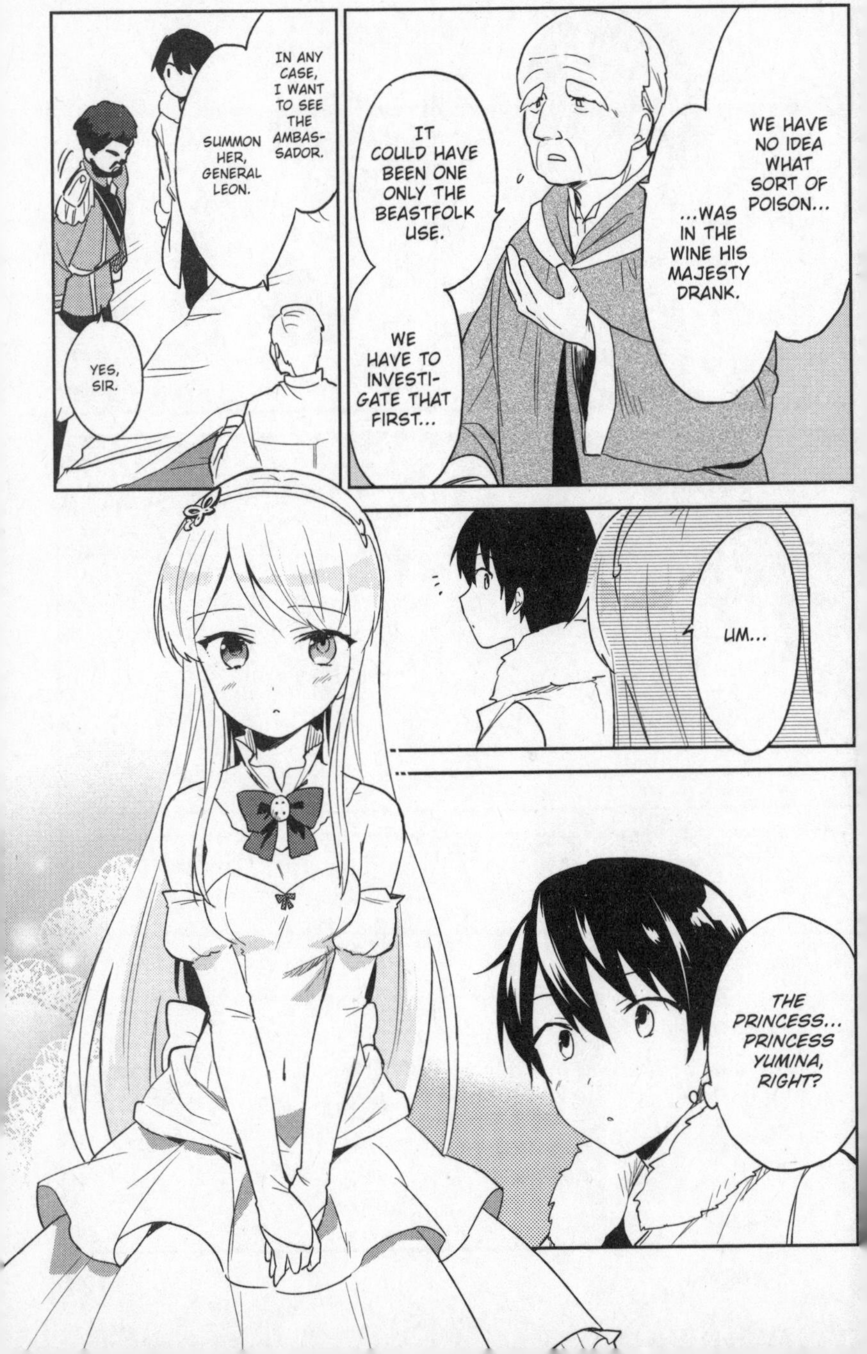
WE HAVE NO IDEA WHAT SORT OF POISON...
...WAS IN THE WINE HIS MAJESTY DRANK.
IT COULD HAVE BEEN ONE ONLY THE BEASTFOLK USE.
WE HAVE TO INVESTIGATE THAT FIRST...
IN ANY CASE, I WANT TO SEE THE AMBASSADOR.
SUMMON HER, GENERAL LEON.
YES, SIR.
UM...
THE PRINCESS... PRINCESS YUMINA, RIGHT?

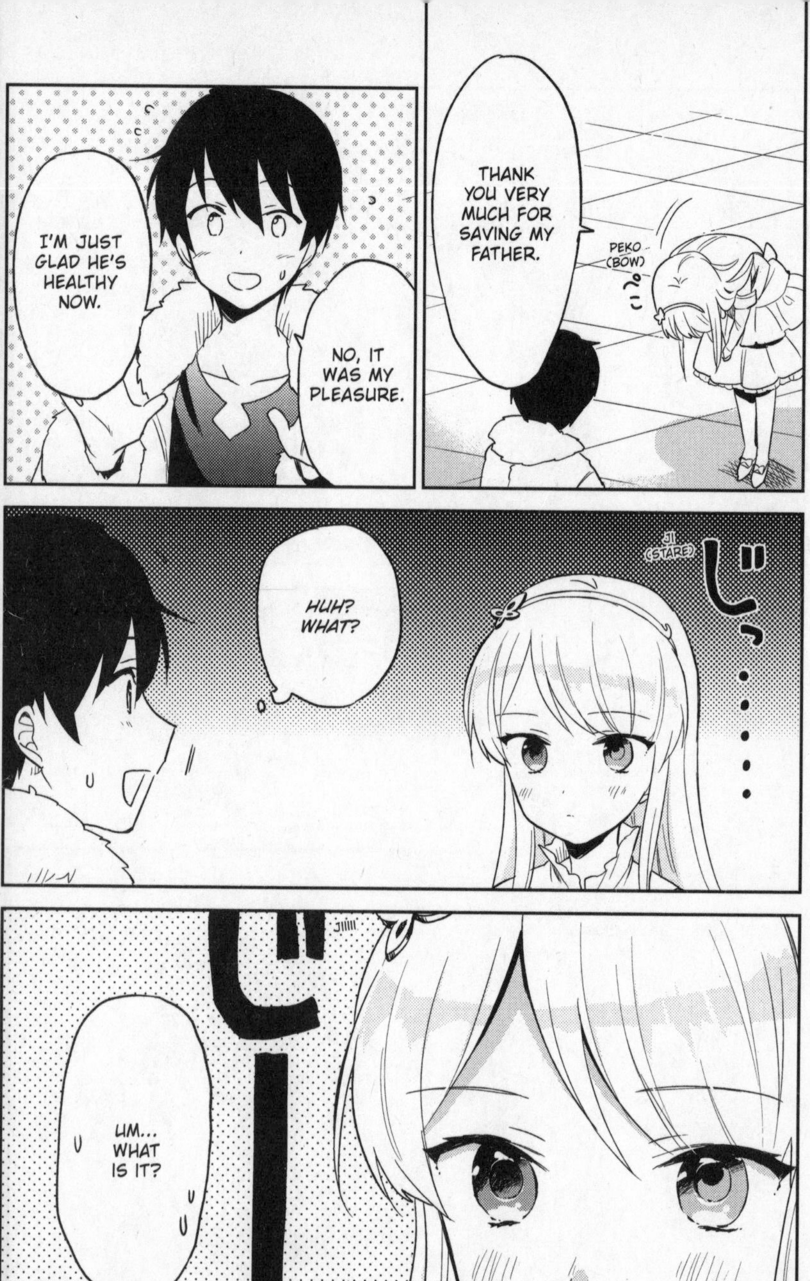
THANK YOU VERY MUCH FOR SAVING MY FATHER.
PEKO (BOW)
NO, IT WAS MY PLEASURE.
I'M JUST GLAD HE'S HEALTHY NOW.
JI (STARE)
HUH? WHAT?
JIIII
UM... WHAT IS IT?

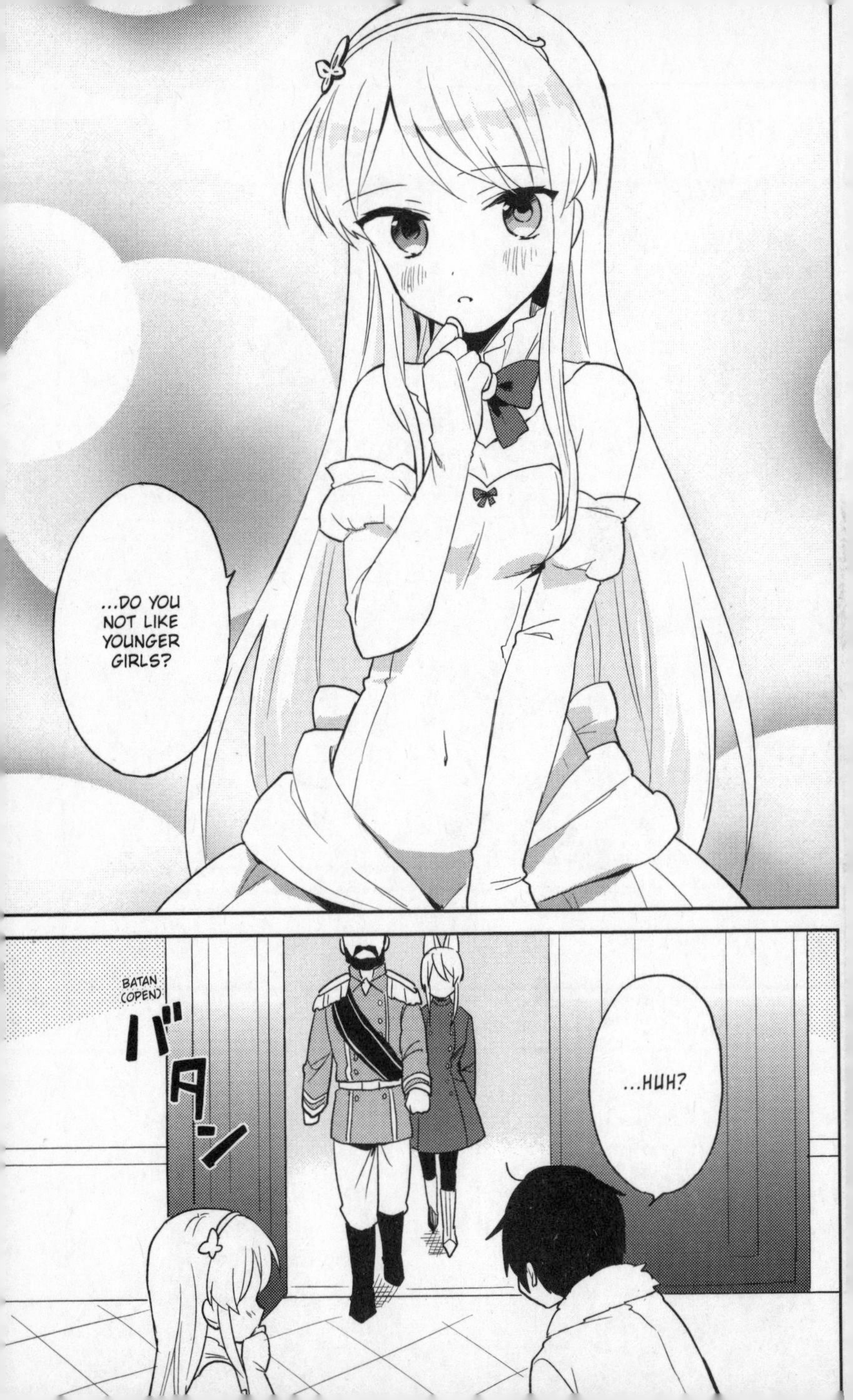
...DO YOU NOT LIKE YOUNGER GIRLS?
...HUH?
BATAN (OPEN)
バタン

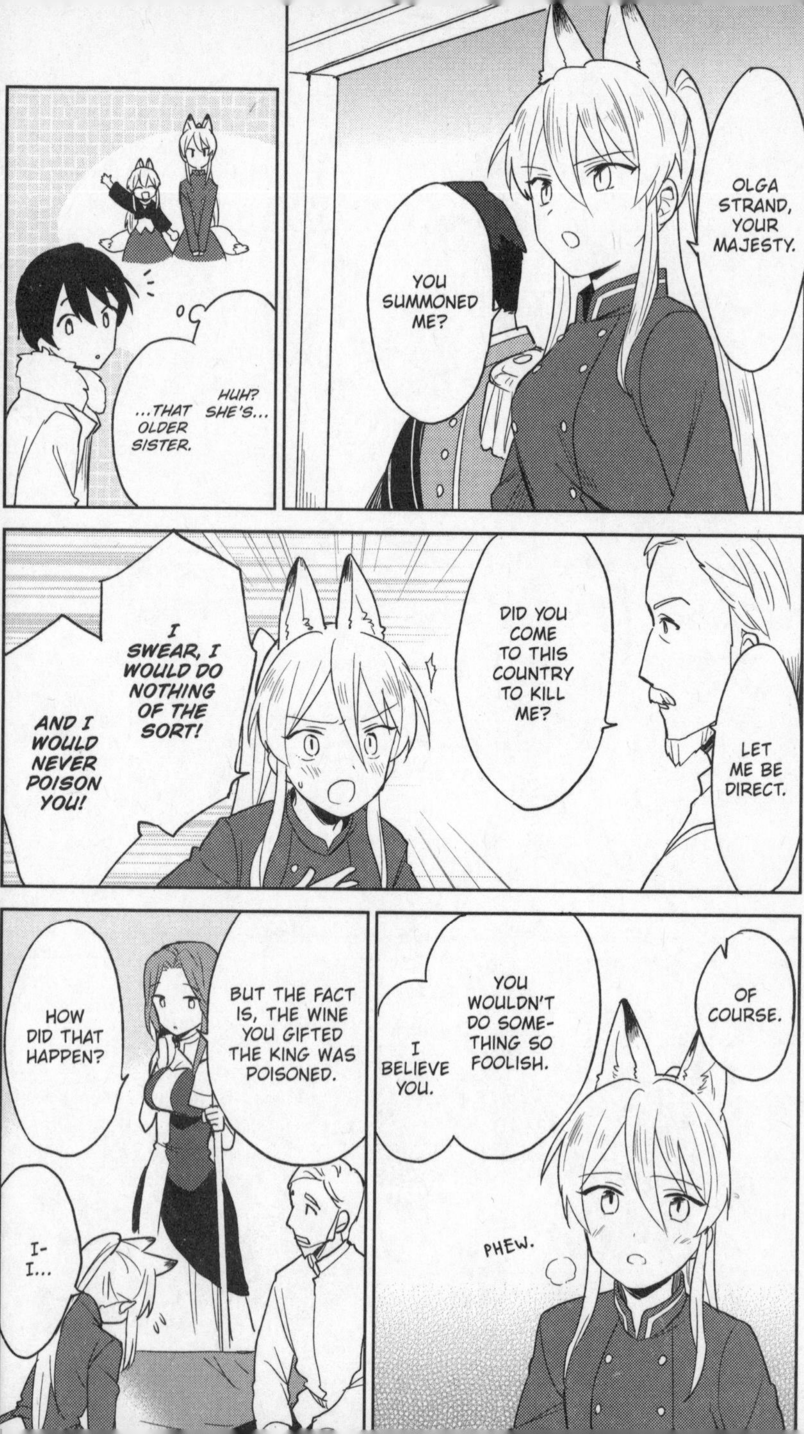
OLGA STRAND, YOUR MAJESTY.
YOU SUMMONED ME?
HUH? SHE'S...
...THAT OLDER SISTER.
LET ME BE DIRECT.
DID YOU COME TO THIS COUNTRY TO KILL ME?
I SWEAR, I WOULD DO NOTHING OF THE SORT!
AND I WOULD NEVER POISON YOU!
OF COURSE.
YOU WOULDN'T DO SOME-THING SO FOOLISH.
I BELIEVE YOU.
PHEW.
BUT THE FACT IS, THE WINE YOU GIFTED THE KING WAS POISONED.
HOW DID THAT HAPPEN?
I- I...

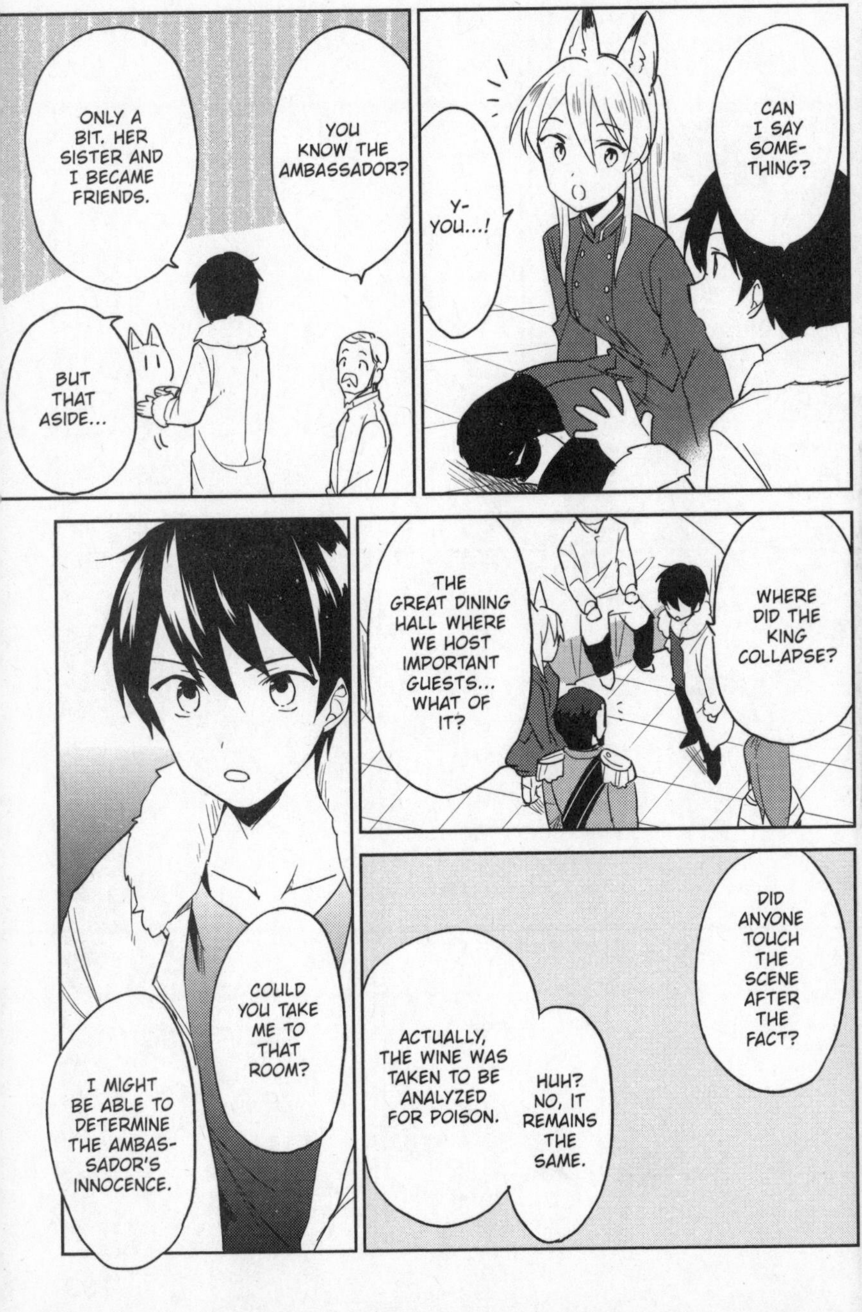
CAN I SAY SOMETHING?
Y-YOU...!
YOU KNOW THE AMBASSADOR?
ONLY A BIT. HER SISTER AND I BECAME FRIENDS.
BUT THAT ASIDE...
WHERE DID THE KING COLLAPSE?
THE GREAT DINING HALL WHERE WE HOST IMPORTANT GUESTS... WHAT OF IT?
DID ANYONE TOUCH THE SCENE AFTER THE FACT?
HUH? NO, IT REMAINS THE SAME.
ACTUALLY, THE WINE WAS TAKEN TO BE ANALYZED FOR POISON.
COULD YOU TAKE ME TO THAT ROOM?
I MIGHT BE ABLE TO DETERMINE THE AMBASSADOR'S INNOCENCE.

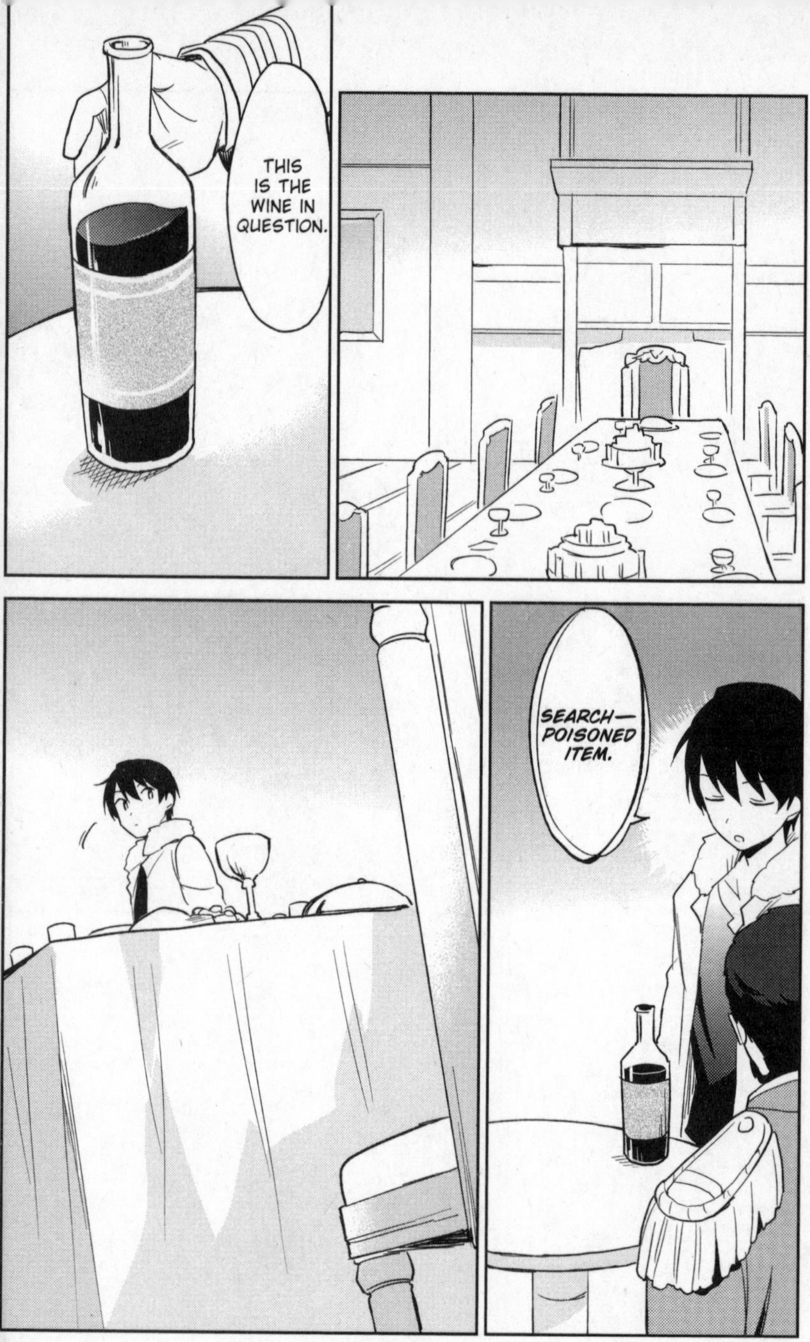
THIS IS THE WINE IN QUESTION.
SEARCH—POISONED ITEM.

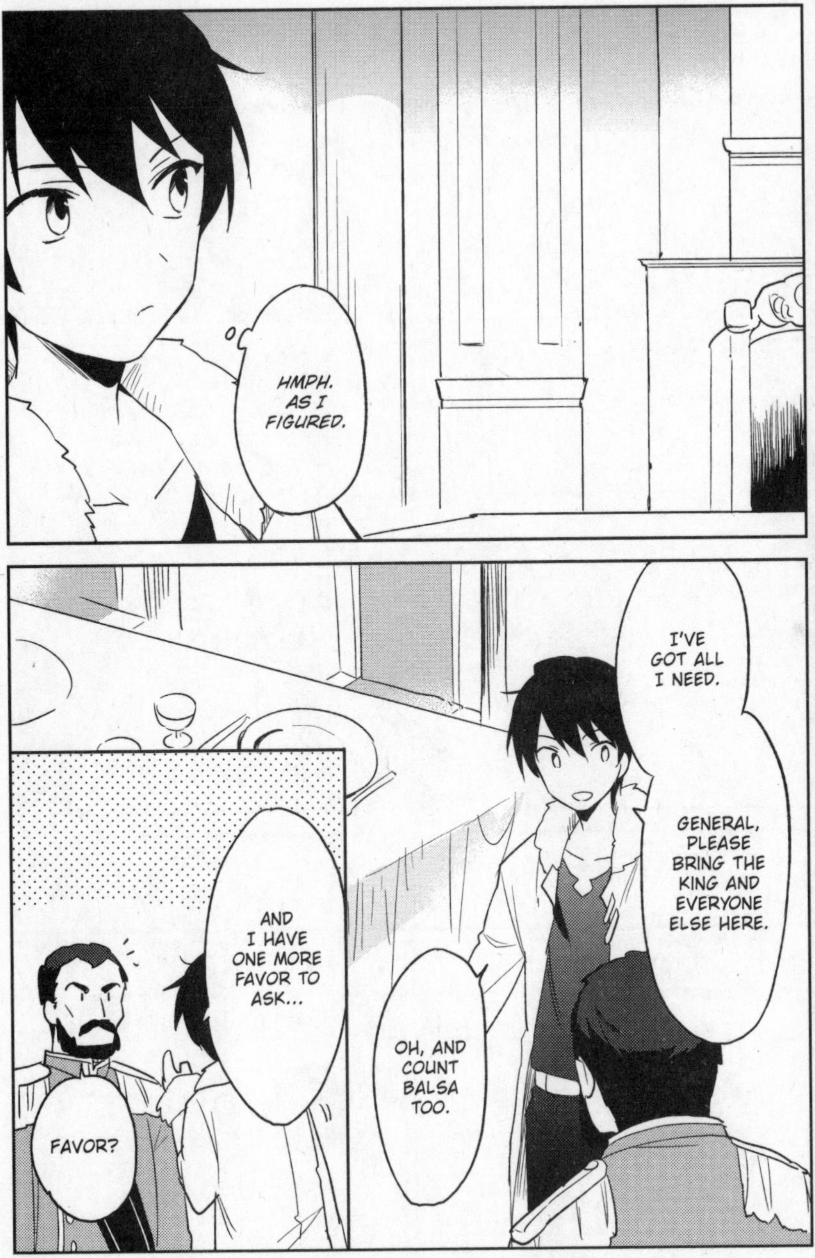
HMPH. AS I FIGURED.
I'VE GOT ALL I NEED.
GENERAL, PLEASE BRING THE KING AND EVERYONE ELSE HERE.
OH, AND COUNT BALSA TOO.
AND I HAVE ONE MORE FAVOR TO ASK...
FAVOR?

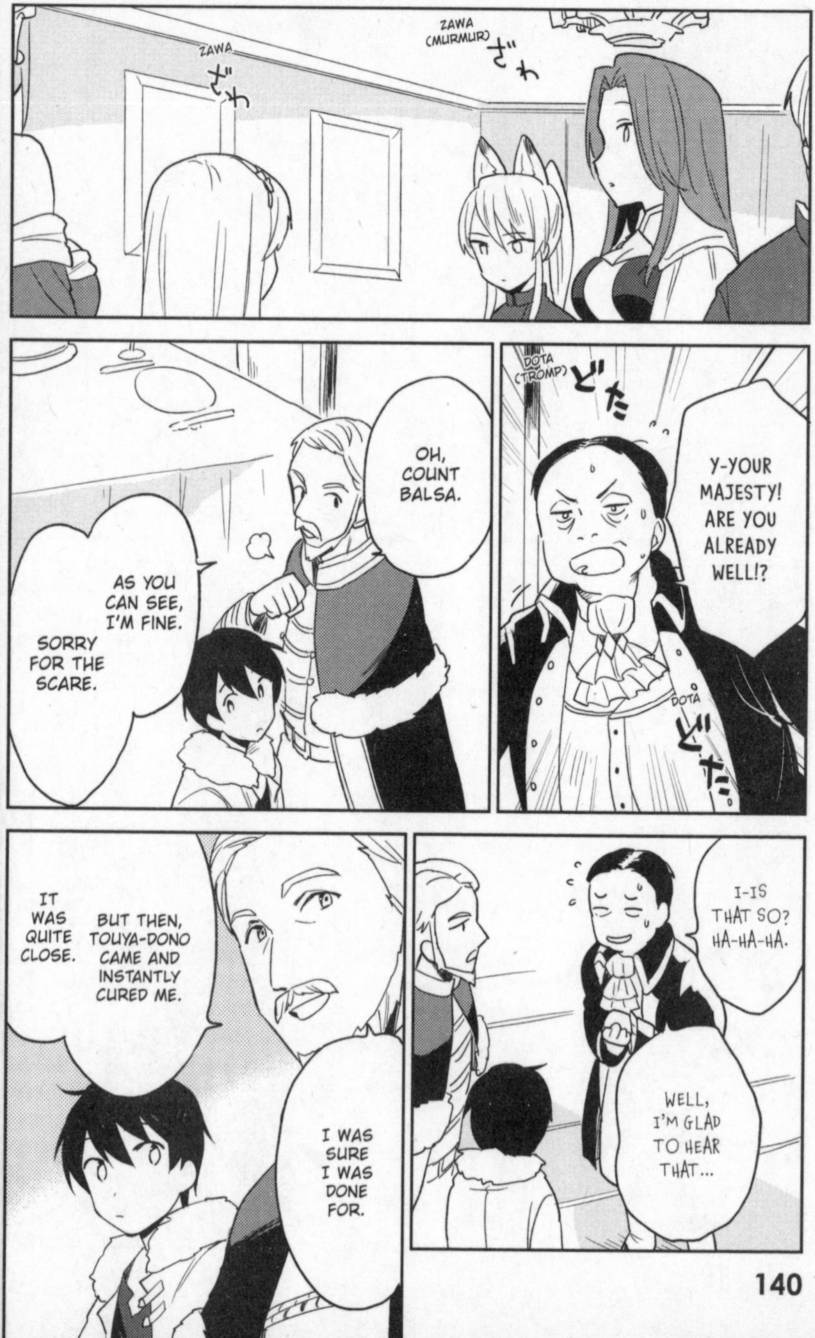
ZAWA (MURMUR) ざわ
ZAWA ざわ
DOTA (TROMP) どた
Y-YOUR MAJESTY! ARE YOU ALREADY WELL!?
DOTA どた
OH, COUNT BALSA.
AS YOU CAN SEE, I'M FINE.
SORRY FOR THE SCARE.
I-IS THAT SO? HA-HA-HA.
WELL, I'M GLAD TO HEAR THAT...
IT WAS QUITE CLOSE.
BUT THEN, TOUYA-DONO CAME AND INSTANTLY CURED ME.
I WAS SURE I WAS DONE FOR.

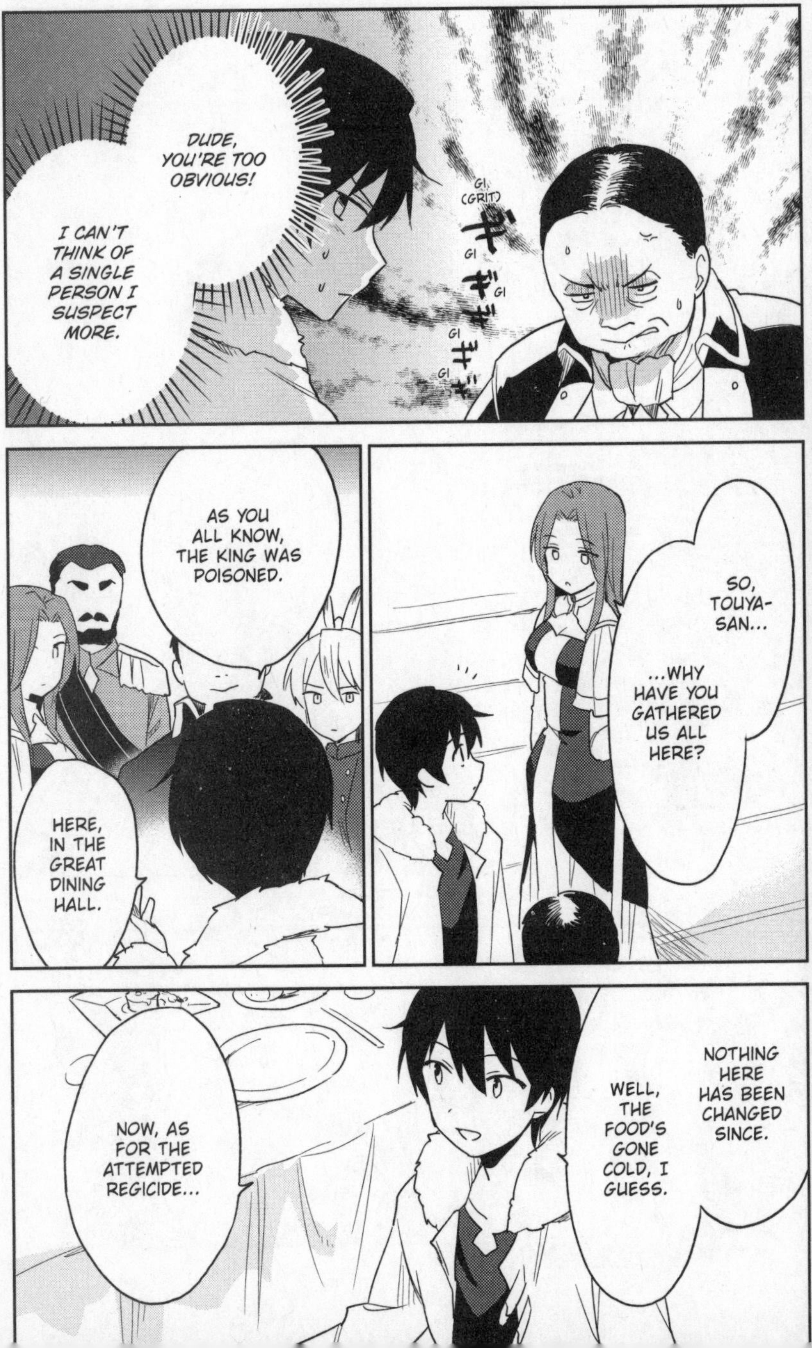
GI (GRIT)
GI
GI
GI
GI
DUDE, YOU'RE TOO OBVIOUS!
I CAN'T THINK OF A SINGLE PERSON I SUSPECT MORE.
SO, TOUYA-SAN...
...WHY HAVE YOU GATHERED US ALL HERE?
AS YOU ALL KNOW, THE KING WAS POISONED.
HERE, IN THE GREAT DINING HALL.
NOTHING HERE HAS BEEN CHANGED SINCE.
WELL, THE FOOD'S GONE COLD, I GUESS.
NOW, AS FOR THE ATTEMPTED REGICIDE...

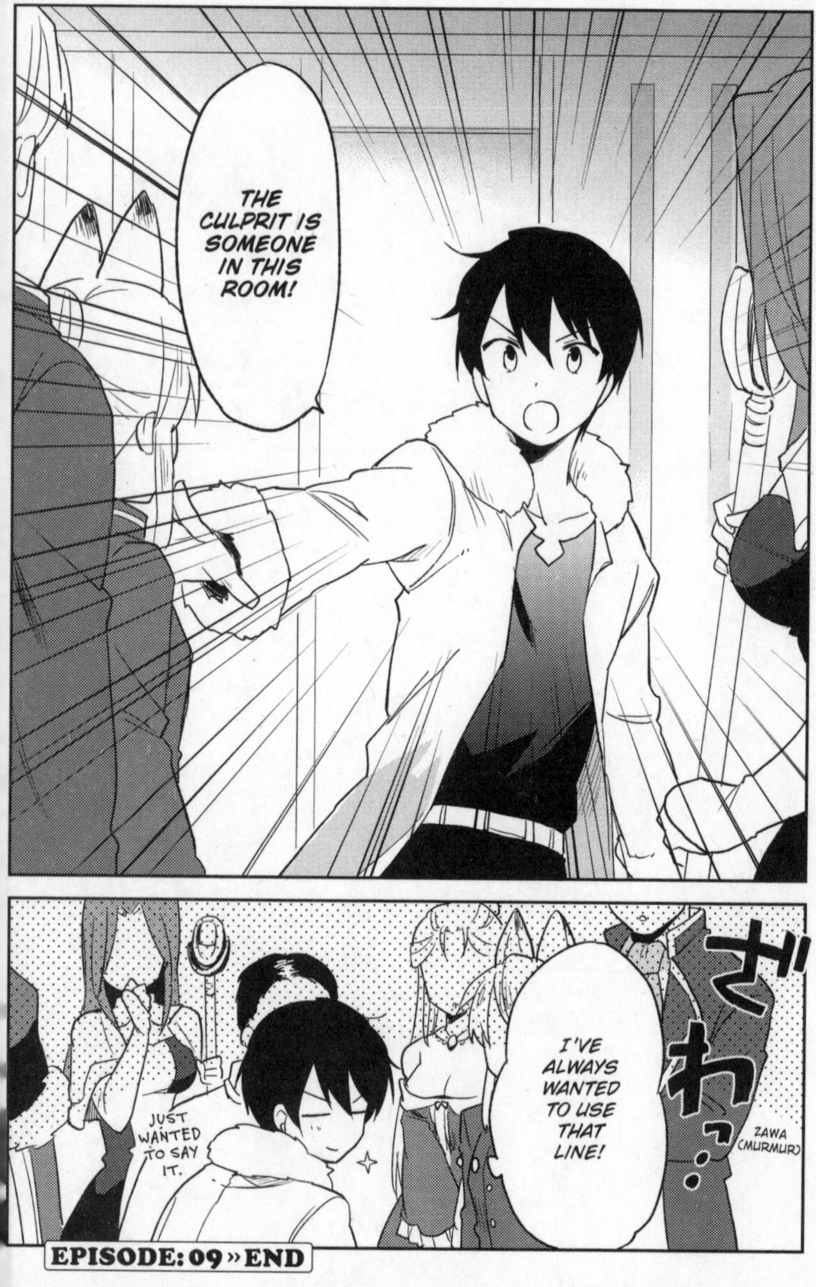
THE CULPRIT IS SOMEONE IN THIS ROOM!
ざわっ・・
ZAWA (MURMUR)
I'VE ALWAYS WANTED TO USE THAT LINE!
JUST WANTED TO SAY IT.

**EPISODE: 09 » END**

In Another World with
My Smartphone

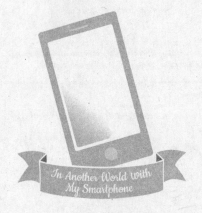

# In Another World with My Smartphone 2

### Art • Soto    Original Story • Patora Fuyuhara

**Character Design: Eiji Usatsuka**

**Translation: Alexander Keller-Nelson | Lettering: Chiho Christie**

ISEKAI WA SMART PHONE TO TOMONI. Vol. 2
©Soto 2017
©Patora Fuyuhara
First published in Japan in 2017 by KADOKAWA CORPORATION, Tokyo. English translation rights arranged with KADOKAWA CORPORATION, Tokyo through Tuttle-Mori Agency, Inc., Tokyo.

English translation © 2021 by Yen Press, LLC

Yen Press
150 West 30th Street, 19th Floor
New York, NY 10001

Visit us!
yenpress.com • facebook.com/yenpress • twitter.com/yenpress
yenpress.tumblr.com • instagram.com/yenpress

First Yen Press Edition: June 2021

Yen Press is an imprint of Yen Press, LLC.
The Yen Press name and logo are trademarks of Yen Press, LLC.

The publisher is not responsible for websites (or their content) that are not owned by the publisher.

Library of Congress Control Number: 2020951871

ISBNs: 978-1-9753-2105-5 (paperback)
978-1-9753-2106-2 (ebook)

10 9 8 7 6 5 4 3 2 1

WOR

Printed in the United States of America